Clinical Vignettes
for the USMLE Step 2
PreTest® Self-Assessment and Review

NOTICE

Medicine is an ever-changing science. As new research and clinical experience broaden our knowledge, changes in treatment and drug therapy are required. The editors and the publisher of this work have checked with sources believed to be reliable in their efforts to provide information that is complete and generally in accord with the standards accepted at the time of publication. However, in view of the possibility of human error or changes in medical sciences, neither the editors nor the publisher nor any other party who has been involved in the preparation or publication of this work warrants that the information contained herein is in every respect accurate or complete, and they are not responsible for any errors or omissions or for the results obtained from use of such information. Readers are encouraged to confirm the information contained herein with other sources. For example and in particular, readers are advised to check the product information sheet included in the package of each drug they plan to administer to be certain that the information contained in this book is accurate and that changes have not been made in the recommended dose or in the contraindications for administration. This recommendation is of particular importance in connection with new or infrequently used drugs.

Clinical Vignettes
for the USMLE Step 2
PreTest® Self-Assessment and Review

McGraw-Hill
Health Professions Division
PreTest® Series

NEW YORK   ST. LOUIS   SAN FRANCISCO   AUCKLAND
BOGOTÁ   CARACAS   LISBON   LONDON   MADRID
MEXICO CITY   MILAN   MONTREAL   NEW DELHI
SAN JUAN   SINGAPORE   SYDNEY   TOKYO   TORONTO

McGraw-Hill

A Division of The McGraw·Hill Companies

Clinical Vignettes for the USMLE Step 2: PreTest® Self-Assessment and Review

1 2 3 4 5 6 7 8 9 0   DOCDOC   9 9

ISBN 0-07-135558-8

This book was set in Berkeley by V & M Graphics.
The editors were John J. Dolan and Peter McCurdy.
Project development was by Joanna V. Pomeranz, V & M Graphics.
The production supervisor was Helene G. Landers.
The text designer was Jim Sullivan/RepoCat Graphics & Editorial Services.
The cover designer was Li Chen Chang / Pinpoint.
R.R. Donnelley & Sons was printer and binder.

This book is printed on acid-free paper.

CONTENTS

PREFACE

The current format of the United States Medical Licensing Exam for Step 2 emphasizes clinical vignettes as the primary test question. The exam is approximately 400 questions, broken up into 8 blocks of 50 questions each. Students have one hour to finish each block.

Clinical Vignettes for the USMLE Step 2 parallels this format. The book is 400 clinical vignette questions covering the clinical sciences. The questions are divided into 8 blocks of 50 questions. As in the Step 2 exam, each block tests the student in all clinical areas. Halfway through each block, a stopwatch set at 30 minutes is included to remind the student of the one hour limit. Answers are in the second half of the book and are comprehensive and referenced to major texts and journals, a trademark of the PreTest® series.

The questions were taken from the 8 PreTest® Clinical Science books and were edited as needed to reflect the current USMLE format. The Publisher acknowledges and thanks the following authors for their contributions to this book:

Surgery, Peter L Geller and Richard S. Nitzberg
Preventive Medicine and Public Health, Sylvie Ratelle
Obstetrics and Gynecology, Mark I. Evans
Pediatrics, Robert J. Yetman
Physical Diagnosis, Tyson K. Cobb
Psychiatry, Sherwyn M. Woods
Medicine, Steven L. Berk
Neurology, Richard Lechtenberg

McGraw-Hill
March, 1999

Clinical Vignettes
for the USMLE Step 2

PreTest® Self-Assessment and Review

BLOCK 1

YOU HAVE **60** MINUTES
TO COMPLETE **50** QUESTIONS.

BLOCK 1

YOU HAVE *60 MINUTES*
TO COMPLETE *50 QUESTIONS.*

Questions

1-1. A 4-year-old child is brought in by her mother because of a painful, honey-colored, crusted lesion on her face. The most likely diagnosis is

(A) miliaria
(B) impetigo
(C) cellulitis
(D) seborrheic dermatitis
(E) chickenpox

1-2. A 70-year-old man with unresectable carcinoma of the lung metastatic to liver and bone has developed progressive weight loss, anorexia, and shortness of breath. The patient has executed a valid living will, which prohibits the use of a feeding tube in the setting of terminal illness. The patient becomes lethargic and stops eating altogether. The patient's wife of 30 years insists on enteral feeding for her husband. Since he has become unable to take in adequate nutrition, you would

(A) respect the wife's wishes because she is a reliable surrogate decision maker
(B) resist the placement of a feeding tube in accordance with the living will
(C) call a family conference to get broad input from others
(D) place a feeding tube until such time as the matter can be discussed with the patient

1-3. A 48-year-old woman develops pain of the right lower quadrant while playing tennis. The pain progresses and she presents to the emergency room later that day with a low-grade fever, a white blood count of 13,000, and complaints of anorexia and nausea as well as persistent, sharp pain of the right lower quadrant. On examination she is tender in the right lower quadrant with muscular spasm and there is a suggestion of a mass effect. An ultrasound is ordered and shows an apparent mass in the abdominal wall. Which of the following is the most likely diagnosis?

(A) Acute appendicitis
(B) Cecal carcinoma
(C) Hematoma of the rectus sheath
(D) Torsion of an ovarian cyst
(E) Cholecystitis

1-4. A 22-year-old man was being treated with fluoxetine (Prozac) for depression, while his twin brother was being treated for depression with an monoamine oxidase (MAO) inhibitor. Because of his increasing despair, the first man began to add his brother's MAO inhibitor to his daily fluoxetine. He soon began having visual hallucinations, became confused, and developed severe myoclonic jerks. On examination he was noted to be flushed and diaphoretic and to have a temperature of 39.44°C (103°F). The most likely diagnosis would be

(A) meningitis
(B) cerebral vascular incident
(C) neuroleptic malignant syndrome
(D) serotonin syndrome
(E) anticholinergic syndrome

I-5. A 70-year-old woman has nausea, vomiting, abdominal distention, and episodic, crampy mid-abdominal pain. She has no history of previous surgery but has a long history of cholelithiasis for which she has refused surgery. Her abdominal radiograph reveals spherical density in the right lower quadrant. Correct treatment should consist of

(A) ileocolectomy
(B) cholecystectomy
(C) ileotomy and extraction
(D) nasogastric tube decompression
(E) intravenous antibiotics

I-6. A 53-year-old man, who has a 40-pack-year history of cigarette smoking, presents with the complaint that he was awakened suddenly from sleep with palpitations and shortness of breath. He was afraid that he was having a "heart attack" and hurried to the hospital. The symptoms are now gone and he claims never to have had exertional angina. The most likely diagnosis is

(A) myocardial infarction
(B) atrial fibrillation
(C) Prinzmetal's angina
(D) stable angina
(E) pulmonary edema

I-7. A 45-year-old man with Parkinson's disease has macular areas of erythema and scaling behind the ears and on the scalp, eyebrows, glabella, nasal labial folds, and central chest. The diagnosis is

(A) tinea versicolor
(B) psoriasis
(C) seborrheic dermatitis
(D) atopic dermatitis
(E) dermatophyte infection

I-8. A 28-year-old, nulligravid patient complains of bleeding between her periods and of increasingly heavy menses. Over the past 2 years she has had two dilation and curettages (D & C's) which have failed to resolve her symptoms. Oral contraceptives and antiprostaglandins have not decreased the abnormal bleeding. It would be appropriate at this time to

(A) perform a hysterectomy
(B) perform hysteroscopy
(C) perform endometrial ablation
(D) treat with a GnRH agonist
(E) start the patient on a high-dose progestational agent

1-9. An 80-year-old man is found to have an asymptomatic abdominal mass and an arteriogram is obtained, which is pictured below. This patient should be advised that

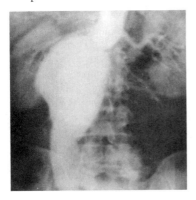

(A) surgery should be performed, but a mortality of 20 percent is to be anticipated

(B) surgery should be performed only if symptoms develop

(C) surgery will improve his 5-year survival

(D) surgery this extensive should not be performed in a patient of his age

(E) surgery should be performed only if follow-up ultrasound demonstrates increasing size

1-10. A 6-month-old male infant with leukokoria and onset of strabismus is brought to the U.S. from a developing country. The family history reveals that his father had an eye and a leg removed. The most likely diagnosis is

(A) coloboma of the choroid
(B) retinal detachment
(C) nematode endophthalmitis
(D) retinoblastoma
(E) persistent hyperplastic primary vitreous

1-11. A 15-month-old boy is brought to the emergency room because of fever and a rash. Six hours earlier he had been seen by another physician who diagnosed otitis media and prescribed ampicillin. After his first dose of antibiotic, the child developed a pinpoint erythematous rash on his face, trunk, and extremities. On physical examination the child is very irritable and he does not interact well with the examiner. Temperature is 39.5°C (103.1°F). Positive findings include scattered erythematous lesions, some of which do not blanch on pressure, and injected, immobile tympanic membranes. The most appropriate next step in the management of this infant is to

(A) begin administration of intravenous ampicillin
(B) begin diphenhydramine
(C) discontinue administration of ampicillin and begin trimethoprim with sulfamethoxazole
(D) perform bilateral myringotomies
(E) perform a lumbar picture

Items 1-12 through 1-14

A 19-year-old male presents with a 1-week history of malaise and anorexia followed by fever and sore throat. On physical examination, the throat is inflamed without exudate. There are a few palatal petechiae. Cervical adenopathy is present. The liver is percussed at 12 cm and the spleen is palpable. Laboratory findings are as follows:

Throat culture: negative for group A streptococci
Hct: 38 percent
Hgb: 12 g/dL
Reticulocytes: 4 percent
WBC: 14,000/mm^3
Segmented: 30 percent
Lymphocytes: 60 percent
Monocytes: 10 percent
Bilirubin total: 2.0 mg/dL
        (n 0.2 to 1.2)
Lactic dehydrogenase (LDH) serum: 260 IU/L (n 20 to 220)
Aspartate (AST, SGOT): 40 U/L (n 8 to 20)
Alanine (ALT, SGPT): 35 U/L (n 8 to 20)
Alkaline phosphatase: 40 IU/L (n 35 to 125)

1-12. The most important initial test would be

(A) liver biopsy
(B) streptococcus screen
(C) peripheral blood smear
(D) toxoplasmosis IgG
(E) lymph node biopsy

1-13. The most important serum test is

(A) heterophil antibody
(B) hepatitis B IgM
(C) hepatitis C antibody
(D) antistreptolysin-O (ASLO) titer
(E) cytomegalovirus IgG

1-14. Corticosteroids would be indicated if

(A) hepatitis is present
(B) fatigue lasts more than 1 week
(C) severe hemolytic anemia is demonstrated
(D) hepatitis B is confirmed by serology

I-I5. A 68-year-old patient presents with severe pruritus that is worse at night and reports similar symptoms among other family members. Upon examination, areas of excoriated papules are observed in the interdigital area. This history is most consistent with the diagnosis of

(A) dermatitis herpetiformis
(B) cutaneous larva migrans
(C) contact dermatitis
(D) scabies
(E) impetigo

I-I6. A 19-year-old college student presents to the university student health center complaining of severe coughing spells for the last 4 days, following initial symptoms of coryza and malaise. She is afebrile. Her medical history is uneventful, and immunizations are up to date. She is a member of the basketball team. During weekends, she babysits a 10-month-old and a 2-year-old. In terms of management of contacts, which etiological agent is the most important to include in the differential diagnosis?

(A) *Streptococcus pneumoniae*
(B) *Mycoplasma pneumoniae*
(C) *Bordetella pertussis*
(D) Influenza virus
(E) *Legionella pneumophila*

I-I7. A patient with decreased visual acuity as determined by a Snellen chart should have which of the following tests done to rule out refraction error?

(A) Slit-lamp examination
(B) Pinhole test
(C) Pseudochromatic plate test
(D) Schiotz tonometry
(E) Visual field examination

I-I8. A 34-year-old woman has recurrent fainting spells induced by fasting. Her serum insulin levels during these episodes are markedly elevated. Correct statements regarding this patient's condition include which of the following?

(A) The underlying lesion is probably an alpha-cell tumor of the pancreas
(B) The underlying lesion is usually multifocal
(C) These lesions are usually malignant
(D) Serum calcium levels may be elevated
(E) She should be screened for a coexistent pheochromocytoma

1-19. A 4-year-old falls from the back of a three-wheeled vehicle, hitting his head. He experiences no loss of consciousness. In the emergency room he is alert and oriented without focal findings on examination. He has blood behind his left tympanic membrane. CT scan of the skull is likely to show

(A) subdural hematoma
(B) epidural hematoma
(C) intraventricular hemorrhage
(D) basilar skull fracture
(E) hydrocephalus

1-20. A patient is constantly critical of the psychiatrist and the psychiatric treatment. The physician is not legally bound to continue treatment if

(A) dismissed by the patient, who is believed to be competent
(B) the patient is given ample medication to last until a new therapist can be found
(C) the psychiatrist recommends the patient seek a new therapist
(D) the patient is uncooperative with the treatment
(E) the doctor explains the action to the family

1-21. A 10-year-old child presents with vesicular lesions on the hands and face, some of which have ruptured and expressed a serous exudate. A Tzanck preparation is negative for multinucleated giant cells, but Gram stain shows grampositive cocci. The most likely diagnosis is

(A) cellulitis
(B) folliculitis
(C) impetigo
(D) Kawasaki's disease
(E) staphylococcal scalded-skin syndrome

1-22. A 27-year-old woman with multiple sclerosis developed paroxysmal pains in the face. The pain was stabbing and rarely lasted more than 1 or 2 s at a time. It occurred several times daily and was occasionally triggered by chewing or brushing the teeth. Pain management should start with

(A) lidocaine injections into the face
(B) ACTH intravenously for 7 days
(C) oral methylprednisolone
(D) destruction of the gasserian ganglion
(E) oral carbamazepine

1-23. A 21-year-old man who recently suffered through the mumps now presents to his physician complaining of a swollen and painful left testicle. The most likely diagnosis is

(A) orchitis
(B) epididymitis
(C) testicular tumor
(D) varicocele
(E) spermatocele

YOU SHOULD HAVE COMPLETED APPROXIMATELY 25 QUESTIONS AND HAVE 30 MINUTES REMAINING.

Items I-24 through I-28

For each of the clinical scenarios, pick from the following list the diagnosis that best explains the clinical picture.

(A) Classic migraine
(B) Cluster headache
(C) Common migraine
(D) Trigeminal neuralgia
(E) Sinusitis
(F) Temporal arteritis
(G) Vertebrobasilar migraine
(H) Hemiplegic migraine
(I) Atypical facial pain
(J) Postherpetic neuralgia

I-24. A 22-year-old dance instructor routinely developed headaches on the weekend. The headache was almost always limited to the right side of her head and was centered about the right temple. She would know that a headache was coming because of changes in her vision that preceded the headache by 20 to 30 min. She would see scintillating lights just to the left of her center of vision. This visual aberration would expand and interfere with her vision. The blindspot it created would appear to have a scintillating margin. As the blindspot cleared, the headache would start. It rarely lasted more than an hour but was usually associated with nausea and vomiting.
(SELECT 1 DIAGNOSIS)

I-25. A 29-year-old woman went to the emergency room with complaints of facial pain of new onset. She had stabbing pains on the left side of her face just below her eye. These lasted less than a second at a time, but were so severe that she winced involuntarily with each pain. The pain seemed to be triggered by drinking cold fluids. The only other problems that she had noticed were clumsiness in her right hand and blurred vision in her right eye. Both of these had been present for more than 2 years and did not interfere with her normal activities.
(SELECT 1 DIAGNOSIS)

I-26. A 35-year-old man complained of severe, throbbing pain waking him from sleep at night and persisting into the day. This pain is usually centered about his left eye and appears on a nearly daily basis for several weeks or months each year. It occurs most prominently at night within a few hours of falling asleep and is associated with a striking personality change. This man becomes combative and agitated. He never vomits or develops focal weakness.
(SELECT 1 DIAGNOSIS)

I-27. A 76-year-old man complained of dull, left-sided head pain with some radiation of the discomfort to the right side of the head. He had no nausea or vomiting with the pain, but had lost 10 pounds over the previous 2 months. His erythrocyte sedimentation rate was 102 mm/h, and he was mildly anemic. An extensive investigation for malignancy revealed no signs of lymphoma, carcinoma, or leukemia.
(SELECT 1 DIAGNOSIS)

I-28. An 81-year-old man with chronic lymphocytic leukemia developed pain and burning over the right side of his face. Within a few days, he developed a vesiculopapular rash in the distribution of the first division of the trigeminal nerve. The vesicles became encrusted and the burning associated with the rash abated. Within a month the rash had largely resolved, but he was left with a dull ache over the area of the rash that was periodically punctuated by shooting pains. Imipramine 100 mg nightly helped reduce the intensity of the chronic pain.
(SELECT 1 DIAGNOSIS)

1-29. A very concerned mother brings a 2-year-old child to your office. You have been following this child in your practice since birth and know that the child is a product of a normal pregnancy and delivery, has been growing and developing normally, and has no acute medical problems. The mother relates that the first episode in question occurred immediately after the mother refused to give the child some juice. The episode consisted of a brief, shrill cry followed by a prolonged expiration and apnea. The child became cyanotic and unconscious and had generalized clonic jerks. A few moments later the child awakened and had no residual effects. A second episode of identical nature occurred at the grocery store when the father of the child refused to purchase a toy for the child. Your physical examination reveals a totally delightful and normal child. The most likely diagnosis in this case is

(A) seizure disorder
(B) drug ingestion
(C) hyperactivity with attention deficit
(D) pervasive development disorder
(E) breath-holding spell

1-30. A 25-year-old woman presents to the emergency room complaining of redness and pain in the right foot up to the level of the mid-calf. She reports that her right leg has been swollen for at least 15 years, but her left leg has been normal. On physical examination she has a temperature of 39°C (102.2°F). Her left leg is normal. The right leg is not tender, but it is swollen from the inguinal ligament down and she has an obvious cellulitis of her foot. Her underlying problem is

(A) popliteal entrapment syndrome
(B) acute arterial insufficiency
(C) primary lymphedema
(D) deep venous thrombosis
(E) none of the above

1-31. A 50-year-old salesman is on a yacht with a client when he has a severe vomiting and retching spell punctuated by a sharp substernal pain. He arrives in your emergency room 4 h later and has a chest film in which the left descending aorta is outlined by air density. Optimum strategy for his care would be

(A) immediate thoracotomy
(B) serial ECGs and CPKs to rule out myocardial ischemia
(C) left chest tube and spit fistula (cervical esophagostomy)
(D) flexible esophagogastroscopy to establish diagnosis
(E) nasogastric tube, antibiotics, close monitoring

Items I-32 through I-34

A 22-year-old woman is admitted to the hospital because of right-hand anesthesia that developed after an argument with her brother. She is in good spirits and seems unconcerned about her problem. There is no history of physical trauma. The neurologic examination is negative except for reduced sensitivity to pain in a glove-like distribution over the right hand. Her entire family is in attendance and is expressing great concern and attentiveness. She ignores her brother and seems unaware of the chronic jealousy and rivalry described by her family.

I-32. The most likely diagnosis is

(A) body dysmorphic disorder
(B) histrionic personality disorder
(C) parietal brain tumor
(D) conversion disorder
(E) hysteria

I-33. The absence of anxiety in association with her lack of awareness of the psychological conflict with her brother is most likely due to

(A) marginal intellectual function
(B) hypochondriasis
(C) organic mental dysfunction
(D) primary gain
(E) psychosis

I-34. The patient's seeming enjoyment of the attention and concern of her family is most likely due to

(A) primary gain
(B) secondary gain
(C) tertiary gain
(D) indifference reaction
(E) suppression

I-35. A 30-year-old woman with Graves' disease has been started on propylthiouracil. She complains of low-grade fever, chills, and sore throat. The most important initial step in evaluating this patient's fever is

(A) measurement of serum TSH
(B) measurement of serum T_3
(C) CBC
(D) blood cultures
(E) chest x-ray

I-36. A 40-year-old white man complains of weakness, weight loss, and abdominal pain. On examination the patient has diffuse hyperpigmentation and a palpable liver edge. A polyarthritis of wrist and hips is also noted. Fasting blood sugar is 185 mg/dL. The most likely diagnosis is

(A) insulin-dependent diabetes mellitus
(B) pancreatic carcinoma
(C) Addison's disease
(D) hemochromatosis

1-37. A 25-year-old man presents with morning back pain, stiffness and tenderness over the sacroiliac joints, and diminished chest expansion. The most likely diagnosis is

(A) rheumatoid arthritis
(B) ankylosing spondylitis
(C) Sjögren's syndrome
(D) systemic lupus erythematosus

1-38. A 35-year-old woman with a history of type I diabetes mellitus is brought to the emergency room after not taking her routine insulin. The most likely type of respiration that she would be experiencing is

(A) Biot's
(B) severe panting
(C) Kussmaul's
(D) Cheyne-Stokes
(E) periodic

1-39. A 28-year-old previously healthy woman arrives in the emergency room complaining of 24 h of anorexia and nausea and lower abdominal pain that is more intense in the right lower quadrant than elsewhere. On examination she has peritoneal signs of the right lower quadrant and a rectal temperature of 38.3°C (101°F). At exploration through incision of the right lower quadrant, she is found to have a small, contained perforation of a cecal diverticulum. Which of the following statements regarding this situation is true?

(A) Cecal diverticula are acquired disorders
(B) Cecal diverticula are usually multiple
(C) Cecal diverticula are mucosal herniations through the muscularis propria
(D) Diverticulectomy, closure of the cecal defect, and appendectomy may be indicated
(E) An ileocolectomy is indicated even with well-localized inflammation

1-40. A 29-year-old, gravida 3, para 2, black woman in the 33rd week of gestation is admitted to the emergency room because of acute abdominal pain that developed and is increasing during the past 24 h. The pain is severe and is radiating from the epigastrium to the back. She vomited a few times and has not eaten or had a bowel movement since the pain started.

On examination you observe an acutely ill patient lying on the bed with her knees drawn up. Her blood pressure is 150/100 mmHg, her pulse is 110 beats per minute, and her temperature is 38.1°C (100.6°F). On palpation the abdomen is somewhat distended and tender, mainly in the epigastric area, and the uterine fundus reaches 31 cm above the symphysis. Hypotonic bowel sounds are noted. Fetal monitoring reveals a normal pattern of fetal heart rate (FHR) without uterine contractions. On ultrasonography the fetus is in vertex presentation and appropriate in size for gestational age; fetal breathing and trunk movements are noted and the volume of amniotic fluid is normal. The placenta is located on the anterior uterine wall and of grade 2–3.

Laboratory values show mild leukocytosis (12,000 cells/mm^3); a hematocrit of 43; mildly elevated SGOT, SGPT, and bilirubin; and serum amylase of 180 U/dL. Urinalysis is normal.

The most probable diagnosis in this patient is

(A) acute degeneration of uterine leiomyoma
(B) acute cholecystitis
(C) acute pancreatitis
(D) acute appendicitis
(E) severe preeclamptic toxemia

1-41. A 65-year-old man undergoes a technically difficult abdominoperineal resection for a rectal cancer during which he receives three units of packed red blood cells. Four hours later in the intensive care unit he is bleeding heavily from his perineal wound. Emergency coagulation studies reveal normal prothrombin, partial thromboplastin, and bleeding times. The fibrin degradation products are not elevated but the serum fibrinogen content is depressed and the platelet count is 70,000/mm^3. The most likely cause of the bleeding is

(A) delayed blood transfusion reaction
(B) autoimmune fibrinolysis
(C) a bleeding blood vessel in the surgical field
(D) factor VIII deficiency
(E) hypothermic coagulopathy

1-42. A 4-week-old boy presents with a 10-day history of vomiting that has increased in frequency and forcefulness. The vomitus is not bile-stained. The child feeds avidly and looks well, but he has been losing weight. The most likely diagnosis is

(A) pyloric stenosis
(B) small intestinal obstruction
(C) gastroenteritis
(D) intussusception
(E) brain tumor

1-43. A 23-year-old, previously healthy man presents to the emergency room after sustaining a single gunshot wound to the left chest. The entrance wound is 3 cm inferior to the nipple and the exit wound just below the scapula. A chest tube is placed and drains 400 mL of blood and continues to drain 50 to 75 mL/h during the initial resuscitation. Initial blood pressure of 70/0 mmHg responds to 2 L crystalloid and is now 100/70 mmHg. Abdominal examination is unremarkable. Chest x-ray reveals a reexpanded lung and no free air under the diaphragm. The next management step should be

(A) admission and observation
(B) peritoneal lavage
(C) exploratory thoracotomy
(D) exploratory celiotomy
(E) local wound exploration

1-44. A 40-year-old woman undergoes wide excision of a pigmented lesion of her thigh. Pathologic examination reveals malignant melanoma that is Clark's level IV. Findings on examination of the groin are normal. The patient should be advised that

(A) radiotherapy will be an important part of subsequent therapy
(B) the likelihood of groin node metastases is remote
(C) immunotherapy is an effective form of adjunctive treatment for metastatic malignant melanoma
(D) groin dissection is not indicated unless and until groin nodes become palpable
(E) intralesional bacille Calmette-Guérin (BCG) administration has been found to aid in local control in the majority of patients

1-45. A 25-year-old woman is admitted for hypertensive crisis. In the hospital, blood pressure is labile and responds poorly to anti-hypertensive therapy. The patient complains of palpitations and apprehension. Her past medical history shows that she developed hypotension during surgery for appendicitis. The following laboratory values were obtained:

> Hct: 49 percent (n 37–48)
> WBC: 11 × 10³/mm³ (n 4.3–10.8)
> Plasma glucose: 160 mg/dL
>   (n 75–115)
> Plasma calcium: 11 mg/dL
>   (n 9–10.5)

The most likely diagnosis is

(A) pheochromocytoma
(B) renal artery stenosis
(C) essential hypertension
(D) insulin-dependent diabetes mellitus

1-46. A 42-year-old woman presents to the emergency room complaining of abdominal pain. While you are palpating under her right costal margin, she abruptly arrests her inspiration and pulls away because of sharp pain. The most likely diagnosis at this time is

(A) pulmonary embolism
(B) acute pancreatitis
(C) alcoholic cirrhosis
(D) acute gastritis
(E) acute cholecystitis

1-47. A 3-year-old has had a "cold" for 14 days. In the 2 days prior to the visit to your office, she has developed a fever to 39°C (102.2°F), purulent nasal discharge, facial pain, and a daytime cough. Examination of the nose after topical decongestants shows pus in the middle meatus. The most likely diagnosis is

(A) brain abscess
(B) maxillary sinusitis
(C) streptococcal throat infection
(D) frontal sinusitis
(E) middle ear infection

1-48. A 43-year-old woman develops acute renal failure following an emergency resection of a leaking abdominal aortic aneurysm. Three days after surgery, the following laboratory values are obtained:

Serum electrolytes (meq/L): Na^+ 127; K^+ 5.9; Cl^- 92; HCO_3^- 15

Blood urea nitrogen: 82 mg/dL

Serum creatinine: 6.7 mg/dL

The patient has gained 4 kg since surgery and is mildly dyspneic at rest. Eight hours after these data are reported, the electrocardiogram shown below is obtained. The initial treatment for this patient should be

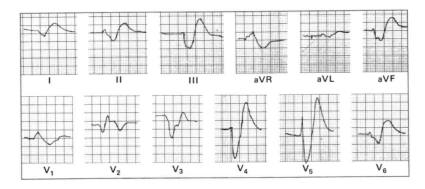

(A) 10% calcium gluconate, 10 mL
(B) digoxin, 0.25 mg every 3 h for three doses
(C) oral Kayexalate
(D) lidocaine, 100 mg
(E) emergent hemodialysis

I-49. A 2-year-old boy is having trouble breathing. The mother states that he has had a cough since he was born, and that this visit for breathing difficulty is one of many. The neonatal history includes that the boy did not defecate for quite some time after delivery. You chart his growth and find that he is in less than the fifth percentile. With this information, what additional test are you going to order?

(A) HIV test
(B) Immunoglobulin electrophoresis
(C) Urine drug screen
(D) Sweat test
(E) Rectal biopsy

I-50. A child has a history of spiking fevers, which have been as high as 40°C (104°F). She has spindle-shaped swelling of finger joints and complains of upper sternal pain. The most likely diagnosis is

(A) rheumatic fever
(B) juvenile rheumatoid arthritis
(C) toxic synovitis
(D) septic arthritis
(E) osteoarthritis

BLOCK 2

**YOU HAVE *60* MINUTES
TO COMPLETE *50* QUESTIONS.**

BLOCK 2

YOU HAVE **60** MINUTES
TO COMPLETE **50** QUESTIONS.

Questions

2-1. A 37-year-old man who works in a fish market presents with a burning pain in his right hand of 1 week's duration. Physical examination reveals a large, violaceous plaque on his finger. Gram stain reveals no organism. The likely diagnosis is

(A) erythrasma
(B) erysipeloid
(C) ecthyma
(D) erysipelas
(E) purpura

2-2. A 23-year-old woman undergoes total thyroidectomy for carcinoma of the thyroid gland. On the second postoperative day, she begins to complain of tingling sensation in her hands. She appears quite anxious and later complains of muscle cramps. Initial therapy should consist of

(A) 10 mL of 10% magnesium sulfate intravenously
(B) oral vitamin D
(C) 100 μg of oral synthroid
(D) continuous infusion of calcium gluconate
(E) oral calcium gluconate

2-3. The most likely diagnosis in a 30-year-old woman with evidence of bilateral injury to the medial longitudinal fasciculus (MLF) is

(A) progressive supranuclear palsy
(B) multiple sclerosis
(C) subacute sclerosing panencephalitis
(D) progressive multifocal leukoencephalopathy
(E) botulism

2-4. A 58-year-old woman complains of the gradual worsening of severe, burning, chest pain that is unilateral and linear in character. Examination reveals a low-grade fever and a tender, reddened band around the right chest. The most likely diagnosis is

(A) pericarditis
(B) rheumatoid lung disease
(C) contact dermatitis
(D) rib fracture
(E) shingles

2-5. A 40-year-old man presents for an annual physical examination. He has not been seen by a physician for 10 years and presently has no complaints. Which of the following tests is indicated regardless of history and findings on physical examination?

(A) Serum cholesterol
(B) Lipoprotein electrophoresis
(C) Electrocardiogram
(D) Serum electrolytes

2-6. As an epidemiological investigation officer for the Centers for Disease Control and Prevention, you are contacted by a local health department. They inform you that a large number of persons have acquired mild symptoms of influenza despite being vaccinated for the appropriate strain being cultured. You find that the cultured strain is the same as that incorporated into the trivalent vaccine administered throughout the world. You also note that the strain had a high case fatality rate in previous epidemics in China, where most new strains are isolated and identified for vaccine preparations. The most likely explanation for the outbreak noted by the local health department is

(A) vaccine failure
(B) antigenic drift
(C) antigenic shift
(D) herd immunity
(E) incomplete immunity from previous rhinovirus infections

2-7. A 28-year-old female reports that she has become depressed with the onset of winter every year for the past 6 years. A diagnosis of major depressive disorder with seasonal pattern is made. It is likely that the patient would have a trial of treatment with

(A) phototherapy
(B) biofeedback
(C) electroconvulsive therapy
(D) benzodiazepines
(E) steroid medication

2-8. A previously healthy 2-year-old black child has developed a chronic cough over the previous 6 weeks. He has been seen in different emergency rooms on two occasions during this period and placed on antibiotics for pneumonia. Upon auscultation you hear normal breath sounds on the left. On the right side, you hear decreased air movement during inspiration but none upon expiration. The routine chest radiograph shows no infiltrate, but the heart is shifted slightly to the left. The appropriate next step in making the diagnosis in this patient is to

(A) measure the patient's sweat chloride
(B) obtain inspiratory and expiratory chest radiographs
(C) prescribe broad-spectrum oral antibiotics
(D) initiate a trial of inhaled beta-agonists
(E) prescribe appropriate doses of oral prednisone

2-9. On physical examination of a 3-month-old child you detect a thrill and a machinery-type murmur at the left upper sternal border. A widened systemic pulse pressure and bounding peripheral pulses are also noted. Based on these findings the most probable diagnosis is

(A) familial hypercholesterolemia
(B) patent ductus arteriosus
(C) tetralogy of Fallot
(D) Marfan's syndrome
(E) aortic stenosis

2-10. A 55-year-old diabetic woman suddenly develops weakness of the left side of her face as well as of her right arm and leg. She also has diplopia on left lateral gaze. The responsible lesion is probably located in the

(A) right cerebral hemisphere
(B) left cerebral hemisphere
(C) right side of the brainstem
(D) left side of the brainstem
(E) right medial longitudinal fasciculus

2-11. A 16-year-old boy is hospitalized on the adolescent ward of a mental hospital. He consistently avoids bathing and personal hygiene and is resistant to changing his behavior. A system is established wherein the patient earns "points" for accomplishing various aspects of personal hygiene. Points can be redeemed at the snack shop, or they can "purchase" extra activity passes. This is an example of a treatment method called

(A) token economy
(B) social skills training
(C) authoritarian psychotherapy
(D) self-psychology
(E) cognitive remediation

2-12. A previously healthy 8-year-old boy has a 3-week history of low-grade fever of unknown source, fatigue, weight loss, myalgia, headaches, and other nonspecific symptoms. Results have been normal on repeated examinations during this period, but now he has developed a heart murmur, petechiae, and mild splenomegaly. The most likely diagnosis is

(A) rheumatic fever
(B) Kawasaki disease
(C) scarlet fever
(D) endocarditis
(E) tuberculosis

Items 2-13 through 2-16

Select the appropriate surgical procedure for each patient.

(A) Vagotomy and antrectomy
(B) Antrectomy alone
(C) Vagotomy and pyloroplasty
(D) Vagotomy and gastrojejunostomy
(E) Proximal gastric vagotomy

2-13. A 72-year-old patient with an intractable type I ulcer along the incisura with a significant amount of scarring along the entire length of the lesser curvature
(SELECT 1 PROCEDURE)

2-14. A 46-year-old patient with gastric outlet obstruction secondary to ulcer disease and severe inflammation around the pylorus and first and second portions of the duodenum
(SELECT 1 PROCEDURE)

2-15. A 90-year-old patient with a bleeding duodenal ulcer
(SELECT 1 PROCEDURE)

2-16. A 36-year-old patient with a type III (pyloric) ulcer that is refractory to medical treatment
(SELECT 1 PROCEDURE)

2-17. An obese 50-year-old woman undergoes a laparoscopic cholecystectomy. In the recovery room she is found to be hypotensive and tachycardic. Her arterial blood gases reveal a pH of 7.29, partial pressure of oxygen is 60 torr, and the partial pressure of CO_2 is 54 torr. The most likely cause of this woman's problem is

(A) acute pulmonary embolism
(B) CO_2 absorption from induced pneumoperitoneum
(C) alveolar hypoventilation
(D) pulmonary edema
(E) atelectasis from high diaphragm

Items 2-18 through 2-21

A 22-year-old, male abuser of intravenous heroin complained of severe headache while having sexual intercourse. Within a few minutes of that complaint, he developed right-sided weakness and became stuporous. His neurologic examination revealed neck stiffness, as well as right arm and face weakness. An unenhanced, emergency CT scan revealed a lesion of 3 to 4 cm in the cortex of the left parietal lobe. The addition of contrast enhancement revealed two other smaller lesions in the right frontal lobe but did not alter the appearance of the lesion in the left parietal lobe.

2-18. The diagnostic study most likely to establish the basis for his neurologic deficits is

(A) HIV antibody testing
(B) cerebrospinal fluid (CSF) examination
(C) electroencephalography
(D) nerve conduction studies
(E) cardiac catheterization

2-19. His HIV antigen test is positive, but he has no depression of his CD4 (helper) T-lymphocyte count. His nerve conduction studies reveal generalized slowing in the legs and his EEG exhibits depressed voltage over the left parietal lobe. Cardiac catheterization suggested aortic valve disease, and his CSF is xanthochromic (yellow). The probable site of injury in the CNS is

(A) an arterial wall
(B) the ventricular endothelium
(C) the pia arachnoid
(D) the dura mater
(E) the perivenular space

2-20. Within a day of admission, the right-sided weakness began to abate and within a week it completely resolved. The CT scan was unchanged from that obtained on admission, despite the rapidly improving clinical picture. The focal weakness was most likely attributable to

(A) a spontaneously resolving encephalitis
(B) thrombolysis in the left middle cerebral artery
(C) remission of vasospasm
(D) diuresis of cerebral edema
(E) spontaneous abscess drainage

2-21. On the fourth day of hospitalization, the patient abruptly lost consciousness and exhibited clonic movements starting on his right side and generalizing to his left side. The movements stopped within 3 min, but he had residual right-sided weakness for half an hour. The most appropriate treatment to institute involves

(A) heparin
(B) recombinant tissue plasminogen activator (r-tPA)
(C) urokinase
(D) phenytoin
(E) warfarin

2-22. A tine test administered at a routine visit of a 2½-year-old boy is positive. The child is asymptomatic and thriving. Your initial course of action would be to

(A) admit the child and perform a workup for tuberculosis
(B) start the child on isoniazid
(C) repeat the tine test
(D) screen all contacts with a tuberculin test and x-ray
(E) administer a Mantoux test

2-23. A 15-year-old boy complains of worsening scrotal pain. On palpation you find a pea-sized, tender mass at the upper pole of the testis. With transillumination it appears as a "blue dot." The most likely diagnosis is

(A) testicular torsion
(B) epididymitis
(C) hernia with hydrocele
(D) appendix testis torsion
(E) orchitis with hydrocele

2-24. A 65-year-old man with diabetes mellitus, bronzed skin, and cirrhosis of the liver is being treated for hemochromatosis previously confirmed by liver biopsy. The patient experiences increasing pain of the right upper quadrant, and his serum alkaline phosphatase is now elevated. There is a weight loss of 15 pounds. The next step in management would be to

(A) increase frequency of phlebotomy for worsening hemochromatosis
(B) obtain a CT scan to rule out hepatoma
(C) obtain hepatitis B serology
(D) obtain antimitochondrial antibody to rule out primary biliary cirrhosis

2-25. A 6-year-old child is brought to the emergency room by her parents on a Friday night because they are concerned about rabies. A bat was present in the child's bedroom when they arrived at their country home that evening. It started flying around the head of the girl when she entered her room and it ruffled her hair. The parents heard her scream, ran up to her room, and shooed the bat out the window. Upon examination, there is no visible bite or scratch marks. Which is the most appropriate intervention?

(A) Reassure the parents that there is no risk of rabies given the history and examination
(B) Consult public health authorities to determine the epidemiology of rabies in that area
(C) Administer rabies vaccine and immunoglobulin
(D) Administer rabies immunoglobulin only
(E) Administer rabies vaccine only

YOU SHOULD HAVE COMPLETED APPROXIMATELY
25 QUESTIONS AND HAVE 30 MINUTES REMAINING.

2-26. A 35-year-old woman appears for psychiatric consultation and demands that her husband be present during the interview. He complains that he has trouble doing anything by himself because of her clinging. She at times idolizes him and, at other times, denounces him as worthless. She has a history of impulsivity with respect to spending and sexuality, and there is a conviction for reckless driving. She acknowledges chronic feelings of emptiness, fits of anger and rage when her husband "abandons" her, and lability of mood. The most likely diagnosis is

(A) borderline personality disorder
(B) narcissistic personality disorder
(C) paranoid personality disorder
(D) antisocial personality disorder
(E) dependent personality

2-27. A psychiatrist is traveling in Southeast Asia and is asked to consult on a young Chinese man who is terrified that his penis is shrinking and may recede into his abdomen and is convinced that this will result in death. He is certain that his condition has been caused by excessive masturbation. The most likely diagnosis is

(A) schizophrenia
(B) major depressive episode
(C) substance abuse
(D) koro
(E) amok

2-28. A 3-year-old boy's parents complain that their child has difficulty walking. The child rolled, sat, and first stood at essentially normal ages and first walked at 13 months of age. The family has noticed over the past several months an increased inward curvature of the lower spine as he walks and that his gait has become more "waddling" in nature. On examination you confirm these later findings and also notice that he has enlargement of his calves. This child most likely has

(A) occult spina bifida
(B) muscular dystrophy
(C) brain tumor
(D) Guillain-Barré syndrome
(E) botulism

Items 2-29 through 2-30

A 45-year-old woman is explored for a perforated duodenal ulcer 6 h after onset of symptoms. She has a history of chronic peptic ulcer disease treated medically with minimal symptoms.

2-29. The procedure of choice is

(A) simple closure with omental patch
(B) truncal vagotomy and pyloroplasty
(C) antrectomy and truncal vagotomy
(D) highly selective vagotomy
(E) hemigastrectomy

2-30. Six weeks after surgery, the patient returns complaining of postprandial weakness, sweating, light-headedness, crampy abdominal pain, and diarrhea. The best management would be

(A) antispasmodic medications (e.g., Lomotil)
(B) dietary advice and counseling that symptoms will probably abate within 3 months of surgery
(C) dietary advice and counseling that symptoms will probably not abate but are not dangerous
(D) workup for neuroendocrine tumor (e.g., carcinoid)
(E) preparation for revision to Roux-en-Y gastrojejunostomy

2-31. A pregnancy of approximately 10 weeks' gestation is confirmed in a 30-year-old woman (gravida 5, para 4) with an IUD in place. The patient expresses a strong desire for the pregnancy to be continued. On examination the strings of the IUD are protruding from the cervical os. The most appropriate course of action would be to

(A) leave the IUD in place without any other treatment
(B) leave the IUD in place and continue prophylactic antibiotics throughout pregnancy
(C) remove the IUD immediately
(D) terminate the pregnancy because of the near certain risk of infection, abortion, or both
(E) perform laparoscopy to rule out an ectopic pregnancy

2-32. While examining the male genitalia, you are unable to retract the foreskin of an uncircumcised patient. There is no evidence of erythema. This condition is known as

(A) balanitis
(B) phimosis
(C) escutcheon
(D) smegma
(E) priapism

2-33. While auscultating a patient's abdomen, the examiner hears a systolic bruit in the midepigastric area. It occurs at a fixed interval after the impulse palpated at the cardiac apex. The most likely source of this bruit is

(A) the hepatic artery
(B) the splenic artery
(C) the abdominal aorta
(D) one of the renal arteries
(E) a transmitted heart murmur

2-34. A 55-year-old woman who has a history of severe depression and who had radical mastectomy for carcinoma of the breast 1 year previously develops polyuria, nocturia, and excessive thirst. Laboratory values are as follows:

Serum electrolytes (meq/L):
    Na^+ 149; K^+ 3.6
Serum calcium: 9.5 mg/dL
Blood glucose: 110 mg/dL
BUN: 30 mg/dL
Urine osmolality: 150
    mOsm/kg

The most likely diagnosis is

(A) psychogenic polydipsia
(B) renal glycosuria
(C) hypercalciuria
(D) diabetes insipidus
(E) inappropriate antidiuretic hormone syndrome (IADHS)

Items 2-35 through 2-36

An 18-year-old male complains of fever and transient pain in both knees and elbows. The right knee was red and swollen for 1 day the week prior to presentation. On physical examination, the patient has a low-grade fever but appears generally well. There is an aortic diastolic murmur heard at the base of the heart. A nodule is palpated over the extensor tendon of the hand. There are pink, erythematous lesions over the abdomen, some with central clearing. The following laboratory values are obtained:

Hct: 42
WBC: 12,000/mm^3
Polymorphonuclear leukocytes: 20 percent
Lymphocytes: 80 percent
ESR: 60 mm/h

The patient's ECG is shown on the following page.

2-35. Which of the following tests is most critical to diagnosis?

(A) Blood cultures
(B) Antistreptolysin O antibody
(C) Echocardiogram
(D) Antinuclear antibodies
(E) Creatinine phosphokinase

2-36. Based on the data available, the best approach to therapy would be

(A) ceftriaxone
(B) corticosteroids
(C) acetaminophen
(D) penicillin plus streptomycin
(E) ketoconazole

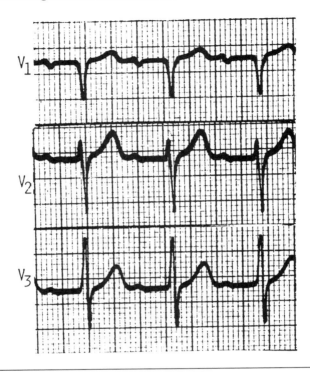

2-37. A 5-year-old boy comes to the emergency department at midnight with a complaint of severe scrotal pain since 7 P.M. There is no history of trauma. Your first step is to

(A) call an appropriate surgeon immediately
(B) order a radioisotope scan as an emergency
(C) order a urinalysis and Gram's stain for bacteria
(D) arrange for an ultrasound examination
(E) order a Doppler examination

2-38. A full-term newborn infant is having episodes of cyanosis and apnea, which are worse when he is attempting to feed, but he seems better when he is crying. The most important diagnosis to establish quickly is

(A) ventricular septal defect
(B) Ondine's curse (primary alveolar hypoventilation syndrome)
(C) choanal atresia
(D) sickle cell anemia
(E) floppy palate syndrome

2-39. A 40-year-old woman is found to have a 1- to 2-cm, slightly tender cystic mass in her breast; she has no perceptible axillary adenopathy. What course would you follow?

(A) Reassurance and reexamination in the immediate postmenstrual period
(B) Immediate excisional biopsy
(C) Aspiration of the mass with cytologic analysis
(D) Fluoroscopically guided needle localization biopsy
(E) Mammography and reevaluation of options with new information

2-40. A 2-year-old boy is brought into the emergency room with a complaint of fever for 6 days and development of a limp. On examination he is found to have an erythematous macular exanthem over his body, ocular conjunctivitis, dry and cracked lips, a red throat, and cervical lymphadenopathy. The skin around his nails is peeling. There is a grade II/VI vibratory systolic ejection murmur at the lower left sternal border. He refuses to bear weight on his left leg. A white blood cell count and differential show predominant neutrophils with increased platelets on smear. The most likely diagnosis is

(A) scarlet fever
(B) rheumatic fever
(C) Kawasaki disease
(D) juvenile rheumatoid arthritis
(E) infectious mononucleosis

2-41. A 30-year-old man is stabbed in the arm. There is no evidence of vascular injury, but he cannot flex his three radial digits. He has injured the

(A) flexor pollicis longus and flexor digitus medius tendons
(B) radial nerve
(C) median nerve
(D) thenar and digital nerves at the wrist
(E) ulnar nerve

2-42. A 27-year-old woman seeks evaluation for her "depression" in an outpatient clinic. She reports episodic feelings of sadness since adolescence. Occasionally she feels good, but these periods seldom last more than 2 weeks. She is able to work but thinks she is not doing as well as she should. In describing her problems, she seems to focus more on repeated disappointments in her life and her low opinion of herself than on discrete depressive symptoms. In your differential diagnosis at this point, the most likely diagnosis is

(A) major depression with melancholia
(B) adjustment disorder with depressed mood
(C) cyclothymia
(D) childhood depression
(E) dysthymia

2-43. A man was stabbed and arrived at the emergency room within 30 min. You notice that the trachea is deviated away from the side of the chest that suffered the puncture. Which of the following would you find upon physical examination of the traumatized side?

(A) Increased fremitus
(B) Increased breath sounds
(C) Dullness to percussion
(D) Hyperresonant percussion
(E) Wheezing and stridor

2-44. A 22-year-old man sustains a gunshot wound to the abdomen. At exploration, an apparently solitary distal small-bowel injury is treated with resection and primary anastomosis. On postoperative day 7, he drains small-bowel fluid through his operative incision. The fascia remains intact. The fistula output is 300 mL/day and there is no evidence of intraabdominal sepsis. Correct treatment includes

(A) early reoperation to close the fistula tract
(B) broad-spectrum antibiotics
(C) total parenteral nutrition
(D) somatostatin to lower fistula output
(E) loperamide to inhibit gut motility

2-45. A 6-year-old boy presents to your office with a history of neck stiffness following an upper respiratory infection. On examination you note that the patient's head is leaning toward the left shoulder and slightly rotated. The most likely diagnosis is

(A) acute meningitis
(B) thoracic spinal deformity
(C) torticollis
(D) scoliosis
(E) goiter

2-46. Five days after an uneventful cholecystectomy, an asymptomatic middle-aged woman is found to have a serum sodium level of 120 meq/L. Proper management would be

(A) administration of hypertonic saline solution
(B) restriction of free water
(C) plasma ultrafiltration
(D) hemodialysis
(E) observation

2-47. A 15-year-old boy presents with complaints of pain in the left hip. The pain has been present for approximately 3 weeks and is increasing in severity. It is worse at night and is relieved by aspirin. There is no history of trauma or previous hip problems. This history is most consistent with

(A) osteoarthritis
(B) septic joint
(C) osteoid osteoma
(D) avascular necrosis
(E) muscle strain

2-48. A 34-year-old black woman presents to your office with symptoms of cough, dyspnea, and lymphadenopathy. Physical examination shows cervical adenopathy and hepatomegaly. Her chest radiograph is shown in the figure below. How would you pursue diagnosis?

(A) Open lung biopsy
(B) Liver biopsy
(C) Bronchoscopy and transbronchial lung biopsy
(D) Scalene node biopsy
(E) Serum angiotensin-converting enzyme (ACE) level

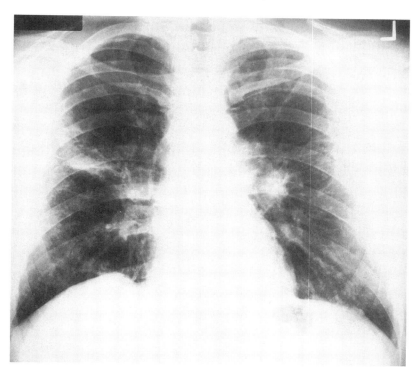

2-49. A 7-year-old girl hospitalized for a tonsillectomy awakens and cries out in fright that a "big bear" is in her room. She is relieved when a nurse, responding to her cry, enters the room and turns on the light, revealing the bear to be an armchair covered with a coat. This experience would be an example of

(A) a delusion
(B) a hallucination
(C) an illusion
(D) deja vu
(E) dissociative reaction

2-50. A 30-year-old male patient has complained of fever and sore throat for several days. The patient presents to you today with additional complaints of hoarseness, difficulty breathing, and drooling. On examination, the patient is febrile and has inspiratory wheezes. Which of the following would be the best course of action?

(A) Begin outpatient treatment with ampicillin
(B) Culture throat for beta-hemolytic streptococci
(C) Admit to intensive care unit and obtain otolaryngologic consultation
(D) Schedule for chest x-ray

BLOCK 3

YOU HAVE **60** MINUTES
TO COMPLETE **50** QUESTIONS.

BLOCK 3

YOU HAVE **60** MINUTES
TO COMPLETE **50** QUESTIONS.

Questions

3-1. A 23-year-old woman (gravida 2, para 2) calls her physician 7 days post partum because she is concerned that she is still bleeding from the vagina. It would be appropriate to tell this woman that it is normal for bloody lochia to last up to

(A) 2 days
(B) 5 days
(C) 8 days
(D) 11 days
(E) 14 days

3-2. A 60-year-old man presents with a history of stomping his feet as he walks. The patient also has noticed that he continually hits things with his feet accidentally. Physical examination reveals loss of vibratory and position sense without loss of pain or temperature perception. The most likely diagnosis is

(A) lesion of the medulla
(B) anterior spinal artery syndrome
(C) posterior column syndrome
(D) lesion of the thalamic nucleus ventralis posterolateralis
(E) syringomyelic syndrome

3-3. A healthy 6-year-old girl has been referred because a reducing substance was found in her urine during a routine examination. Physical examination and the results of glucose tolerance testing are normal; her urine reacts with Clinitest tablets but not with Clinistix. The most likely diagnosis is

(A) diabetes mellitus
(B) renal glycosuria
(C) hereditary fructose intolerance
(D) essential fructosuria
(E) deficiency of fructose-1,6-diphosphatase activity

3-4. A 55-year-old man with recent onset of atrial fibrillation presents with a cold, pulseless left lower extremity. He complains of left leg paresthesia and is unable to dorsiflex his toes. Following a successful popliteal embolectomy, with restoration of palpable pedal pulses, he is still unable to dorsiflex his toes. The next step in his management should be

(A) electromyography (EMG)
(B) measurement of anterior compartment pressure
(C) elevation of the left leg
(D) immediate fasciotomy
(E) application of a posterior splint

3-5. A heavy cigarette smoker is determined to quit and asks for your assistance. He has attempted to quit on his own on several occasions but has been unsuccessful. The most effective approach to management of this patient would be to

(A) set up a behavioral modification program
(B) prescribe nicotine gum or patch
(C) set up behavioral program and prescribe nicotine gum or patch
(D) encourage patient to just stop smoking

3-6. A 66-year-old patient presents to you with a complaint of a swelling in the neck. Upon examination you note a 2-cm hard, firm nodule in the posterior triangle of the left side of the neck. Which of the following would you do next?

(A) Examine the lung fields
(B) Examine the oral cavity
(C) Perform a Weber test
(D) Perform a visual acuity test
(E) Reassure the patient that the mass will go away

3-7. A 9-month-old infant accidentally ingests an unknown quantity of digitalis. The most important noncardiac manifestation of toxicity in this infant is

(A) fever
(B) dizziness
(C) vomiting
(D) visual disturbances
(E) urticaria

3-8. A 20-year-old woman presents with a 2-week history of 1- to 3-cm areas of scaly plaques on the knees and trunk. They are noted to be pruritic, and upon examination, there are erythematous lesions with small bleeding points when scraped (Auspitz's sign). The patient is suffering from

(A) Kaposi's sarcoma
(B) pemphigus
(C) psoriasis
(D) systemic lupus erythematosus (SLE)
(E) hairy leukoplakia

Items 3-9 through 3-10

An 18-year-old high school football player is kicked in the left flank. Three hours later he develops hematuria. His vital signs are stable.

3-9. Initial diagnostic tests in the emergency room should include which of the following?

(A) Retrograde urethrography
(B) Retrograde cystography
(C) Arteriography
(D) High-dose infusion urography
(E) Diagnostic peritoneal lavage

3-10. The diagnostic tests performed reveal extravasation of contrast into the renal parenchyma. Treatment should consist of

(A) resumption of normal daily activity excluding sports
(B) exploration and suture of laceration
(C) exploration and wedge resection of left kidney
(D) nephrostomy
(E) antibiotics and serial monitoring of blood count and vital signs

3-11. A 33-year-old fair-skinned woman has telangiectasias of the cheeks and nose along with red papules and occasional pustules. She also appears to have a conjunctivitis because of dilated scleral vessels. She reports frequent flushing and blushing. Drinking red wine produces a severe flushing of the face. There is a family history of this condition. The diagnosis is

(A) carcinoid syndrome
(B) porphyria cutanea tarda
(C) lupus vulgaris
(D) acne rosacea
(E) seborrheic dermatitis

3-12. The workup of this patient is most likely to show

(A) acellular spinal fluid with high protein
(B) abnormal electromyogram (EMG) that shows axonal degeneration
(C) positive Tensilon test
(D) elevated creatine phosphokinase (CPK)
(E) respiratory alkalosis by arterial blood gases

Items 3-13 through 3-16

A 55-year-old man presents with the chief complaint of feelings of helplessness, hopelessness, loss of interest, and poor sleep for the past 3 weeks. He is about 25 pounds overweight, smokes a pack of cigarettes a day, and has multiple physical complaints. He was fired from his job of 20 years 6 weeks ago. One month ago it was discovered that he has hypertension, and he was started on antihypertensive medication.

3-13. The patient's differential diagnosis should include all the following EXCEPT

(A) dysthymia
(B) adjustment disorder with depressed mood
(C) major depressive disorder
(D) mood disorder due to medical condition or treatment
(E) substance abuse

3-14. If this patient began complaining of impotence for the first time, the most likely cause would be

(A) disorder of core gender identity
(B) drug effect
(C) primary impotence
(D) penile steal syndrome
(E) dementia

3-15. If psychopharmacological intervention was prescribed for his symptoms, the most likely medication would be

(A) fluoxetine
(B) phenobarbital
(C) lithium
(D) buspirone
(E) phenytoin

3-16. It is unlikely that the patient's mood changes are secondary to schizophrenia, which is characterized by all the following EXCEPT

(A) the dysphoric mood is usually apathetic or empty
(B) there is a more gradual onset
(C) hallucinations and delusions are constant
(D) there is often more deterioration of general functioning
(E) psychotic symptoms tend to persist after mood symptoms remit

3-17. You are asked to evaluate a patient in the emergency room. He was brought by the rescue squad in a comatose state. Serum electrolytes drawn on admission show the following: Na^+ 133 meq/L, K^+ 8.0 meq/L, Cl^+ 98 meq/L, HCO_3^+ 13 meq/L. An electrocardiogram shows a rhythm with absence of P waves, a widened QRS complex, and peaked T waves. Which would be the most appropriate initial step?

(A) Repeat electrolyte measurements and observe
(B) Attempt cardioversion
(C) Administer intravenous calcium gluconate
(D) Administer hydrochlorothiazide, 25 mg orally
(E) Administer intravenous potassium chloride, 20 meq over 1 h

3-18. A 71-year-old woman with a history of coronary artery disease presents to her family physician for a routine check-up. The physician notices that she has lost 20 pounds since her last visit 6 months ago. When questioned, she gives a history of intermittent periumbilical pain that always begins about 30 min after eating and lasts about 2 h. She claims that the pain is worse after large meals and so she has begun to eat less out of fear of the pain. The most likely diagnosis is

(A) pancreatitis
(B) cholecystitis
(C) small bowel obstruction
(D) intestinal ischemia
(E) peptic ulcer disease

3-19. A 15-year-old high school boy sustained an abrasion of the knee after a fall while roller blading in the school yard. School records reveal that his last DPT booster was at age 6. In this situation, which of the following is appropriate?

(A) Tetanus toxoid
(B) Adult tetanus and diphtheria toxoid (Td)
(C) DPT booster
(D) Tetanus toxoid and tetanus immune globulin
(E) No immunization

3-20. A 14-year-old girl awakens with a mild sore throat, low-grade fever, and a diffuse maculopapular rash. During the next 24 h she develops tender swelling of her wrists and redness of her eyes. In addition, her physician notes mild tenderness and marked swelling of her posterior cervical and occipital lymph nodes. Four days after the onset of her illness the rash has vanished. The most likely diagnosis of this girl's condition is

(A) rubella
(B) rubeola
(C) roseola
(D) erythema infectiosum
(E) erythema multiforme

Items 3-21 through 3-25

For each clinical description select the appropriate stage of breast cancer.

(A) Stage I
(B) Stage II
(C) Stage III
(D) Stage IV
(E) Inflammatory carcinoma

3-21. Tumor not palpable, clinically positive lymph nodes fixed to one another, no evidence of metastases
(SELECT 1 STAGE)

3-22. Tumor 5.0 cm; clinically positive, movable ipsilateral lymph nodes; no evidence of metastases
(SELECT 1 STAGE)

3-23. Tumor 2.1 cm, clinically negative lymph nodes, no evidence of metastases
(SELECT 1 STAGE)

3-24. Tumor not palpable but breast diffusely enlarged and erythematous, clinically positive supraclavicular nodes, and evidence of metastases
(SELECT 1 STAGE)

3-25. Tumor 0.5 cm, clinically negative lymph nodes, pathological rib fracture
(SELECT 1 STAGE)

YOU SHOULD HAVE COMPLETED APPROXIMATELY
25 QUESTIONS AND HAVE 30 MINUTES REMAINING.

3-26. A 30-year-old man is evaluated for a thyroid nodule. The patient reports that his father died from "thyroid cancer" and that a brother had a history of recurrent renal stones. Blood calcitonin concentration is 2000 pg/mL (normal: less than 100); serum calcium and phosphate levels are normal. Before referring the patient to a surgeon, the physician should

(A) obtain a liver scan
(B) perform a calcium infusion test
(C) measure urinary catecholamines
(D) administer suppressive doses of thyroxine and measure levels of thyroid-stimulating hormone
(E) treat the patient with radioactive iodine

3-27. A 9-year-old girl with papilledema and precocious puberty is most likely to have

(A) a pineal region tumor
(B) an oligodendroglioma
(C) a Kernohan class II astrocytoma
(D) a brainstem glioma
(E) an ependymoma

3-28. A 16-year-old patient presents to the emergency room with extreme penile pain. The ER physician notes that this uncircumcised patient has his foreskin retracted and that his glans penis is enlarged and bluish in color. The patient suffers extreme pain when the physician attempts to reposition the foreskin. The most likely diagnosis is

(A) hypospadias
(B) balanitis
(C) priapism
(D) paraphimosis
(E) phimosis

3-29. Following blunt abdominal trauma, a 12-year-old girl develops upper abdominal pain, nausea, and vomiting. An upper gastrointestinal series reveals a total obstruction of the duodenum with a "coiled spring" appearance in the second and third portions. Appropriate management is

(A) gastrojejunostomy
(B) nasogastric suction and observation
(C) duodenal resection
(D) TPN to increase size of retroperitoneal fat pad
(E) duodenojejunostomy

3-30. Two weeks after a viral syndrome a 9-year-old girl presents to your clinic with a complaint of several days of drooping of her mouth. In addition to the drooping of her mouth on the left side, you note that she is unable to shut completely her left eye. Her smile is asymmetric, but her examination is otherwise normal. This girl likely has

(A) Guillain-Barré syndrome
(B) botulism
(C) cerebral vascular accident
(D) brainstem tumor
(E) Bell's palsy

3-31. A patient is found to have an unexpectedly high value for diffusing capacity. This finding is consistent with which of the following disorders?

(A) Anemia
(B) Cystic fibrosis
(C) Emphysema
(D) Intrapulmonary hemorrhage
(E) Pulmonary emboli

3-32. You are a physician in charge of the patients that reside in a nursing home. Several of the patients have developed influenza-like symptoms, and the community is in the midst of an influenza A outbreak. None of the nursing home residents have received the influenza vaccine. What course of action would be most appropriate?

(A) Give the influenza vaccine to all residents of the nursing home who do not have a contraindication to the vaccine (allergy to eggs)
(B) Give the influenza vaccine to all residents of the nursing home who do not have a contraindication to the vaccine and also give amantadine for a 2-week period
(C) Give amantadine alone to all nursing home residents
(D) Do not give any prophylactic regimen

3-33. A 30-year-old man took a can of beer out of his refrigerator at the end of the day and rapidly swallowed a mouthful of its contents before he realized that it was not beer. Within a few minutes he developed severe abdominal cramps, blurred vision, twitching, and loss of consciousness. His wife notified emergency medical personnel that she had placed some roach spray in the beer can for storage and had left it in the refrigerator to deal with roaches that were nesting there. She claimed that she had forgotten to advise her husband. Emergency personnel checked the insecticide brand and determined that it was an organophosphate. To counteract the cholinesterase inhibiting activity of the organophosphate poison, this man should receive

(A) methacholine
(B) pyridostigmine
(C) physostigmine
(D) edrophonium
(E) atropine

3-34. A 60-year-old man involved in an automobile accident suffered multiple long-bone fractures and injury to the pelvis. Two days following his admission, he was febrile with sinus tachycardia, axillary and conjunctival petechiae, and a P_{O_2} of 64 mmHg. Your working diagnosis is

(A) gram-negative sepsis with ARDS
(B) fat embolism syndrome
(C) lower lobe pneumonia
(D) acute exacerbation of COPD
(E) anemia

Items 3-35 through 3-36

A 68-year-old hypertensive man underwent successful repair of a ruptured abdominal aortic aneurysm. He received 9 L Ringer's lactate solution and 4 units of whole blood during the operation. Two hours after transfer to the surgical intensive care unit, the following hemodynamic parameters are obtained:

Systemic blood pressure (BP): 90/60 mmHg

Pulse rate: 110 beats per minute

Central venous pressure (CVP): 7 mmHg

Pulmonary artery pressure: 28/10

Pulmonary capillary wedge pressure: 8 mmHg

Cardiac output: 1.9 L/min

Systemic vascular resistance: 35 Woods units (normal 24 to 30 Woods units)

Pa_{O_2}: 140 torr (F_{IO_2} 0.45)

Urine output: 15 mL/h (specific gravity 1.029)

Hematocrit: 35 percent

3-35. Proper management would now call for

(A) administration of a diuretic to increase urine output

(B) administration of a vasopressor agent to increase the systemic blood pressure

(C) administration of a fluid challenge to increase the urine output

(D) administration of a vasodiluting agent to decrease the elevated systemic vascular resistance

(E) a period of observation to obtain more data

3-36. The patient then has an improvement in all hemodynamic parameters. However, 6 h later he develops ST-segment depression, and a 12-lead cardiogram shows anterolateral ischemia. New hemodynamic parameters are obtained:

Systemic BP: 70/40 mmHg

Pulse rate: 100 beats per minute

Central venous pressure (CVP): 18 cmH$_2$O

Pulmonary capillary wedge pressure (PCWP): 25 mmHg

Cardiac output: 1.5 L/min

Systemic vascular resistance: 25 Woods units

The single best pharmacologic intervention would be

(A) sublingual nitroglycerin
(B) intravenous nitroglycerin
(C) a short-acting beta blocker
(D) sodium nitroprusside
(E) dobutamine

3-37. A 6-year-old child has a somewhat unsteady but nonspecific gait and is irritable. Physical examination reveals a very mild left facial weakness, brisk stretch reflexes in all four extremities, bilateral extensor plantar responses, and mild hypertonicity of the left upper and lower extremities; there is no muscular weakness. The most likely diagnosis is

(A) pontine glioma
(B) cerebellar astrocytoma
(C) tumor of the right cerebral hemisphere
(D) subacute sclerosing panencephalitis
(E) subacute necrotizing leukoencephalopathy

3-38. A 60-year-old female cigarette smoker complains of fatigue and dyspnea. The most specific evidence for congestive heart failure in this patient would be

(A) ankle edema
(B) wheezes
(C) S_3 gallop
(D) weight gain

3-39. A 62-year-old woman complained of limb discomfort and trouble getting off the toilet. She was unable to climb stairs and noticed a rash on her face about her eyes. On examination she was found to have weakness about the hip and shoulder girdle. Not only did she have a purplish-red discoloration of the skin about the eyes, but she also had erythematous discoloration over the finger joints and purplish nodules over the elbows and knees. Which of the following is the most probable diagnosis?

(A) Systemic lupus erythematosus
(B) Psoriasis
(C) Myasthenia gravis
(D) Dermatomyositis
(E) Rheumatoid arthritis

3-40. A 6-week-old girl is constantly coughing. She is afebrile and began coughing about 10 days ago with increasing regularity. There were no complications during the pregnancy, labor, or delivery. When the infant was 10 days old a mild conjunctivitis developed, which responded successfully to 10 days of topical erythromycin. The respiratory rate is 55 breaths per minute, there are supraclavicular and intercostal retractions, the cough is paroxysmal and staccato in character, and auscultation reveals bilateral rales. Chest roentgenograph shows a diffuse interstitial infiltrate. The most likely diagnosis is

(A) group B streptococcal sepsis
(B) chlamydial pneumonia
(C) pertussis
(D) respiratory syncytial viral pneumonia
(E) aspiration pneumonia

3-41. A 55-year-old man with an 80-pack-year smoking history would most likely have what type of respiratory pattern?

(A) Biot's
(B) Sighing
(C) Cheyne-Stokes
(D) Rapid and shallow
(E) Kussmaul's

3-42. This 40-year-old alcoholic develops cough and fever. Chest x-ray shows an air fluid level in the superior segment of the right lower lobe. The most likely etiologic agent is

(A) *S. pneumoniae*
(B) *H. influenzae*
(C) *Legionella*
(D) An anaerobe

3-43. One of your patients, a 30-year-old businessman, tells you he is planning a trip to the Dominican Republic the following month. Which is the most appropriate intervention for malaria prophylaxis for this patient?

(A) No prophylaxis
(B) Chloroquine
(C) Mefloquine
(D) Doxycycline
(E) Primaquine

3-44. A 65-year-old woman has a life-threatening pulmonary embolus 5 days following removal of a uterine malignancy. She is immediately heparinized and maintained in good therapeutic range for the next 3 days, then passes gross blood from her vagina and develops tachycardia, hypotension, and oliguria. During resuscitation, an abdominal CT scan reveals a major retroperitoneal hematoma. You should now

(A) immediately reverse heparin by a calculated dose of protamine and place a vena cava filter (e.g., a Greenfield filter)
(B) reverse heparin with protamine, explore and evacuate hematoma, and ligate vena cava below the renal veins
(C) switch to low-dose heparin
(D) stop heparin and observe closely
(E) stop heparin, give fresh frozen plasma (FFP), and begin warfarin therapy

3-45. A 50-year-old patient with long-standing chronic obstructive pulmonary disease (COPD) develops the insidious onset of aching in the distal extremities, particularly the wrist bilaterally. There is a 10-pound weight loss. Skin over the wrists is warm and erythematous. There is bilateral clubbing. Plain film is read as "periosteal thickening, possible osteomyelitis." You would

(A) aspirate both wrists
(B) obtain a chest x-ray
(C) start ciprofloxacin
(D) start gold therapy

3-46. A 3-year-old child presents with a petechial rash but is otherwise well and without physical findings. Platelet count is 20,000/mm^3; hemoglobin and WBC count are normal. The most likely diagnosis is

(A) immune thrombocytopenic purpura (ITP)
(B) Henoch-Schönlein purpura
(C) disseminated intravascular coagulopathy (DIC)
(D) acute lymphoblastic leukemia
(E) systemic lupus erythematosus (SLE)

3-47. A 6-month-old infant has eaten a diet with the following content and intake for the past 5 months: protein 4 percent of calories, fat 50 percent of calories, carbohydrates 46 percent of calories, calories 105 per kilogram of body weight per day. The patient's disturbance is

(A) rickets
(B) marasmus
(C) obesity
(D) tetany
(E) kwashiorkor

3-48. A mother brings her 10-year-old son to your office because he lost consciousness the day before while running. She says that he has had similar episodes in the past and that he does not seem to be able to play as long as most of his friends. He has been observed squatting down periodically while in the midst of activity. On physical examination you detect a low-pitched systolic ejection murmur and find that the point of maximal impulse is deviated laterally. The most likely diagnosis is

(A) mitral valve stenosis
(B) aortic stenosis
(C) coarctation of the aorta
(D) aortic insufficiency
(E) patent ductus arteriosus

3-49. A previously healthy 18-month-old has been in a separate room from his family. The family notices the sudden onset of coughing, which resolves over a few minutes. Subsequently, the patient appears to be normal except for increased amounts of drooling and refusal to take foods orally. The most likely explanation for this toddler's condition is

(A) severe gastroesophageal reflux
(B) foreign body in the airway
(C) croup
(D) epiglottitis
(E) foreign body in the esophagus

3-50. During a physical examination for participation in a sport, a 16-year-old girl is noted to have a late apical systolic murmur, which is preceded by a click. The rest of the cardiac examination is normal. She states that her mother also has some type of heart "murmur" but knows nothing else about it. The most likely diagnosis is

(A) atrial septal defect
(B) aortic stenosis
(C) tricuspid regurgitation
(D) mitral valve prolapse
(E) ventricular septal defect

BLOCK 4

**YOU HAVE *60* MINUTES
TO COMPLETE *50* QUESTIONS.**

BLOCK 4

YOU HAVE **60** MINUTES
TO COMPLETE **50** QUESTIONS.

Questions

4-1. A 15-year-old girl is brought to the pediatric emergency room by the lunchroom teacher, who observed her sitting alone and crying. On questioning the teacher learned that the girl had taken five tablets after having had an argument with her mother about a boyfriend of whom the mother disapproved. Toxicology studies are negative and physical examination is normal. The most appropriate course of action would be to

(A) hospitalize the teenager on your adolescent ward

(B) get a psychiatry consultation

(C) get a social service consultation

(D) arrange a family conference that includes the boyfriend

(E) prescribe an antidepressant and arrange for a prompt clinic appointment

4-2. A 10-year-old boy presents to the emergency room with testicular pain of 5 h duration. His pain was of acute onset and woke him from sleep. On physical examination, he is noted to have a high-riding, indurated, and markedly tender left testis. Pain is not diminished by elevation. Urinalysis is unremarkable. Which of the following statements regarding the patient's diagnosis and treatment is true?

(A) There is a strong likelihood that this patient's father or brother has had or will have a similar event
(B) Operation should be delayed until a technetium scan clarifies the diagnosis
(C) The majority of testicles that have undergone torsion can be salvaged if surgery is performed within 24 h
(D) If torsion is found, both testes should undergo orchiopexy
(E) The differential diagnosis includes spermatocele

4-3. A 28-year-old woman presents complaining that she feels tired when chewing food. Further questioning reveals intermittent diplopia. The most likely diagnosis to pursue is

(A) muscular dystrophy
(B) thyrotoxicosis
(C) myasthenia gravis
(D) multiple sclerosis
(E) primary aldosteronism

4-4. A 25-year-old man seeks psychiatric consultation because of anxiety, conflict with his new wife, and a chaotic work history. Examination reveals the presence of an underlying paranoid personality. Psychotherapy is suggested as part of the recommended treatment. Which of the following therapies is most likely to be CONTRAINDICATED?

(A) Hypnosis
(B) Cognitive therapy
(C) Family therapy
(D) Supportive psychotherapy
(E) Psychodynamic psychotherapy

Items 4-5 through 4-9

A 35-year-old man was involved in a motor vehicle accident during which he lost consciousness for more than 10 minutes. Although his airbag deployed, he had extensive bruising about the head. The police at the scene noticed that he was confused and lethargic. He was taken to an emergency room.

4-5. The physician on call found slight right-sided weakness and decided to observe the accident victim for a few hours. Within an hour of arrival, the patient was unresponsive to verbal stimuli and periodically flexed his right arm while extending his left leg when a key was pressed into his supraorbital notch. The physician should immediately perform which of the following?

(A) EEG
(B) Skull x-ray
(C) Precontrast CT scan of the head
(D) Postcontrast CT scan of the head
(E) Lumbar puncture

4-6. The emergency room physician obtained a skull x-ray and was told by the radiologist on call that there appeared to be a fracture of the squamous portion of the temporal bone on the left side of the skull. The patient stopped breathing shortly after returning from the x-ray suite and was intubated. The physician should immediately administer which of the following?

(A) Furosemide 80 mg IV
(B) Dexamethasone 2 mg IV
(C) Phenytoin 1000 mg IV
(D) Phenobarbital 300 mg IM
(E) Mannitol 50 g IV

4-7. The radiologist contacted a neurosurgeon, and the patient had an epidural hematoma removed from the left side of his head. Herniation under the falx cerebri had already begun, but the patient still had good cardiac function after the surgery. As part of the management of the increased intracranial pressure, the neurosurgeon should do which of the following?

(A) Place a cardiac pacemaker
(B) Place a ventricular drain in the left lateral ventricle
(C) Initiate weaning from the ventilator
(D) Administer penicillin G 2 million IU IV every 6 h
(E) Start on phenytoin 300 mg daily

4-8. Although the patient's intracranial pressure remains below 15 mmHg and his arterial blood gases are normal, he fails to show substantial improvement by the second day after surgery. There is no evidence of infection in his lungs or urine, but he has developed a fever and has neck stiffness. The most reasonable procedure to further investigate the source of the fever is which of the following?

(A) Culture fluid from the ventricular drain
(B) Culture gastric aspirate
(C) Culture bronchoscopy aspirate
(D) Perform a biopsy of the rectal wall
(E) Perform cytologic studies of the CSF

4-9. No organisms appear on Gram stain. While awaiting culture results, the physician should do which of the following?

(A) Place the patient on cooling blankets
(B) Replace the ventricular drain
(C) Reexplore the site of hematoma evacuation
(D) Start on penicillin G IV
(E) Start on metronidazole

Items 4-10 through 4-13

A 25-year-old college student is admitted to a psychiatric ward with a history of "personality change, strange behavior, and weird ideas" for 6 months, and bizarre paranoid delusions and hallucinations for the past 6 weeks. During the past month he displayed pressured and disorganized speech. He was also grandiose, talked incessantly, was hyperactive and distractible, and went for long periods without sleep. He has been unable to accomplish his academic work and has been disruptive in class.

4-10. With this patient, it would be important to investigate the possibility of substance abuse, and the most likely substance would be

(A) alcohol
(B) stimulants, such as cocaine or amphetamine
(C) benzodiazepines, such as diazepam (Valium)
(D) narcotics
(E) tricyclic antidepressants

4-11. The most likely diagnosis would be

(A) schizophrenia
(B) schizoaffective disorder
(C) delusional disorder
(D) bipolar I disorder
(E) schizoid personality disorder

4-12. The patient's medical condition would require evaluation, in that any of the following medical illnesses can result in psychotic symptoms EXCEPT

(A) cerebral neoplasm
(B) hypothyroidism
(C) hyperthyroidism
(D) asthma
(E) hepatic or renal disease

4-13. Any of the following drugs might be used to treat the patient's psychotic symptoms EXCEPT

(A) benzodiazepines
(B) lithium
(C) chlorpromazine
(D) olanzapine
(E) haloperidol

4-14. A 14-year-old boy complains of the gradual worsening of scrotal swelling and pain. He also complains of dysuria. On examination you note an edematous and erythematous scrotum. When you elevate the testicle, he feels much relief of his pain. The most likely diagnosis is

(A) orchitis
(B) epididymitis
(C) testicular torsion
(D) varicocele
(E) hydrocele

4-15. An elderly, diabetic, steroid-dependent, bronchospastic woman has had an ileocolectomy for a perforated cecum. She is recovering well in the ICU, intubated on triple antibiotics and a rapid steroid taper, and making adequate urine on renal-dose dopamine. On postoperative day 2 she develops a fever of 39.2°C (102.5°F), hypotension, lethargy, and laboratory values remarkable for hypoglycemia and hyperkalemia. The most likely diagnosis of this acute event is

(A) sepsis
(B) hypovolemia
(C) adrenal insufficiency
(D) acute tubular necrosis
(E) diabetic ketoacidosis

Items 4-16 through 4-20

A 43-year-old man presents with signs and symptoms of peritonitis in the right lower quadrant. The clinical impression and supportive data suggest acute appendicitis. At exploration, however, a tumor is found; frozen section suggests carcinoid features. For each tumor described, choose the most appropriate surgical procedure.

(A) Appendectomy
(B) Segmental ileal resection
(C) Cecectomy
(D) Right hemicolectomy
(E) Hepatic wedge resection and appropriate bowel resection

4-16. A 2.5-cm tumor at the base of the appendix
(SELECT 1 PROCEDURE)

4-17. A 1.0-cm tumor at the tip of the appendix
(SELECT 1 PROCEDURE)

4-18. A 0.5-cm tumor with serosal umbilication in the ileum
(SELECT 1 PROCEDURE)

4-19. A 1.0-cm tumor of the mid-appendix; 1-cm firm, pale lesion at the periphery of the right lobe of the liver
(SELECT 1 PROCEDURE)

4-20. A 3.5-cm tumor encroaching onto the cecum and extensive liver metastases
(SELECT 1 PROCEDURE)

4-21. A woman presents with a pathologic process that involves the hip joint. When asked to identify the site of pain, she would most likely point to the

(A) groin
(B) knee
(C) posterior aspect of the greater trochanter
(D) buttock
(E) calf

4-22. A 65-year-old woman who has a 12-year history of symmetric polyarthritis is admitted to the hospital. Physical examination reveals splenomegaly, ulcerations over the lateral malleoli, and synovitis of the wrists, shoulders, and knees. Splenomegaly, but no hepatomegaly, is noted. Laboratory values demonstrate a white blood cell count of 2500/mm^3 and a rheumatoid factor titer of 1:4096. This patient's white blood cell differential count is likely to reveal

(A) pancytopenia
(B) lymphopenia
(C) granulocytopenia
(D) lymphocytosis
(E) basophilia

4-23. A previously healthy 4-year-old child presents to the emergency room with a 2-day history of a brightly erythematous rash and temperature to 40°C (104°F). The exquisitely tender, generalized rash is worse in the flexural and perioral areas. The child is admitted and over the next day develops crusting and fissuring around the eyes, mouth, and the nose. Sheets of skin tear away with gentle traction. This child most likely has

(A) epidermolysis bullosa
(B) staphylococcal scalded skin syndrome
(C) erythema multiforme
(D) drug eruption
(E) scarlet fever

4-24. A 22-year-old woman, gravida 3, para 2 (one abortion), is brought to the hospital because she says she has been raped by a 35-year-old man whom she knows to have had a vasectomy 2 years ago. Both persons have an A-positive blood type. Which of the following would be most useful to her in the prosecution of this case?

(A) Accurate description of the introitus
(B) Smear for sperm from the cervix
(C) Vaginal washings for acid phosphatase
(D) Specific typing of vaginal washings
(E) Examination of her pubic hair

YOU SHOULD HAVE COMPLETED APPROXIMATELY
25 QUESTIONS AND HAVE 30 MINUTES REMAINING.

Items 4-25 through 4-27

A 28-year-old man is brought to the emergency room for a severe head injury after a fall. Initially lethargic, he becomes comatose and does not move his right side. His left pupil is dilated and responds only sluggishly.

4-25. The most common initial manifestation of increasing intra-cranial pressure in the victim of head trauma is

(A) change in level of consciousness
(B) ipsilateral (side of hemorrhage) pupillary dilatation
(C) contralateral pupillary dilatation
(D) hemiparesis
(E) hypertension

4-26. Initial emergency reduction of intracranial pressure is most rapidly accomplished by

(A) saline-furosemide (Lasix) infusion
(B) urea infusion
(C) mannitol infusion
(D) intravenous dexamethasone (Decadron)
(E) hyperventilation

4-27. In the patient described, compression of the affected nerve is produced by

(A) infection within the cavernous sinus
(B) herniation of the uncal process of the temporal lobe
(C) laceration of the corpus callosum by the falx cerebri
(D) occult damage to the superior cervical ganglion
(E) cerebellar hypoxia

4-28. A 2-year-old boy was just admitted to the hospital because of a convulsion 6 h ago followed by coma. The emergency room doctor ordered a CT scan with contrast, which showed enhancement of the basal cisterns by the contrast material. No other history is available. The most likely diagnosis is

(A) battered child syndrome
(B) malformation of the vein of Galen
(C) meningococcal meningitis
(D) tuberculous meningitis
(E) eastern equine encephalitis

4-29. A 40-year-old man is found to have a uric acid level of 9 mg/dL on routine screening of blood chemistry. The patient has never had gouty arthritis, renal disease, or kidney stones. He has no evidence on history or physical examination of underlying chronic or malignant disease. Which of the following is correct?

(A) The risk of urolithiasis requires the institution of prophylactic therapy
(B) Asymptomatic hyperuricemia is associated with an increased risk of gouty arthritis, but benefits of prophylaxis do not outweigh risks in this patient
(C) The presence or absence of lymphoproliferative disease does not affect the decision to use prophylaxis in hyperuricemia
(D) Lowering serum uric acid will have a direct cardiovascular benefit to the patient in lowering the risk of coronary artery disease

4-30. A renal biopsy is performed on a 10-year-old boy with hematuria and proteinuria; a micrograph from the biopsy is shown below. The most likely diagnosis is

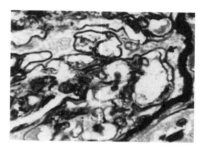

(A) segmental glomerulosclerosis
(B) focal global glomerulosclerosis
(C) membranoproliferative glomerulonephritis
(D) crescentic glomerulonephritis
(E) postinfectious glomerulonephritis

4-31. A 13-year-old boy has a 3-day history of low-grade fever, upper respiratory symptoms, and a sore throat. A few hours before his presentation to the emergency room, he has an abrupt onset of high fevers, difficulty swallowing, and poor handling of his secretions. He indicates he has a marked worsening in the severity of his sore throat. His pharynx has a fluctuant bulge in the posterior wall. Appropriate initial therapy for this patient would be

(A) narcotic analgesics
(B) trial of oral penicillin V
(C) surgical consultation for incision and drainage under general anesthesia
(D) rapid streptococcal screen
(E) monospot test

4-32. A 45-year-old woman presents to her physician with an 8-month history of gradually increasing limb weakness. She first noticed difficulty climbing stairs, then problems rising from chairs, walking more than half a block, and finally, lifting her arms above shoulder level. Aside from some difficulty swallowing, she has no ocular, bulbar, or sphincter problems and no sensory complaints. Family history is negative for neurologic disease. Examination reveals significant proximal limb and neck muscle weakness with minimal atrophy, normal sensory findings, and intact deep tendon reflexes. The most likely diagnosis in this patient is

(A) polymyositis
(B) cervical myelopathy
(C) myasthenia gravis
(D) mononeuropathy multiplex
(E) limb girdle muscular dystrophy

4-33. A 42-year-old man presents with a history of burning epigastric pain that begins 1 to 4 h postprandially. He reports that this pain is relieved either by food or antacid tablets. The most likely diagnosis is

(A) cholecystitis
(B) acute pancreatitis
(C) a peptic ulcer
(D) intestinal angina
(E) celiac sprue

Items 4-34 through 4-36

Match each patient with the correct diagnosis.

(A) Hepatorenal syndrome
(B) Acute tubular necrosis
(C) Interstitial nephritis
(D) Prerenal azotemia
(E) Polycystic kidney disease
(F) Acute obstruction
(G) Poststreptococcal glomerulonephritis

4-34. A 30-year-old woman complains of nausea and vomiting with associated diarrhea. Her urine sodium is 8 meq/L and her urine-specific gravity is 1.03. **(SELECT 1 DIAGNOSIS)**

4-35. An elderly man has been recently hospitalized for confusion and treated with thorazine. He complains of mild lower abdominal pain. The patient has voided only 200 mL in 24 h. **(SELECT 1 DIAGNOSIS)**

4-36. A hospitalized elderly woman is treated for gram-negative sepsis with ticarcillin and tobramycin. Her BUN is 80 meq/L, creatinine 8 meq/L, and urine sodium 45 meq/L. **(SELECT 1 DIAGNOSIS)**

4-37. A 20-month-old child presents to your office with a mild viral infection. The results of examination are normal except for a temperature of 37.2°C (99°F) and clear nasal discharge. Review of her vaccination records reveals that she received only two doses of oral polio vaccine (OPV) and diphtheria-tetanus-pertussis vaccine (DTP), and that she did not receive the measles-mumps-rubella vaccine (MMR). The mother is 20 weeks pregnant. Her brother is undergoing chemotherapy for leukemia. Which of the following is the most appropriate intervention?

(A) Schedule a visit in 2 weeks for DTP
(B) Administer inactivated polio vaccine (IPV) and DTP
(C) Administer DTP, OPV, and MMR
(D) Administer DTP, IPV, and MMR
(E) Administer DTP and OPV and schedule a visit in 3 months for MMR

4-38. A 19-year-old woman with complaints of headaches and visual blurring had prominent bulging of both optic nerve heads with obscuration of all margins of both optic discs. Her physician was reluctant to pursue neurologic studies because the patient was 8 months pregnant and had similar complaints during the last month of another pregnancy. Her physical and neurologic examination was otherwise unrevealing. If neuroimaging studies had been performed on this woman, they probably would have revealed

(A) a subfrontal meningioma
(B) intraventricular blood
(C) slitlike ventricles
(D) transtentorial herniation
(E) metastatic breast carcinoma

4-39. A 73-year-old woman with a long history of heavy smoking undergoes femoral artery–popliteal artery bypass for resting pain in her left leg. Because of serious underlying respiratory insufficiency, she continues to require ventilatory support for 4 days after her operation. As soon as her endotracheal tube is removed, she begins complaining of vague upper abdominal pain. She has daily fever spikes to 39°C (102.2°F) and a leukocyte count of 18,000/mm³. An upper abdominal ultrasonogram reveals a dilated gallbladder, but no stones are seen. A presumptive diagnosis of acalculous cholecystitis is made. You would recommend

(A) nasogastric suction and broad-spectrum antibiotics
(B) immediate cholecystectomy with operative cholangiogram
(C) percutaneous drainage of the gallbladder
(D) endoscopic retrograde cholangio-pancreatography (ERCP) to visualize and drain the common bile duct
(E) provocation of cholecystokinin release by cautious feeding of the patient

4-40. A previously well 1-year-old infant has had a runny nose and has been sneezing and coughing for 2 days. Two other members of the family had similar symptoms. Four hours ago his cough became much worse. On physical examination he is in moderate respiratory distress with nasal flaring, hyperexpansion of the chest, and easily audible wheezing without rales. The most likely diagnosis is

(A) bronchiolitis
(B) viral croup
(C) asthma
(D) epiglottitis
(E) diphtheria

4-41. A 14-year-old boy presents with a history of chronic sinusitis and frequent pneumonias. You note that the heart sounds are best heard on the right side of the chest, and percussion shows the heart to be right-sided. The most likely diagnosis is

(A) cystic fibrosis
(B) Kartagener's syndrome
(C) empyema
(D) pulmonary dysplasia
(E) tracheoesophageal fistula

4-42. On physical examination of a 15-year-old boy, you find a blood pressure of 140/55 mmHg at rest. You also notice a large, well-healed scar over the medial aspect of his left thigh. On questioning he states that he acquired the scar by impaling his thigh on a large nail after falling. Auscultation of the scar reveals a bruit and there is a palpable thrill. Most likely the patient has

(A) premature atherosclerosis
(B) an arteriovenous fistula
(C) scar tissue compressing the femoral artery
(D) congenital duplication of the femoral artery
(E) a bone tumor

4-43. During a regular checkup on an 8-year-old child, you note a loud first heart sound with a fixed and widely split second heart sound at the upper left sternal border that does not change with respirations. The patient is otherwise active and healthy. The mostly likely heart lesion to explain these findings is

(A) atrial septal defect
(B) ventricular septal defect
(C) isolated tricuspid regurgitation
(D) tetralogy of Fallot
(E) mitral valve prolapse

4-44. A 32-year-old woman has a 3-year history of oligomenorrhea that has progressed to amenorrhea during the past year. She has observed loss of breast fullness, reduced hip measurements, acne, increased body hair, and deepening of her voice. Physical examination reveals frontal balding, clitoral hypertrophy, and a male escutcheon. Urinary free cortisol and dehydroepiandrosterone sulfate (DHEAS) are normal. Her plasma testosterone level is 6 ng/mL (normal: 0.2 to 0.8). The most likely diagnosis of this patient's disorder is

(A) hilar cell tumor
(B) Cushing's syndrome
(C) arrhenoblastoma
(D) polycystic ovary syndrome
(E) granulosa-theca cell tumor

4-45. A 37-year-old man complained of difficulty relaxing his grip on his golf club after putting. He also complained of problems with excessive somnolence. Examination revealed early cataract development, testicular atrophy, and baldness. His family noted that he had become increasingly stubborn and hostile over the past 3 years. His electrocardiogram (ECG) revealed a minor conduction defect. An electromyogram (EMG) of this man will probably reveal

(A) repetitive discharges with minor stimulation
(B) polyphasic giant action potentials
(C) fasciculations
(D) fibrillations
(E) positive waves

4-46. A 64-year-old woman is found to have a left-sided pleural effusion on chest x-ray. Analysis of the pleural fluid reveals a ratio of concentration of total protein in pleural fluid to serum of 0.38, a lactic dehydrogenase (LDH) level of 125 IU, and a ratio of LDH concentration in pleural fluid to serum of 0.46. Which of the following disorders is most likely in this patient?

(A) Uremia
(B) Congestive heart failure
(C) Pulmonary embolism
(D) Sarcoidosis
(E) Systemic lupus erythematosus

4-47. A 58-year-old man presents to your office with a history of having an episode of sudden visual loss in his right eye. The patient describes the loss of vision as similar to someone pulling a cover over his right eye. Vision returned to the right eye after 10 min. This visual field defect is

(A) scotoma
(B) amaurosis fugax
(C) strabismus
(D) esotropia
(E) night blindness

4-48. Aunt Mary is helping her family move to a new apartment. During the confusion, 3-year-old Jimmy is noted to be stumbling about, his face flushed, his speech slurred. The contents of Aunt Mary's purse are strewn about on the floor. In the ER, Jimmy is found to have a rapid heart beat, blood pressure of 42/20, and dilated pupils. ECG shows prolonged QRS and QT intervals. Jimmy suddenly starts to convulse. His condition is most likely to be the result of poisoning with

(A) barbiturates
(B) tricyclic antidepressants
(C) diazepam
(D) organophosphates
(E) arsenic

4-49. A 30-year-old man is admitted to the hospital after a motorcycle accident that resulted in a fracture of the right femur. The fracture is managed with traction. Three days later he becomes confused and tachypneic. A petechial rash is noted over the chest. Lungs are clear to auscultation. Arterial blood gases show a P_{O_2} 50, P_{CO_2} 28, and pH 7.49. The most likely diagnosis is

(A) unilateral pulmonary edema
(B) hematoma of chest
(C) fat embolism
(D) pulmonary embolism
(E) early *Staphylococcus aureus* pneumonia

4-50. A 20-year-old ataxic woman with a family history of Friedreich's disease developed polyuria and excessive thirst over the course of a few weeks. She noticed that she fatigued easily and had intermittently blurred vision. The most likely explanation for her complaints is

(A) inappropriate antidiuretic hormone
(B) diabetes mellitus
(C) panhypopituitarism
(D) progressive adrenal insufficiency
(E) hypothyroidism

BLOCK 5

*YOU HAVE **60** MINUTES
TO COMPLETE **50** QUESTIONS.*

BLOCK 5

YOU HAVE **60** MINUTES
TO COMPLETE **50** QUESTIONS.

Questions

5-1. A 43-year-old woman presents with large hands, a large mandible, and coarse, leathery facial skin. The most likely diagnosis is

(A) Marfan's syndrome
(B) hypothyroidism
(C) scleroderma
(D) acromegaly
(E) Cushing's syndrome

Items 5-2 through 5-3

A previously healthy 55-year-old man undergoes elective right hemicolectomy for a Dukes' A cancer of the cecum. His postoperative ileus is somewhat prolonged, and on the fifth postoperative day his nasogastric tube is still in place. Physical examination reveals diminished skin turgor, dry mucous membranes, and orthostatic hypotension. Pertinent laboratory values are as follows:

Arterial blood gases: pH 7.56; P_{O_2} 85 torr; P_{CO_2} 50 torr

Serum electrolytes (meq/L): Na^+ 132; K^+ 3.1; Cl^- 80; HCO_3^- 42

Urine electrolytes (meq/L): Na^+ 2; K^- 5; Cl^- 6

5-2. The values given above allow the descriptive diagnosis of

(A) uncompensated metabolic alkalosis
(B) respiratory acidosis with metabolic compensation
(C) combined metabolic and respiratory alkalosis
(D) metabolic alkalosis with respiratory compensation
(E) "paradoxical" metabolic respiratory alkalosis

5-3. The most appropriate therapy for the patient described would be

(A) infusion of 0.9% NaCl with supplemental KCl until clinical signs of volume depletion are eliminated
(B) infusion of isotonic (0.15 N) HCl via a central venous catheter
(C) clamping the nasogastric tube to prevent further acid losses
(D) administration of acetazolamide to promote renal excretion of bicarbonate
(E) intubation and controlled hypoventilation on a volume-cycled ventilator to further increase the P_{CO_2}

5-4. A 43-year-old woman with a 1-year history of episodic leg edema and dyspnea is noted to have clubbing of the fingers. Her ECG is shown below. The correct diagnosis is

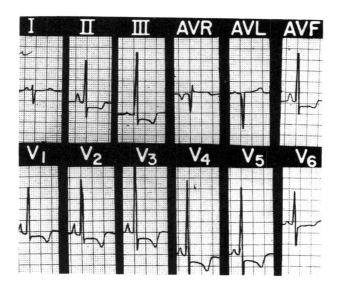

(A) inferior wall myocardial infarction
(B) right bundle branch block
(C) anterior wall myocardial infarction
(D) Wolff-Parkinson-White syndrome
(E) cor pulmonale

5-5. A 10-year-old boy is admitted to the hospital because of bleeding. Pertinent laboratory findings include a platelet count of 50,000/mm³, pro-thrombin time (PT) of 15 s (control 11.5 s), activated partial thrombo-plastin time (aPTT) of 51 s (control 36 s), thrombin time (TT) of 13.7 s (control 10.5 s), and factor VIII level of 14 percent (normal 38 to 178 per-cent). The most likely cause of his bleeding is

(A) immune thrombocytopenic purpura (ITP)
(B) vitamin K deficiency
(C) disseminated intravascular coagulation (DIC)
(D) hemophilia A
(E) hemophilia B

5-6. A 50-year-old man with a 60-pack-year history of smoking presents with what appears to be enlarged and spongy fingertips that are slightly blue in color. Of the following, which is the most likely disease?

(A) Graves' disease
(B) Ulcerative colitis
(C) Crohn's disease
(D) Biliary cirrhosis
(E) Bronchogenic carcinoma

5-7. A nursing student has just completed her hepatitis B vaccine series. On reviewing her laboratory studies and assuming she has no prior exposure to hepatitis B, you would expect

(A) a positive test for hepatitis B surface antigen (HBsAg)
(B) antibody against HBsAg alone
(C) antibody against hepatitis B core antigen (HBcAg)
(D) antibody against both HBsAg and HBcAg
(E) antibody against hepatitis B e antigen (HBeAg)

5-8. A 7-year-old girl is brought to your office by her mother because of a rash that appeared 3 days ago. Her temperature is 37.2°C (99°F) and her face has an intense rash with a slapped-cheek appearance. The most likely etiologic agent is

(A) adenovirus
(B) rotavirus
(C) parvovirus
(D) coxsackievirus
(E) echovirus

5-9. A patient with a family history of Huntington's disease wishes to select his nephew as the person to make decisions about health care if he should become incompetent. The necessary document is called a

(A) last testament
(B) durable power of attorney
(C) informed consent
(D) competency document
(E) contract

5-10. A 32-year-old woman, gravida 3, para 3, presents with abdominal pain. Her last menstrual period was 6 weeks ago, and a pregnancy test is positive. The specimen shown below is obtained at laparotomy. The most likely diagnosis is

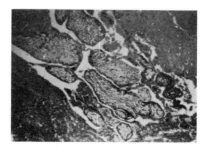

(A) incomplete abortion
(B) missed abortion
(C) hydatidiform mole
(D) tubal ectopic pregnancy
(E) ovarian pregnancy

Items 5-11 through 5-12

For each description below, select the type of vascular event with which it is most likely to be associated.

(A) Subdural hematoma
(B) Epidural hematoma
(C) Carotid dissection
(D) Brain contusion
(E) Ruptured intracranial aneurysm

5-11. While watching a golf tournament, a 37-year-old man is struck on the side of the head by a golf ball. He is conscious and talkative after the injury, but several days later he is noted to be increasingly lethargic, somewhat confused, and unable to move his right side.
(SELECT 1 DIAGNOSIS)

5-12. A 42-year-old woman complains of the sudden onset of a severe headache, stiff neck, and photophobia. She loses consciousness. She is later noted to have a dilated pupil.
(SELECT 1 DIAGNOSIS)

5-13. A 92-year-old woman with non-insulin-dependent diabetes mellitus has developed cellulitis and gangrene of her left foot. She requires a life-saving amputation but has refused to give consent for the surgery. She has been ambulatory in her nursing home but states that she would be so dependent after surgery that life would not be worth living for her. She has no living relatives; she enjoys walks and gardening. She is competent and of clear mind. You would

(A) perform emergency surgery
(B) consult a psychiatrist
(C) request permission for surgery from a friend of the patient
(D) follow the patient's wishes

5-14. A 4-year-old boy is brought to the emergency room soon after developing a fever of 39.44°C (103°F) and complaining to his mother that "it hurts to swallow." His voice sounds "weak and throaty." The boy has increasing difficulty with breathing, and it appears to the mother that "he can't get air in." Vital signs include a pulse of 156 beats per minute and a respiratory rate of 36 breaths per minute. The child appears anxious, his face is flushed, and he has saliva coming out of his mouth. He is holding his neck in an immobile, rigid manner. On auscultation, there is a very loud, high-pitched sound with each inspiration, heard best over the neck. The most appropriate diagnosis is

(A) asthma
(B) epiglottitis
(C) laryngotracheobronchitis
(D) tonsillitis
(E) pneumonia

5-15. Your 6-year-old son awakens at 1:00 A.M. screaming. You note that he is hyperventilating, is tachycardic, and has dilated pupils. He cannot be consoled, does not respond, and is unaware of his environment. After a few minutes, he returns to normal sleep. He recalls nothing the following morning. The most likely diagnosis is

(A) seizure disorder
(B) night terrors
(C) drug ingestion
(D) psychiatric disorder
(E) migraine headache

5-16. A 46-year-old woman presents with drooping eyelids, but no other significant findings. Which of the following diagnoses should be considered?

(A) Bell's palsy
(B) Metastatic tumor impinging upon the cervical sympathetic trunk
(C) Hyperthyroidism
(D) Myasthenia gravis
(E) Reiter's syndrome

Items 5-17 through 5-18

A 25-year-old male student presents with a chief complaint of rash. There is no headache, fever, or myalgia. A slightly pruritic maculopapular rash is noted over the abdomen, trunk, palms of hands, and soles of feet. Inguinal, occipital, and cervical lymphadenopathy is also noted. Hypertrophic, flat, wartlike lesions are noted around the anal area. Laboratory studies show the following:

HCT: 40 percent
Hgb: 14 g/dL
WBC: 13,000/mm^3
Segmented neutrophils: 50 percent
Lymphocytes: 50 percent

5-17. The most useful laboratory test in this patient is

(A) Weil-Felix titer
(B) Venereal Disease Research Laboratory (VDRL) test
(C) *Chlamydia* titer
(D) Blood cultures

5-18. The treatment of choice for this patient is

(A) Penicillin
(B) Ceftriaxone
(C) Tetracycline
(D) Interferon alpha
(E) Erythromycin

5-19. A mother calls you on the telephone and says that her 4-year-old son had bitten the hand of her 2-year-old son 2 days previously and now the area around the laceration is red, stiff, and swollen and he has a temperature of 103°F (39.4°C). Your immediate response should be to

(A) arrange for a plastic surgery consultation to be scheduled in 3 days
(B) admit the child to the hospital immediately for surgical and antibiotic treatment
(C) prescribe penicillin over the telephone and have the mother apply warm soaks for 15 min qid
(D) suggest purchase of bacitracin ointment to apply to the lesion tid
(E) see the patient in the emergency room to suture the laceration

5-20. A 5-year-old girl cut her face on broken glass. Initially the injury appeared superficial except for a small area of deeper penetration just above the right eyebrow. Within 4 days, the child complained of periorbital pain and double vision. The tissues about the eye were erythematous and the eye appeared to bulge slightly. The optic disc was sharp and no afferent pupillary defect was apparent. Visual acuity in the affected eye was preserved. This child probably has

(A) orbital cellulitis
(B) cavernous sinus thrombosis
(C) transverse sinus thrombosis
(D) optic neuritis
(E) diphtheritic polyneuropathy

Items 5-21 through 5-22

Several days following esophagectomy a patient complains of dyspnea and chest tightness. A large pleural effusion is noted on chest radiograph and thoracentesis yields milky fluid consistent with chyle.

5-21. Initial management of this patient consists of which of the following procedures?

(A) Immediate operation to repair the thoracic duct
(B) Immediate operation to ligate the thoracic duct
(C) Tube thoracostomy and low-fat diet
(D) Observation and low-fat diet
(E) Observation and antibiotics

5-22. Two weeks following the initial management of this patient's chylothorax there is persistent accumulation of chyle in the pleural space. Appropriate management at this time includes which of the following procedures?

(A) Neck exploration and ligation of the thoracic duct
(B) Subdiaphragmatic ligation of the thoracic duct
(C) Thoracotomy and repair of the thoracic duct
(D) Thoracotomy and ligation of the thoracic duct
(E) Thoracotomy and abrasion of the pleural space

5-23. A 24-year-old patient has returned from a yearlong stay in the tropics. Four weeks ago she noted a small vulvar ulceration that spontaneously healed. Now there is painful, inguinal adenopathy with malaise and fever. You are considering the diagnosis of lymphogranuloma venereum (LGV). The diagnosis can be established by

(A) staining for Donovan bodies
(B) the presence of antibodies to *Chlamydia trachomatis*
(C) positive Frei skin test
(D) culturing *Haemophilus ducreyi*
(E) culturing *Calymmatobacterium granulomatis*

5-24. A 3-day-old infant's left side of the scrotum is larger than the right. Palpation reveals a tense, fluid-filled area surrounding the right testicle. The scrotum transilluminates well and the amount of fluid does not vary with mild pressure. The appropriate approach to this condition is to

(A) request a surgical consultation
(B) begin furosemide orally
(C) administer prophylactic antibiotics
(D) observe only
(E) perform a chromosome determination

5-25. A 22-year-old man presents 1 day after having been a restrained driver involved in a moderate-speed automobile accident. He is complaining only of a discolored (blue) scrotum. There was no trauma to the scrotum. You note that the discoloration is gravity-dependent. The most likely diagnosis is

(A) fat necrosis
(B) testicular torsion
(C) inguinal hernia
(D) hematocele
(E) hydrocele

YOU SHOULD HAVE COMPLETED APPROXIMATELY
25 QUESTIONS AND HAVE 30 MINUTES REMAINING.

5-26. A 15-year-old girl complains of a low-grade fever, malaise, conjunctivitis, coryza, and cough. After this prodromal phase, a rash of discrete pink macules begins on her face and extends to her hands and feet. She is also noted to have small, red spots on her palate. The cause of her rash is

(A) toxic shock syndrome
(B) gonococcal bacteremia
(C) Reiter's syndrome
(D) rubeola (measles)
(E) rubella (German measles)

5-27. A 32-year-old woman undergoes a cholecystectomy for acute cholecystitis and is discharged home on the sixth postoperative day. She returns to the clinic 8 months after the operation for a routine visit and is noted by the surgeon to be jaundiced. Laboratory values on readmission show total bilirubin 5.6 mg/dL, direct bilirubin 4.8 mg/dL, alkaline phosphatase 250 IU (normal 21 to 91 IU), SGOT 52 KU (normal 10 to 40 KU), and SGPT 51 KU (normal 10 to 40 KU). An ultrasonogram shows dilated intrahepatic ducts. She undergoes the transhepatic cholangiogram seen below. Appropriate management is

(A) choledochoplasty with insertion of a T tube
(B) end-to-end choledochocholedochal anastomosis
(C) Roux-en-Y choledochojejunostomy
(D) percutaneous transhepatic dilatation
(E) choledochoduodenostomy

5-28. A 25-year-old man is brought reluctantly to a psychiatrist by his parents, who are concerned about his inability to hold a job. They state that since adolescence, he has been impulsive, constantly in conflict in all his interpersonal relationships, and always sees the world and himself differently than do other people. He states he does not use drugs and has no psychiatric symptoms. The mental status examination shows no cognitive deficits and no abnormality of mood, affect, or thinking. The most likely diagnosis is

(A) posttraumatic stress disorder
(B) major depression
(C) schizophrenia
(D) obsessive-compulsive disorder
(E) personality disorder

5-29. A 10-year-old boy has been having bellyaches for about 2 years. They occur at night as well as during the day. Occasionally he vomits after the onset of pain. Occult blood has been found in his stool. His father also gets frequent stomachaches. The most likely diagnosis is

(A) peptic ulcer
(B) appendicitis
(C) Meckel's diverticulum
(D) intussusception
(E) pinworm infestation

Items 5-30 through 5-33

A 39-year-old woman had diplopia several times a day for 6 weeks. She consulted a physician when the double vision became unremitting and also complained of dull pain behind her right eye. When a red glass was placed over the right eye and she was asked to look at a flashlight off to her left, she reported seeing a white light and a red light. The red light appeared to her to be more to the left than the white light. Her right pupil was more dilated than her left pupil and responded less briskly to a bright light directed at it than did the left pupil.

5-30. Before any further investigations could be performed, this young woman developed the worst headache of her life and became stuporous. Her physician discovered that she had marked neck stiffness and photophobia. The physician performed a transfemoral angiogram. This radiologic study is expected to reveal that the woman has

(A) an arteriovenous malformation
(B) an occipital astrocytoma
(C) a sphenoidal meningioma
(D) a pituitary adenoma
(E) a saccular aneurysm

5-31. The cranial nerve injury likely to be responsible for all of these observations is one involving

(A) the second cranial nerve
(B) the third cranial nerve
(C) the fourth cranial nerve
(D) the sixth cranial nerve
(E) none of the above

5-32. The site of the lesion responsible for this woman's symptoms and signs is most probably the

(A) anterior communicating artery
(B) posterior communicating artery
(C) anterior cerebral artery
(D) middle cerebral artery
(E) posterior cerebral artery

5-33. Three days after developing neck stiffness and photophobia, this woman developed left-sided weakness and hyperreflexia. Her left plantar response was upgoing. Her physician presumed that these deficits were a delayed effect of the subarachnoid blood and so would treat her with

(A) heparin
(B) warfarin
(C) nimodipine
(D) phenytoin
(E) carbamazepine

5-34. A spry octogenarian who has never before been hospitalized is admitted with signs and symptoms typical of a small bowel obstruction. Which of the following clinical findings would give most help in ascertaining the diagnosis?

(A) Coffee-grounds aspirate from the stomach
(B) Aerobilia
(C) A leukocyte count of 40,000/mm^3
(D) A pH of 7.5 P$_{CO_2}$ 50 torr, and paradoxically acid urine
(E) A palpable mass in the pelvis

5-35. While you are on duty in the emergency room, a 12-year-old boy arrives with pain and inflammation over the ball of his left foot and red streaks extending up the inner aspect of his leg. He remembers removing a wood splinter from the sole of his foot on the previous day. The most likely infecting organism is

(A) *Clostridium perfingens*
(B) *Clostridium tetanus*
(C) *Staphylococcus*
(D) *Escherichia coli*
(E) *Streptococcus*

5-36. Because of a psychotic illness, a young man is started on high-potency neuroleptic medication and shortly thereafter develops pacing, an inability to sit still, and restless leg symptoms, which lead to the diagnosis of akathisia. The medication most likely to prove helpful is

(A) barbiturate
(B) propranolol
(C) phenytoin
(D) a neuroleptic of higher potency
(E) anticholinergic medication

5-37. A man complains of soft, raised, reddish lesions on his glans penis, prepuce, and penile shaft. Several excisional biopsies are done to look for possible malignant change. The most likely diagnosis is

(A) lymphogranuloma venereum
(B) Peyronie's disease
(C) condyloma acuminatum
(D) molluscum contagiosum
(E) syphilitic chancre

5-38. A 50-year-old construction worker continues to have an elevated blood pressure of 160/95 mmHg even after a third agent is added to his hypertension regimen. Results of physical examination are normal, electrolytes are normal, and the patient is taking no over-the-counter medications. The next helpful step in this patient is

(A) check pill count
(B) evaluate for Cushing's disease
(C) check chest x-ray for coarctation of the aorta
(D) obtain a renal angiogram

5-39. A 6-year-old boy is brought to the emergency room with a 3-h history of fever to 39.5°C (103.1°F) and sore throat. The child appears alert but anxious and he has mild inspiratory stridor. You should immediately

(A) examine the throat and obtain a culture
(B) obtain an arterial blood gas and start an IV line
(C) order a chest x-ray and lateral view of the neck
(D) prepare to establish an airway
(E) admit the child and place him in a mist tent

5-40. A newborn infant has mild cyanosis, diaphoresis, poor peripheral pulses, hepatomegaly, and cardiomegaly. Respiratory rate is 60 breaths per minute, and heart rate is 230 beats per minute. The child most likely has congestive heart failure caused by

(A) a large atrial septal defect and valvular pulmonic stenosis
(B) a ventricular septal defect and transposition of the great vessels
(C) atrial flutter and partial atrioventricular block
(D) hypoplastic left heart syndrome
(E) paroxysmal atrial tachycardia

5-41. The most likely diagnosis in a patient with hypertension, hypokalemia, and a 7-cm suprarenal mass is

(A) hypernephroma
(B) Cushing's disease
(C) adrenocortical carcinoma
(D) pheochromocytoma
(E) carcinoid syndrome

5-42. 35-year-old man stumbles into the emergency room. His pulse is 100 beats per minute, his blood pressure is 170/95 mmHg, and he is diaphoretic. He is tremulous and has difficulty relating a history. He does admit to insomnia the past two nights and thinks a curtain is a ghost in the room. He also states he has been a drinker since age 19, but has not had a drink in 4 days. The most likely diagnosis is

(A) adjustment disorder
(B) atypical psychosis
(C) alcohol withdrawal delirium (delirium tremens)
(D) alcohol intoxication
(E) alcohol idiosyncratic intoxication

5-43. A 68-year-old man presents with a chief complaint that solid food gets stuck in the middle of his chest. In addition, he admits to a 25-pound weight loss over the last 3 months. The most likely diagnosis is

(A) esophagitis
(B) lower esophageal ring
(C) esophageal carcinoma
(D) cerebrovascular accident
(E) myocardial infarction

5-44. A 19-year-old primiparous woman develops toxemia in her last trimester of pregnancy and during the course of her labor is treated with magnesium sulfate. At 38 weeks of gestation, she delivers a 2300-g infant with an Apgar score of 7. Laboratory studies at 18 h of age reveal a hematocrit of 79 percent, glucose 38 mg/dL, and calcium 8.7 mg/L. Soon after this the infant has a generalized convulsion. The most likely cause of the infant's seizure is

(A) polycythemia
(B) hypoglycemia
(C) hypocalcemia
(D) hypermagnesemia
(E) hypomagnesemia

5-45. A 47-year-old man with hypertensive nephropathy develops fever, graft tenderness, and oliguria 4 weeks following cadaveric renal transplantation. Serum creatinine is 3.1 mg/dL. A renal ultrasound reveals mild edema of the renal papillae but normal flow in both the renal artery and renal vein. Nuclear scan demonstrates sluggish uptake and excretion. The next most appropriate step is

(A) perform an angiogram
(B) decrease steroid and cyclosporine dose
(C) begin intravenous antibiotics
(D) perform renal biopsy, steroid boost, and immunoglobulin therapy
(E) begin FK 506

5-46. A 55-year-old married professor without a previous psychiatric history is early in her menopause. In addition to experiencing "hot flashes" and some irritability, she complains of episodes of dizzy spells and memory lapses, which she had experienced on several occasions earlier in life. She denies depressive symptoms either now or in the past. In particular, she should be evaluated for possible

(A) schizophrenia
(B) major depression
(C) temporal lobe epilepsy
(D) dysthymia
(E) panic disorder

5-47. A 21-year-old man presents to the office for a sore throat. On examination, the patient is found to be tall, with gynecomastia and testicular atrophy. Which is the most likely diagnosis?

(A) Testicular feminization syndrome
(B) 45,X (Turner's syndrome)
(C) Trisomy 21 (Down's syndrome)
(D) 47,XXY (Klinefelter's syndrome)
(E) Hepatic cirrhosis

5-48. A 30-year-old black man plans a trip to India and is advised to take prophylaxis for malaria. Three days after beginning treatment, he develops dark urine, pallor, fatigue, and jaundice. Hematocrit is 30 percent (it had been 43 percent) and the reticulocyte count is 7 percent. He stops taking the medication. Which of the following treatments, if any, is advisable?

(A) Splenectomy
(B) Administration of methylene blue
(C) Administration of vitamin E
(D) Exchange transfusions
(E) No additional treatment

5-49. A 16-year-old wrestler sustains an elbow injury when he is thrown to the mat on his outstretched left arm. His elbow seemed to be dislocated, then spontaneously reduced with the help of his coach. Since this event, the patient has noted three additional episodes of instability that reduces with minimal effort by the patient or parent. On examination the elbow is stable to varus and valgus stress. Which test or maneuver will likely diagnose this condition?

(A) Valgus stress radiograph
(B) Varus stress radiograph
(C) Tinel's sign
(D) Finkelstein's test
(E) Posterolateral rotatory instability test

5-50. Following a 2-h fire-fighting episode, a 36-year-old fireman begins complaining of a throbbing headache, nausea, dizziness, and visual disturbances. He is taken to the emergency room where his carboxyhemoglobin (COHb) level is found to be 31 percent. Appropriate treatment would be to

(A) begin an immediate exchange transfusion
(B) transfer the patient to a hyperbaric oxygen chamber
(C) begin bicarbonate infusion and give 250 mg acetazolamide (Diamox) IV
(D) administer 100% oxygen by mask
(E) perform flexible bronchoscopy with further therapy determined by findings

BLOCK 6

YOU HAVE _60_ MINUTES TO COMPLETE _50_ QUESTIONS.

BLOCK 6

YOU HAVE **60** MINUTES
TO COMPLETE **50** QUESTIONS.

Questions

6-1. A patient presents with painless papules that arose following a puncture wound from a rose thorn a few weeks earlier. Physical examination reveals a chain of erythematous nodules along the dorsal aspect of the arm. The most likely diagnosis is

(A) *Candida albicans* infection
(B) blastomycosis
(C) tinea versicolor
(D) sporotrichosis
(E) cutaneous larva migrans

6-2. A 40-year-old cigarette smoker is found on routine physical examination to have a 1-cm white patch on his oral mucosa that does not rub off. There are no other lesions in the mouth. The patient has no risk factors for HIV infection. The lesion is nontender. The next step in management would be to

(A) culture for *Candida albicans*
(B) biopsy the lesion
(C) follow the lesion with an annual physical examination
(D) reassure the patient that this is an insignificant lesion

6-3. An 18-year-old man is admitted to the emergency room following a motorcycle accident. He is alert and fully oriented but witnesses to the accident report an interval of unresponsiveness following the injury. Skull films disclose a fracture of the left temporal bone. Following x-ray the patient suddenly loses consciousness and dilatation of the left pupil is noted. This patient should be considered to have

(A) a ruptured berry aneurysm
(B) acute subdural hematoma
(C) epidural hematoma
(D) intraabdominal hemorrhage
(E) ruptured arteriovenous malformation

6-4. On a routine well-child examination, a 1-year-old boy is noted to be pale. He is in the 75th percentile for weight, and the 25th percentile for length. Results of physical examination are otherwise normal. His hematocrit is 24 percent. Of the following questions, which is most likely to be helpful in making a diagnosis?

(A) What is the child's usual daily diet?
(B) Did the child receive phototherapy for neonatal jaundice?
(C) Has anyone in the family received a blood transfusion?
(D) Is the child on any medications?
(E) What is the pattern and appearance of his bowel movements?

6-5. A psychiatrist is called in to evaluate a wealthy 85-year-old man who is drawing up a new "last will" and is concerned that it might be challenged after his death on the basis of possible reduced mental capacity. The psychiatric evaluation would be for the purpose of determining the patient's

(A) sanity versus insanity
(B) testamentary capacity
(C) ability to distinguish right from wrong
(D) judgmental capacity
(E) insight

6-6. A 13-year-old boy is complaining of heaviness to his scrotum and a vague pain. He states that the pain is worsened by exertion. On palpation you feel dilated veins ("bag of worms") above his left testis. The most likely diagnosis is

(A) orchitis
(B) testicular torsion
(C) epididymitis
(D) varicocele
(E) hematocele

6-7. A 7-year-old boy who had had a mild upper respiratory tract infection for 2 days without fever or change in level of activity awakens with a temperature of 39.7°C (103.5°F), lassitude, and anorexia. He soon struggles to breathe and his parents bring him to the emergency room. On physical examination his vital signs include a pulse of 150 beats per minute and respiratory rate of 36 breaths per minute. The child is holding his arms around the back of a chair and exerting a great effort to breathe. He has a mucoid rhinorrhea, and auscultation reveals high-pitched breath sounds in all lung fields during expiration. The most appropriate diagnosis is

(A) epiglottitis
(B) asthma
(C) laryngotracheobronchitis
(D) tonsillitis
(E) pneumonia

6-8. A 36-year-old man abruptly loses vision in one eye. His retina appears cloudy and grayish yellow with narrowed arterioles. The fovea appears cherry red and the vessels that are obvious appear to have segmented columns of blood. This man probably has

(A) chorioretinitis
(B) occlusion of the central retinal vein
(C) occlusion of the central retinal artery
(D) optic neuritis
(E) Tay-Sachs disease

6-9. A 19-year-old patient has extensive vaginal flat condylomas that have recurred after laser treatment 3 months ago. The best therapy is to

(A) repeat laser treatment
(B) apply podophyllum
(C) apply trichloroacetic acid
(D) apply 5% 5-fluorouracil cream
(E) perform cryotherapy

6-10. One of your patients returns to your office for the results of his HIV test. You inform him that his test is positive for antibodies to HIV. He is married, and sexually active with his wife. In the course of subsequent counseling, you tell him it is important that his wife be advised of the exposure. He refuses to tell his wife or have anyone else inform her of the exposure. At this time, what is the most appropriate management of the situation?

(A) Tell the patient you refuse to continue seeing him unless his wife is informed

(B) Send an anonymous letter to his wife informing her of the exposure

(C) Try to convince him of the importance of informing his wife and offer assistance

(D) Contact public health authorities so they can inform his wife

(E) Call his wife and set up an appointment at your office to inform her of the exposure

6-11. You are called to evaluate a 56-year-old man with chest, jaw, and left arm pain. On physical examination you find an anxious, pale man who is uncomfortable on the examination table. He is perspiring heavily although his extremities are cool. At this point the most likely diagnosis would be

(A) gastric ulcer
(B) angina pectoris
(C) pneumonia
(D) acute myocardial infarct
(E) appendicitis

Items 6-12 through 6-13

A 60-year-old male alcoholic is admitted to the hospital with hematemesis. His blood pressure is 100/60 mmHg, the physical examination reveals splenomegaly and ascites, and the initial hematocrit is 25 percent. Nasogastric suction yields 300 mL of fresh blood.

6-12. After initial resuscitation, this man should undergo

(A) esophageal balloon tamponade
(B) barium swallow
(C) selective angiography
(D) esophagogastroscopy
(E) exploratory celiotomy

6-13. A diagnosis of bleeding esophageal varices is made in this patient. Appropriate initial therapy would be

(A) intravenous vasopressin
(B) endoscopic sclerotherapy
(C) emergency portacaval shunt
(D) emergency esophageal transection
(E) esophageal balloon tamponade

Items 6-14 through 6-16

For each description, select the likely diagnosis.

(A) Tension headache
(B) Cluster headache
(C) Migraine headache
(D) Temporal arteritis
(E) Brain tumor
(F) Sinusitis
(G) Temporomandibular joint dysfunction
(H) Tic douloureux

6-14. A bilateral, bandlike sensation is felt around the head. Dull, steady pain may last days or weeks. The patient may have occipital or nuchal soreness.
(SELECT 1 DIAGNOSIS)

6-15. This unilateral, nonthrobbing headache is more common in men. Nasal stuffiness and lacrimation may be associated.
(SELECT 1 DIAGNOSIS)

6-16. This unilateral headache with localized scalp tenderness is often seen in older patients. They may have transient visual loss.
(SELECT 1 DIAGNOSIS)

6-17. A 7-year-old boy has crampy abdominal pain and a rash mainly on the back of his legs and buttocks as well as on the extensor surfaces of his forearms. Laboratory analysis reveals proteinuria and micro-hematuria. He is most likely to be affected by

(A) systemic lupus erythematosus
(B) anaphylactoid purpura
(C) poststreptococcal glomerulonephritis
(D) Takayasu arteritis
(E) dermatomyositis

Items 6-18 through 6-19

6-18. A noncyanotic 2-day-old child has a systolic murmur along the left sternal border; the examination is otherwise normal. Chest x-ray and electrocardiogram are normal. These findings are most closely associated with which of the following congenital cardiac anomalies?

(A) Tetralogy of Fallot
(B) Ventricular septal defect
(C) Tricuspid atresia
(D) Transposition of the great vessels
(E) Patent ductus arteriosus

6-19. A 3-year-old child with congenital cyanosis most probably is suffering from

(A) tetralogy of Fallot
(B) ventricular septal defect
(C) tricuspid atresia
(D) transposition of the great vessels
(E) patent ductus arteriosus

6-20. A 34-year-old mathematician is in psychoanalytic psychotherapy because of anxiety, depression, and marital problems, which seemed to begin shortly after the death of his mother. They had an intensely dependent and ambivalent relationship with each other. When the patient discusses his mother and her death, it is intellectual, with detachment and an absence of affect. This is an example of

(A) projection
(B) isolation
(C) splitting
(D) reaction-formation
(E) projective-identification

6-21. A 34-year-old man complains of lumps in his scrotal skin. The lumps are found to be small and mobile, and an oily material can be extruded from them. The most likely diagnosis is

(A) scrotal rings
(B) microcarcinoma of the scrotal type
(C) epidermoid cysts
(D) molluscum contagiosum
(E) condyloma acuminatum

6-22. The parents of a 3-year-old child indicate that he seems to be clumsy, engages in hand-wringing, is poorly coordinated, has impaired language development, and a head that seems not to be growing in proportion to the rest of the body. The most likely diagnosis is

(A) Asperger's disorder
(B) porphyria
(C) attention-deficit/hyperactivity disorder
(D) Rett's disorder
(E) conduct disorder

6-23. A previously healthy 15-year-old boy is brought to the emergency room with complaints of about 12 h of progressive anorexia, nausea, and pain of the right lower quadrant. On physical examination, he is found to have a rectal temperature of 38.1°C (100.5°F) and has direct and rebound abdominal tenderness localizing to McBurney's point as well as involuntary guarding in the right lower quadrant. At operation through a McBurney-type incision, his appendix and cecum are found to be normal, but the surgeon is impressed with the marked edema of the terminal ileum, which also has an overlying fibrinopurulent exudate. The correct procedure is to

(A) close the abdomen after culturing the exudate
(B) perform a standard appendectomy
(C) resect the involved terminal ileum
(D) perform the ileocolic resection
(E) perform an ileocolostomy to bypass the involved terminal ileum

6-24. A 50-year-old man presents with jaundice, right upper quadrant tenderness, spider angiomata, and ascites. He takes no medication but has been drinking alcohol heavily. Which of the following would be most likely in this patient?

(A) Jugular venous distention on physical examination
(B) SGPT (ALT) much higher than the SGOT (AST)
(C) Mallory bodies on liver biopsy
(D) Rapid clinical recovery after abstinence

6-25. A 16-year-old girl with complex partial seizures and mild mental retardation had an area of deep red discoloration (port wine nevus) extending over her forehead and left upper eyelid. A CT scan of her brain would be likely to reveal

(A) a hemangioblastoma
(B) a Charcot-Bouchard aneurysm
(C) an arteriovenous malformation
(D) a leptomeningeal angioma
(E) a fusiform aneurysm

YOU SHOULD HAVE COMPLETED APPROXIMATELY 25 QUESTIONS AND HAVE 30 MINUTES REMAINING.

6-26. A 4-year-old presents with sudden onset of sore throat, hoarseness, and difficulty breathing. The patient prefers to lean forward, is drooling, and has a high temperature. The most likely diagnosis is

(A) acute epiglottitis
(B) whooping cough
(C) streptococcal pharyngitis
(D) bronchiolitis
(E) mononucleosis

6-27. A 53-year-old woman presents with complaints of weakness, anorexia, malaise, constipation, and back pain. While being evaluated, she becomes somewhat lethargic. Laboratory studies include a normal chest x-ray, serum albumin of .2 mg/dL, serum calcium of 14 g/dL, serum phosphorus of 2.6 mg/dL, serum chloride of 108 mg/dL, BUN of 32 mg/dL, and creatinine of 2.0 mg/dL. Appropriate initial management would include

(A) intravenous normal saline infusion
(B) administration of thiazide diuretics
(C) administration of intravenous phosphorus
(D) use of mithramycin
(E) neck exploration and parathyroidectomy

6-28. A 72-year-old man undergoes resection of an abdominal aneurysm. He arrives in the ICU with a core temperature of 33°C (91.4°F) and shivering. The physiologic consequence of the shivering is

(A) rising mixed venous oxygen saturation
(B) increased production of carbon dioxide
(C) decreased consumption of oxygen
(D) rising base excess
(E) decreased minute ventilation

6-29. A 17-year-old high-school senior, who is 66 inches tall (168 cm) and weighs 70 lb (31.8 kg), is admitted to the hospital. She talks a great deal about her fears of "losing control" and becoming "even more fat than I am now." Despite her emaciated appearance, she diets and exercises rigorously. She insists her face, hips, and thighs are too fat. Her menstrual periods have ceased. She takes a lot of food, but eats little. The most likely diagnosis is

(A) anorexia nervosa
(B) social phobia
(C) paranoid personality disorder
(D) body dysmorphic disorder
(E) major depressive disorder

6-30. An attractive and well-dressed 22-year-old woman is arrested for prostitution, but on being booked at the jail, she is found to actually be a male. The patient tells the consulting physician that he is a female trapped in a male body and has felt that way since he was a child. He has been taking female hormones and is attempting to find a surgeon who would remove his male genitals and create a vagina. The most likely diagnosis is

(A) homosexuality
(B) gender identity disorder
(C) transvestic fetishism
(D) delusional disorder
(E) schizophrenia

6-31. A 3½-year-old girl is brought to your office by her parents who are concerned about her knock-knees (genu valgum). The parents state she was bowlegged as an infant and has become progressively knock-kneed over the past 6 months. The patient is otherwise healthy and has met all developmental milestones. Height and weight are within the 80th percentile. The femoral-tibial angle measures 14 degrees bilaterally. The intramalleolar distance is 10 cm with the knees just touching. The most likely diagnosis is

(A) Blount's disease
(B) physiologic knock-knees
(C) malunion
(D) rickets
(E) partial physeal arrest

6-32. A 25-year-old man presents with a single, indurated, painless ulcer on the penis that appeared 2 days ago. His last unprotected sexual contact was 21 days before. An immediate rapid plasma reagin (RPR) test is negative. The most likely diagnosis is

(A) syphilis
(B) herpes
(C) chancroid
(D) lymphogranuloma venereum
(E) donovanosis (granuloma inguinale)

6-33. A 26-year-old man sustains a gunshot wound to the left thigh. Exploration reveals that a 5-cm portion of superficial femoral artery is destroyed. Appropriate management includes

(A) debridement and end-to-end anastomosis
(B) debridement and repair with an interposition prosthetic graft
(C) debridement and repair with an interposition arterial graft
(D) debridement and repair with an interposition vein graft
(E) ligation and observation

6-34. A 55-year-old, obese woman develops substernal chest pain of 1 h duration. Her ECG is shown below. The most likely diagnosis is

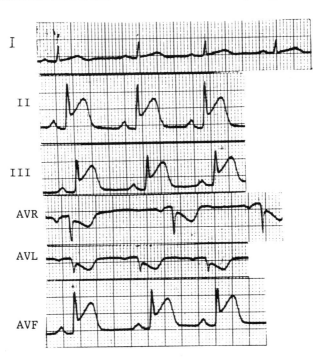

(A) costochondritis
(B) esophageal reflux
(C) acute myocardial infarction
(D) cholecystitis
(E) duodenal ulcer disease

6-35. An obese 60-year-old woman presents with progressive pain and swelling of the right knee of 12 months' duration. Her symptoms are worse after activity and late in the day. She has little pain or stiffness in the mornings. No other joints are involved and she is otherwise in good health. Your working diagnosis is

(A) Reiter's syndrome
(B) gout
(C) rheumatoid arthritis
(D) osteoarthritis
(E) psoriatic arthritis

6-36. A 4-year-old boy presents with a history of constipation since the age of 6 months. His stools, produced every 3 to 4 days, are described as large and hard. Physical examination is normal; rectal examination reveals a large ampulla, poor sphincter tone, and stool in the rectal vault. The most likely diagnosis is

(A) Hirschsprung's disease
(B) functional constipation
(C) hypercalcemia
(D) intestinal obstruction
(E) hypothyroidism

DIRECTIONS: Each group of questions below consists of four lettered options followed by a set of numbered items. For each numbered item select

A	if the item is associated with	(A) only
B	if the item is associated with	(B) only
C	if the item is associated with	**both** (A) and (B)
D	if the item is associated with	**neither** (A) nor (B)

Each lettered option may be used **once, more than once, or not at all.**

Items 6-37 through 6-41

(A) Epiglottitis
(B) Viral croup
(C) Both
(D) Neither

6-37. Most common between 3 months and 3 years of age

6-38. Fall and winter occurrence most common

6-39. Acute onset

6-40. Fever usually greater than 39.44°C (103°F)

6-41. Typical presence of an extremely sore throat

6-42. A 70-year-old man with COPD requires 2 L of nasal O_2 to treat his hypoxia, which is sometimes associated with angina. While receiving nasal O_2, the patient develops pleuritic chest pain, fever, and purulent sputum. He becomes stuporous and develops a respiratory acidosis with CO_2 retention and worsening hypoxia. The next step would be to

(A) observe patient 24 h before changing therapy
(B) stop oxygen
(C) intubate the trachea and begin mechanical ventilation
(D) begin medroxyprogesterone
(E) begin sodium bicarbonate

6-43. A previously healthy, active 18-month-old child presents with unilateral nasal obstruction and foul-smelling discharge. The child's examination is otherwise unremarkable. The most likely diagnosis is

(A) foreign body
(B) nasal polyps
(C) frontal sinusitis
(D) deviated septum
(E) choanal atresia

6-44. A patient with low-grade fever and weight loss has poor excursion, decreased fremitus, flatness to percussion, and decreased breath sounds all on the right side of the chest. The trachea is deviated to the left. The likely diagnosis is

(A) pneumothorax
(B) pleural effusion secondary to histoplasmosis
(C) consolidated pneumonia
(D) atelectasis

6-45. An ill-appearing 2-week-old girl is brought to the emergency room. She is pale and dyspneic with a respiratory rate of 80 breaths per minute. Heart rate is 195 beats per minute, sounds are distant, and there is a suggestion of a gallop. There is cardiomegaly by x-ray. An echocardiogram demonstrates poor ventricular function, dilated ventricles, and dilatation of the left atrium. An electrocardiogram shows ventricular depolarization complexes that have low voltage. The diagnosis suggested by this clinical picture is

(A) myocarditis
(B) endocardial fibroelastosis
(C) pericarditis
(D) aberrant left coronary artery arising from pulmonary artery
(E) glycogen storage disease of the heart

6-46. A 50-year-old patient presents with symptomatic nephrolithiasis. He reports that he underwent a jejunoileal bypass for morbid obesity when he was 39. One would expect to find

(A) pseudohyperparathyroidism
(B) hyperuric aciduria
(C) "hungry-bone" syndrome
(D) hyperoxaluria
(E) sporadic unicameral bone cysts

6-47. A healthy premature infant who weighs 950 g (2 lb, 1 oz) is fed breast milk to provide 120 cal/kg per day. Over ensuing weeks the baby is most apt to develop

(A) hypernatremia
(B) hypocalcemia
(C) blood in the stool
(D) hyperphosphatemia
(E) vitamin D toxicity

6-48. One month after her mother's death from chronic heart disease, a 25-year-old woman with no prior psychiatric history has the onset of irritability, difficulty concentrating, sudden fits of crying, and difficulty falling asleep. The most likely diagnosis would be

(A) major depression
(B) dysthymia
(C) posttraumatic stress disorder
(D) adjustment disorder
(E) uncomplicated bereavement

6-49. A 69-year-old man is suspected of having an acute onset of multiple small cerebral infarcts. The finding on mental status examination that would be most supportive of this diagnosis is

(A) a change in cognitive functioning
(B) depressed mood
(C) inappropriate affect
(D) delusional thinking
(E) anxiety

6-50. A 1-week-old black infant presents to you for the first time with a large, fairly well-defined, purple lesion over the buttocks bilaterally. The lesion is not palpable, nor is it warm or tender. The mother denies trauma and reports that the lesion has been present since birth. This otherwise well-appearing infant is growing and developing normally and appears normal upon physical examination. The most likely diagnosis in this infant is

(A) child abuse
(B) mongolian spot
(C) subcutaneous fat necrosis
(D) vitamin K deficiency
(E) hemophilia

BLOCK 7

**YOU HAVE 60 MINUTES
TO COMPLETE 50 QUESTIONS.**

BLOCK 7

YOU HAVE **60** MINUTES
TO COMPLETE **50** QUESTIONS.

Questions

7-1. After being stung by a yellow-jacket, a 14-year-old develops sudden onset of hoarseness and shortness of breath. An urticarial rash is noted. The most important first step in treatment is

(A) antihistamine
(B) epinephrine
(C) venom immunotherapy
(D) corticosteroids
(E) removal of stinger

7-2. A 15-year-old boy has been immobilized in a double hip spica for 6 weeks after having fractured his femur in a skiing accident. He has become depressed and listless for the past few days and has complained of nausea and constipation. He is found to have microscopic hematuria and a blood pressure of 150/100 mmHg. You should

(A) request a psychiatric evaluation
(B) check blood pressure every 2 h for 2 days
(C) collect urine for measurement of the calcium-creatinine ratio
(D) order a renal sonogram and intravenous pyelogram (IVP)
(E) measure 24-h urinary protein

7-3. During the course of an operation on an unstable, critically ill patient, the left ureter is lacerated through 50 percent of its circumference. If the patient's condition is felt to be too serious to allow time for definitive repair, alternative methods of management include

(A) ligation of the injured ureter and ipsilateral nephrostomy
(B) ipsilateral nephrectomy
(C) placement of a catheter from the distal ureter through an abdominal wall stab wound
(D) placement of a suction drain adjacent to the injury without further manipulation that might convert the partial laceration into a complete disruption
(E) bringing the proximal ureter up to the skin as a ureterostomy

Items 7-4 through 7-7

A 32-year-old man with diabetic nephropathy undergoes an uneventful renal transplant from his sister (2 haplotype match). His immunosuppressive regimen includes azathioprine, steroids, and cyclosporine. For each development in the postoperative period, select the most appropriate next step.

(A) Begin ganciclovir
(B) Administer steroid boost
(C) Withhold steroids
(D) Decrease cyclosporine
(E) Increase cyclosporine
(F) Decrease azathioprine
(G) Obtain renal ultrasound
(H) Begin broad-spectrum antibiotics
(I) Administer filgrastim (Neupogen)
(J) Administer FK50

7-4. On postoperative day 3 he is doing well, but you notice on his routine laboratory tests that his white blood cell count is 2.0 **(SELECT 1 STEP)**

7-5. His WBC count gradually returns to normal, but on postoperative day 7 he develops a fever to 39.44°C (103°F) and a nonproductive cough. A chest x-ray reveals diffuse interstitial infiltrates, and a "buffy coat" is positive for viral inclusions.
(SELECT 1 STEP)

7-6. The patient recovers from the above illness and is discharged home on postoperative day 18. At 3-month follow-up he is doing well, but you notice that his creatinine is 2.8 mg/dL. He has no fever, his graft is not tender, and his renal ultrasound is normal.
(SELECT 1 STEP)

7-7. Six months following his transplant, the patient begins to develop fever, malaise, and pain of the right lower quadrant. Upon palpation the graft is tender. Chest x-ray and urine and blood cultures are normal. Renal ultrasound shows an edematous graft.
(SELECT 1 STEP)

7-8. Two weeks after a viral syndrome a 2-year-old child develops bruising and generalized petechiae, more prominent over the legs. No hepatosplenomegaly nor lymph node enlargement is noted. The child seems remarkably normal except for these findings. Laboratory testing shows the patient to have a normal hemoglobin, hematocrit, and white blood count and differential. The platelet count is 15,000/mm^3. The most likely diagnosis is

(A) von Willebrand disease
(B) acute leukemia
(C) idiopathic thrombocytopenic purpura
(D) aplastic anemia
(E) thrombotic thrombocytopenic purpura

Items 7-9 through 7-10

A 35-year-old man complains of substernal chest pain, aggravated by inspiration and relieved by sitting up. The patient has had a history of tuberculosis. Chest x-ray shows an enlarged cardiac silhouette. Lung fields are clear.

7-9. The next step in evaluation would be

(A) cardiac catheterization
(B) right lateral decubitus film
(C) echocardiogram
(D) serial ECGs
(E) thallium stress test

7-10. The patient develops jugular venous distention. There is an inward movement of the jugular pulse synchronous with the pulse of the carotid artery. The ECG shows electrical alternans. The most likely additional finding would be

(A) basilar rales halfway up both posterior lung fields
(B) S_3 gallop
(C) pulsus paradoxus
(D) strong apical beat

7-11. A 6-year-old child presents complaining of patchy hair loss on the back of the scalp. Examination reveals well-demarcated areas of erythema and scaling, and although there is still some hair in the area, it is noted that the hairs are extremely short and broken in appearance. The patient is most likely suffering from

(A) cutaneous candidiasis
(B) tinea capitis
(C) androgenic hair loss
(D) scalp psoriasis
(E) seborrheic dermatitis

7-12. A 30-year-old man is transferred to the medical service 5 days after undergoing splenectomy for trauma. His blood urea nitrogen has risen to 100 mg/dL and his creatinine to 10 mg/dL. On examination there is normal skin turgor, his chest is clear to auscultation and percussion, and there is no peripheral or sacral edema. The bladder is not distended on percussion. The most important information about this patient will come from

(A) renal biopsy
(B)   24-h urine protein
(C) urine sediment and spot urine sodium
(D) antinuclear antibody and serum complement

7-13. A 54-year-old woman under-goes a laparotomy because of a pelvic mass, which proves to be a unilateral ovarian neoplasm accom-panied by a large omental metastasis. The most appropriate intraoperative course of action would be

(A) omental biopsy
(B) ovarian biopsy
(C) excision of the omental metastasis and unilateral oophorectomy
(D) omentectomy and bilateral salpingo-oophorectomy
(E) omentectomy, total abdominal hysterectomy, and bilateral salpingo-oophorectomy

7-14. A patient is brought to the emergency room after a motor vehicle accident. He is unconscious and has a deep scalp laceration and one dilated pupil. His heart rate is 120 beats per minute, blood pres-sure 80/40 mmHg, and respiratory rate 35 breaths per minute. Despite rapid administration of 2 L normal saline, his vital signs do not change significantly. The injury likely to explain this patient's hypotension is

(A) epidural hematoma
(B) subdural hematoma
(C) intraparenchymal brain hemorrhage
(D) basilar skull fracture
(E) none of the above

7-15. A term, 4200-g female infant is delivered via cesarean section because of cephalopelvic dispropor-tion. The amniotic fluid was clear and the infant cried almost immedi-ately after birth. Within the first 15 min of life, however, the infant's respiratory rate increased to 80 breaths per minute and she began to have intermittent grunting respi-rations. The infant was transferred to the level two nursery and was noted to have an oxygen saturation of 94 percent. The chest radiograph showed fluid in the fissure, over-aeration, and prominent pulmonary vascular markings. The most likely diagnosis in this infant is

(A) diaphragmatic hernia
(B) meconium aspiration
(C) pneumonia
(D) idiopathic respiratory distress syndrome
(E) transient tachypnea of the newborn

7-16. A 23-year-old woman was seen in the emergency room stating that "out-of-the-blue" she was seized by intense fear associated with shortness of breath, a pounding heart, shaking, dizziness, a choking sensation, fear that she was dying or going crazy, and a desire to run away. The attack lasted about 20 min. This was the third occurrence of these symptoms in the past 3 weeks. The most likely diagnosis is

(A) acute psychotic episode
(B) hypochondriasis
(C) panic attack
(D) generalized anxiety disorder
(E) major depression

7-17. A 3-year-old child awakens at night with a fever of 39.6°C (103.3°F), a severe sore throat, and a barking cough. Physical examination of the child, who is drooling, shows a very red throat and inspiratory stridor. The hypopharynx is obscured by yellow mucus. There is no respiratory distress. Optimal management would include

(A) immediate hospitalization for possible intubation
(B) immediate inhalation therapy with racemic epinephrine
(C) treatment with oral ampicillin, 50 mg/kg per day
(D) suctioning of the pharynx and hourly examinations of the hypopharynx
(E) a throat culture and expectorant and mist therapy

7-18. A 12-year-old boy presents with a 3-h history of a painful scrotum. Examination reveals an enlarged, tender, erythematous scrotum. The scrotum does not transilluminate, and the testicle is in a transverse lie. The most likely diagnosis is

(A) spermatocele
(B) hydrocele
(C) epididymitis
(D) varicocele
(E) testicular torsion

7-19. A 32-year-old farmer presents to the emergency room with a crushing injury of the index finger and thumb that occurred while he was working with machinery in his barn. Records show that he received three doses of Td in the past, and that his last dose was given when he was 25 years old. In addition to proper wound cleaning and management, which of the following is the most appropriate intervention to prevent tetanus?

(A) No additional prophylaxis
(B) Administration of tetanus toxoid
(C) Administration of tetanus immunoglobulin only
(D) Administration of tetanus toxoid and immunoglobulin
(E) Administration of tetanus and diphtheria toxoid

7-20. A 16-year-old basketball player complains of pain in his knees. A physical examination reveals, in addition to tenderness, a swollen and prominent tibial tuberosity. Radiographs of the area are unremarkable. The most likely diagnosis is

(A) Osgood-Schlatter disease
(B) popliteal cyst
(C) slipped capital femoral epiphysis
(D) Legg-Calvé-Perthes disease
(E) gonococcal arthritis

7-21. A 64-year-old man afflicted with severe emphysema, who receives oxygen therapy at home, is admitted to the hospital because of upper gastrointestinal bleeding. The bleeding ceases soon after admission, and the patient becomes agitated and then disoriented; he is given intramuscular diazepam (Valium), 5 mg. Twenty minutes later he is unresponsive. Physical examination reveals a stuporous but arousable man who has papilledema and asterixis. Arterial blood gases are pH 7.17 P_{O_2} 42 torr, P_{CO_2} 95 torr. The best immediate therapy would be to

(A) correct hypoxemia with high-flow nasal oxygen
(B) correct acidosis with sodium bicarbonate
(C) administer intravenous dexamethasone, 10 mg
(D) intubate the patient
(E) call for neurosurgical consultation

7-22. A 20-year-old white man has noted an uneven tan on his upper back and chest. On examination he has many circular, lighter macules with a barely visible scale that coalesce into larger areas. The best test procedure to establish the diagnosis is a

(A) punch biopsy
(B) potassium hydroxide (KOH) microscopic examination
(C) dermatophyte test medium (DTM) culture for fungus
(D) serologic test for syphilis
(E) Tzanck smear

7-23. Three weeks after an upper respiratory illness, a 25-year-old man develops weakness of his arms and legs over several days. On physical examination, he is tachypneic with shallow respirations and has symmetric muscle weakness in both arms and legs. There is no obvious sensory deficit, but motor reflexes cannot be elicited. The most likely diagnosis is

(A) myasthenia gravis
(B) multiple sclerosis
(C) Guillain-Barré syndrome
(D) dermatomyositis
(E) diabetes mellitus

7-24. A 75-year-old man complained of malaise and slowly progressive weight loss for the better part of 3 months. Laboratory tests revealed a hematocrit of 32 percent, an erythrocyte sedimentation rate (ESR) of 97 mm/h, and a white blood cell count of 10,700 cells per cubic millimeter. His serum creatine kinase (CK) and thyroxine (T_4) levels were normal. Which of the following is most likely as the explanation for his complaints?

(A) Polymyositis
(B) Dermatomyositis
(C) Polymyalgia rheumatica
(D) Rheumatoid arthritis
(E) Hyperthyroid myopathy

7-25. A stockbroker in his mid-forties consults you with complaints of episodes of severe, often incapacitating chest pain on swallowing. The diagnostic studies on the esophagus you have ordered yield the following: endoscopic examination and biopsy—mild inflammation distally; manometry—prolonged high amplitude contractions from the arch of the aorta distally, lower esophageal sphincter (LES) pressure 20 mmHg with relaxation on swallowing; barium swallow—2-cm epiphrenic diverticulum. You would recommend

(A) myotomy from level of aortic arch to distal sphincter; no disruption of LES
(B) diverticulectomy, myotomy from level of aortic arch to fundus, fundoplication
(C) diverticulectomy, cardiomyotomy of distal 3 cm of esophagus and proximal 2 cm of stomach with antireflux fundoplication
(D) a trial of calcium channel blockers
(E) pneumatic dilation of LES

YOU SHOULD HAVE COMPLETED APPROXIMATELY
25 QUESTIONS AND HAVE 30 MINUTES REMAINING.

7-26. A man who has agitated depression is started on the following medications (in daily doses): imipramine, 150 mg; perphenazine, 32 mg; and benztropine mesylate (Cogentin), 2 mg. One week later, his wife reports that he has been unusually forgetful during the last 4 days and that last night he awoke unusually confused about where he was. On physical examination, the man appears slightly flushed, his skin and palms are dry, and his heart rate is fast. He is slow to remember the date and has trouble concentrating. He showed none of these symptoms during his appointment last week. The diagnosis is

(A) anticholinergic syndrome
(B) neuroleptic syndrome
(C) schizophreniform psychosis
(D) toxic brain syndrome
(E) cerebrovascular accident

7-27. A previously healthy 7-year-old child suddenly complains of a headache and falls to the floor. When examined in the emergency room, he is lethargic and has a left central facial weakness and left hemiparesis with conjugate ocular deviation to the right. The most likely diagnosis is

(A) hemiplegic migraine
(B) supratentorial tumor
(C) Todd's paralysis
(D) acute subdural hematoma
(E) acute infantile hemiplegia

7-28. A young adult male presents with arthritis, skin lesions, and acute tenosynovitis. Which of the following is the most likely diagnosis?

(A) Disseminated gonococcal infection
(B) DeQuervain's stenosing tenosynovitis
(C) Acute pseudogout
(D) Osteoarthritis
(E) Reiter's syndrome

7-29. A patient with small cell carcinoma of the lung develops lethargy. Serum electrolytes are drawn and show a serum sodium of 118 mg/L. There is no evidence of edema, orthostatic hypotension, or dehydration. Urine is concentrated with an osmolality of 320 mmol/kg. Serum BUN, creatinine, and glucose are within the normal range. Which of the following is the next appropriate step?

(A) Normal saline infusion
(B) Diuresis
(C) Fluid restriction
(D) Tetracycline

Items 7-30 through 7-32

A 40-year-old man develops bilateral facial weakness. The patient returned from a camping trip in Wisconsin that had lasted 6 weeks. He gives a history of arthralgias. There is no evidence of arthritis. On examination he cannot close either eye well or raise either eyebrow. The first heart sound is diminished, and the ECG shows first-degree atrioventricular (AV) block. Laboratory findings are as follows:

Hgb: 14 g/dL
WBC: 10,000/mm^3
VDRL test: negative
Fluorescent treponemal antibody-absorption (FTA-ABS) test: positive

7-30. Which of the following would be most useful?

(A) CT scan of head
(B) MRI of head
(C) More detailed history
(D) Kveim test

7-31. The likely cause of these symptoms is

(A) intracranial infection
(B) Lyme disease
(C) endocarditis
(D) herpes simplex

7-32. Treatment of choice would be

(A) penicillin or ceftriaxone
(B) acyclovir
(C) corticosteroids
(D) aminoglycoside

7-33. A 16-year-old boy presents in the emergency room with a history of a football injury to the left flank earlier that day. He reports that at the time of injury he only had the wind knocked out of him and recovered in a few minutes. About 1 h later he began to experience pain in the left upper quadrant and left shoulder and light-headedness on standing. The diagnosis that would best explain these symptoms is

(A) dislocation of the left shoulder
(B) broken rib on the left side
(C) collapsed lung
(D) contusion of the left kidney
(E) ruptured spleen

7-34. An 8-year-old is accidentally hit in the abdomen by a baseball bat. After several minutes of discomfort, he seems to be fine. Over the ensuing 24 h, however, he develops a fever, abdominal pain, and persistent vomiting. On examination the child appears quite uncomfortable. The abdomen is tender with decreased bowel sounds throughout, but especially painful with guarding in the midepigastric region. The test likely to confirm your suspicions is

(A) serum amylase
(B) complete blood count with differential and platelets
(C) serum total and direct bilirubin levels
(D) abdominal radiograph
(E) electrolyte panel

7-35. A 49-year-old man with hypertension and anxiety is attached to an apparatus that measures skin temperature and emits a tone proportional in loudness to the temperature. This is an example of a therapeutic technique called

(A) hypnosis
(B) behavior modification
(C) supportive psychotherapy
(D) placebo therapy
(E) biofeedback

7-36. A 62-year-old woman is admitted to a medical unit because of an 11.4-kg (25-lb) weight loss over the last 3 months. She also reports anorexia, insomnia, fatigue, and decreased sexual interest. She does not have depressed affect, and her mental status is judged to be unimpaired. Extensive medical evaluation is unremarkable. The most likely diagnosis is

(A) senile dementia
(B) occult malignancy
(C) hypochondriasis
(D) chronic anxiety
(E) masked depression

7-37. If a parent has the gene for Huntington's disease,

(A) half the offspring are at risk only if the affected parent is male

(B) half the offspring are at risk only if the affected parent is female

(C) half the offspring are at risk if either parent is symptomatic for the disease before the age of 30

(D) half the offspring are at risk for the disease

(E) one out of four children is at risk for the disease

7-38. A 4-hour-old girl had been doing fine until the nurses attempted to challenge-feed the newborn. She became cyanotic during the attempt, but improved with a return to crying when the attempt at feeding was discontinued. The most likely diagnosis is

(A) hyaline membrane disease

(B) choanal atresia

(C) transient tachypnea of the newborn

(D) meconium aspiration syndrome

(E) tracheoesophageal fistula

7-39. A 60-year-old man presents to your clinic with an 80-pack-year history of cigarette smoking, has an increased anteroposterior thickness of the thorax, and suffers from exertional dyspnea. He most likely suffers from

(A) chylothorax

(B) bronchiectasis

(C) panlobular emphysema

(D) lung abscess

(E) bronchial adenoma

7-40. A teenaged boy falls from his bicycle and is run over by a truck. On arrival in the emergency room, he is awake, alert, and appears frightened but in no distress. The chest radiograph suggests an air fluid level in the left lower lung field and the nasogastric tube seems to coil upward into the left chest. The next best step in management is

(A) placement of a left chest tube

(B) immediate thoracotomy

(C) immediate celiotomy

(D) esophagogastroscopy

(E) removal and replacement of the nasogastric tube; diagnostic peritoneal lavage

7-41. A 46-year-old woman presents with depression, urinary urgency, night sweats, and headaches. On examination she is found to be anovulatory. The most likely diagnosis is

(A) psychosomatic disorder
(B) manic depression
(C) urinary tract infection
(D) tuberculosis with
    renal involvement
(E) menopause

7-42. A 33-year-old married man comes for consultation because of chronic anxiety. He states his marriage is very happy and gives a sexual history that includes daily and satisfying sexual intercourse with his wife. He also masturbates three to four times weekly. He states that his sexual drive has been high ever since he was a teenager. His sexual fantasies are predominantly heterosexual, but there are occasional homosexual fantasies while masturbating. On several occasions as an adult, while traveling alone, he has had both heterosexual and homosexual experiences, which are remembered as having been pleasurable. While describing some transient guilt about "stepping out" on his wife, he is not anxious or troubled about his sexuality and does not consider it to be a problem. On the basis of the patient's sexual history, one could reasonably infer a diagnosis of

(A) schizotypal personality disorder
(B) antisocial personality disorder
(C) narcissistic personality disorder
(D) borderline personality disorder
(E) no personality disorder

7-43. You are awakened in the night by your 2-year-old son, who has developed noisy breathing on inspiration, marked retractions of the chest wall, flaring of the nostrils, and a barking cough. He has a mild upper respiratory infection (URI) for 2 days. The most likely diagnosis is

(A) asthma
(B) epiglottitis
(C) bronchiolitis
(D) viral croup
(E) foreign body in the right mainstem bronchus

7-44. A 22-year-old man from New Jersey has suddenly developed a pruritic vesicular rash on his arms, hands, and face. There are linear areas of blisters. The rash appears to be spreading for 2 days. Four days ago he was working in his yard clearing out a wooded area. The diagnosis is

(A) chickenpox
(B) Lyme disease
(C) blister beetle bites
(D) poison ivy
(E) photosensitivity reaction

7-45. On physical examination of a 21-year-old woman, you auscultate at the apex of her heart a low-pitched mid-to-late diastolic murmur with accentuation of S_1. Upon careful listening you notice a clicking sound just after S_2 and immediately preceding the rumbling murmur. The most likely condition is

(A) aortic insufficiency
(B) atrial myxoma
(C) mitral valve prolapse
(D) mitral valve stenosis
(E) patent foramen ovale

7-46. A cyanotic newborn is suspected of having congenital heart disease. The ECG shows left axis deviation and left ventricular hypertrophy (LVH). The most likely diagnosis is

(A) transposition of the great arteries
(B) truncus arteriosus
(C) tricuspid atresia
(D) tetralogy of Fallot
(E) persistent fetal circulation

7-47. A 30-year-old woman in the last trimester of pregnancy suddenly develops massive swelling of the left lower extremity from the inguinal ligament to the ankle. The correct sequence of workup and treatment should be

(A) venogram, bed rest, heparin
(B) impedance plethysmography, bed rest, heparin
(C) impedance plethysmography, bed rest, vena caval filter
(D) impedance plethysmography, bed rest, heparin, warfarin (Coumadin)
(E) clinical evaluation, bed rest, warfarin

7-48. A 5-year-old boy presents to your office complaining of right ear pain. Upon examination of the ear, pain is elicited with traction of the tragus, the tympanic membrane is not visualized well, and some periauricular lymph nodes are palpable. The most likely diagnosis is

(A) acute otitis media
(B) acute otitis externa
(C) mastoiditis
(D) a blocked eustachian tube
(E) acute viral conjunctivitis

7-49. A young man fractured his humerus in an automobile accident. As the pain from the injury subsided he noticed that he had weakness on attempted flexion at the elbow. He developed paresthesias over the radial and volar aspects of the forearm. During the accident he probably injured his

(A) suprascapular nerve
(B) long thoracic nerve
(C) musculocutaneous nerve
(D) radial nerve
(E) median nerve

7-50. A 22-year-old woman with a history of hypertension, use of oral contraceptives, and sickle cell anemia was involved in a motorcycle accident and is recovering from massive reconstructive surgery to her right leg. During her second week in traction, she develops tachypnea and tachycardia. Auscultation reveals a pleural friction rub, and roentgenographic findings show a raised left diaphragm and basilar atelectasis. The most likely diagnosis is

(A) bacterial pneumonia
(B) pneumothorax
(C) pulmonary embolism
(D) neurogenic shock
(E) hemorrhagic shock

BLOCK 8

**YOU HAVE 60 MINUTES
TO COMPLETE 50 QUESTIONS.**

BLOCK 8

YOU HAVE *60* MINUTES
TO COMPLETE *50* QUESTIONS.

Questions

Items 8-1 through 8-2

A 40-year-old woman with a history of chaotic interpersonal relationships enters psychoanalytic psychotherapy. She alternates between periods in which she idealizes the therapist and the therapy and periods of rageful anger, at which time nothing is good about the therapist or the therapy either now or in the past.

8-1. This is an example of the defense mechanism of

(A) reaction-formation
(B) denial
(C) projection
(D) undoing
(E) splitting

8-2. In which of the following diagnoses is this most commonly encountered?

(A) Schizophrenia
(B) Major depressive episode
(C) Obsessive-compulsive disorder
(D) Schizoid personality disorder
(E) Borderline personality disorder

8-3. A 2-week-old female is noted to have a thin membrane adhering together the upper portion of labia minora. The most appropriate course of action for these labial adhesions is to

(A) apply estrogen cream daily
(B) refer for surgical repair
(C) apply traction to the opposing labia until the adhesion breaks
(D) evaluate the patient for congenital adrenal hyperplasia
(E) do nothing as the lesions are of no consequence

8-4. A 31-year-old man is brought to the emergency room following an automobile accident in which his chest struck the steering wheel. Examination reveals stable vital signs but the patient exhibits multiple palpable rib fractures and paradoxical movement of the right side of the chest. Chest x-ray shows no evidence of pneumothorax or hemothorax, but a large pulmonary contusion is developing. Proper treatment would consist of which of the following?

(A) Tracheostomy, mechanical ventilation, and positive-end-expiratory pressure
(B) Stabilization of the chest wall with sandbags
(C) Stabilization with towel clips
(D) Immediate operative stabilization
(E) No treatment unless signs of respiratory distress develop

8-5. A 40-year-old woman presents with puffiness around the eyes, brittle hair, coarse skin, and complaints of fatigue and cold intolerance. The most likely diagnosis is

(A) hypothyroidism
(B) hyperthyroidism
(C) congestive heart failure
(D) Cushing's disease
(E) nephrotic syndrome

8-6. A 70-year-old patient with long-standing type 2 diabetes mellitus presents with complaints of pain in the left ear with purulent drainage. On physical examination, the patient is afebrile. The pinna of the left ear is tender, and the external auditory canal is swollen and edematous. The peripheral white blood cell count is normal. The organism most likely to grow from the purulent drainage is

(A) *Pseudomonas aeruginosa*
(B) *Staphylococcus aureus*
(C) *Candida albicans*
(D) *Haemophilus influenzae*
(E) *Moraxella catarrhalis*

8-7. A young man is brought to your office with a fracture of the humerus in its distal third. He is unable to extend his wrist. What structure is most likely damaged?

(A) Brachial vessel
(B) Radial nerve
(C) Median nerve
(D) Ulnar nerve
(E) Axillary nerve

8-8. A 18-month-old child presents to the emergency center having had a brief, generalized tonic-clonic seizure. He is now postictal and has a temperature of 40°C (104°F). During the lumbar puncture (which proves to be normal) he has a large, watery stool that has both blood and mucus in it. The most likely diagnosis in this patient is

(A) *Salmonella*
(B) enterovirus
(C) rotavirus
(D) *Campylobacter*
(E) *Shigella*

8-9. A 70-year-old man in the intensive care unit complains of fever and shaking chills. He develops hypotension, and blood cultures are positive for gram-negative bacilli. The patient begins bleeding from venipuncture sites and around his Foley catheter. The following laboratory values are found:

> Hct: 38 percent
> WBC: $15 \times 10^3/mm^3$
> Platelet count: 40,000 per
>   microliter
> Peripheral blood smear:
>   fragmented RBCs
> Prothrombin time (PT):
>   prolonged
> Partial thromboplastin time
>   (PTT): prolonged
> Plasma fibrinogen: 70 mg/dL
>   (n 200 to 400)

The best course of therapy in this patient is to

(A) administer heparin
(B) administer vitamin K
(C) begin RBC transfusion
(D) begin plasmapheresis
(E) treat the underlying disease

Items 8-10 through 8-11

A 26-year-old man is brought to the emergency room after being extricated from the driver's seat of a car involved in a head-on collision in which he was not wearing his seat belt. His ECG is shown below.

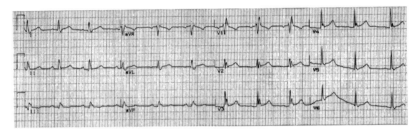

8-10. His ECG is most consistent with

(A) preexisting disease
(B) myocardial ischemia that caused the accident
(C) myocardial contusion that resulted from the accident
(D) Chagas' disease
(E) normal variant

8-11. The best test for establishing the diagnosis and the degree of myocardial dysfunction is

(A) serial ECGs
(B) creatine phosphokinase (CPK-MB) fractionation
(C) echocardiography
(D) radionuclide angiography
(E) coronary angiography

8-12. A 30-year-old nurse is brought to employee health for evaluation following a needle stick injury that occurred at the AIDS clinic. The source patient is known to be infected with HIV. Which of the following factors carries the greatest risk for transmission of HIV to the health care worker?

(A) Depth of the injury
(B) Stage of illness of the source patient
(C) Presence of visible blood on the needle
(D) Use of gloves during the procedure
(E) Entrance of the needle into a vein or artery of the source patient

Items 8-13 through 8-14

A 32-year-old woman with alcoholism and cocaine use dating back at least 10 years came to the emergency room after 48 h of recurrent vomiting and hematemesis. She reported abdominal discomfort that preceded her vomiting by a few days. For at least 36 h she had been unable to keep ethanol in her stomach. Intravenous fluid replacement was started while she was being transported to the emergency room, and while in the emergency room she complained of progressive blurring of vision. Over the course of an hour she became increasingly disoriented, ataxic, and dysarthric.

8-13. The most likely explanation for her rapid deterioration is

(A) dehydration
(B) hypomagnesemia
(C) Wernicke's encephalopathy
(D) hypoglycemia
(E) cocaine overdose

8-14. Emergency administration of what medication is appropriate in this clinical setting?

(A) Glucose
(B) Magnesium sulfate
(C) Pyridoxine
(D) Cyanocobalamin
(E) Thiamine

8-15. A 5-year-old white girl presents with a 14-day history of multiple oval lesions over her back. The rash began with a single lesion over the lower back; the other lesions developed over the next days. These lesions are distributed along the cutaneous cleavage lines and are slightly pruritic. The likely diagnosis is

(A) contact dermatitis
(B) pityriasis rosea
(C) seborrheic dermatitis
(D) lichen planus
(E) psoriasis

8-16. A 9-year-old girl is brought to your office by her mother, who states that the daughter has been losing weight and having difficulty at school. The mother discovered some yellow discharge on the child's underwear. On examination you note erythema to almost all parts of the vulva and to the vagina. There is a yellow discharge, The most likely diagnosis is

(A) müllerian duct tumor
(B) wolffian duct tumor
(C) bubble-bath vaginitis
(D) sexual abuse
(E) straddle injury

8-17. A 17-year-old girl noted a 2-cm, annular, pink, scaly lesion on her thigh. In the next 2 weeks she developed several smaller, oval, pink lesions with a fine collarette of scale. They seem to run in the body folds and mainly involve the trunk, although a few are on the upper arms and thighs. There is no adenopathy and no oral lesions. The most likely diagnosis is

(A) tinea versicolor
(B) psoriasis
(C) lichen planus
(D) pityriasis rosea
(E) secondary syphilis

8-18. An 80-year-old man is admitted to the hospital complaining of nausea, abdominal pain, distention, and diarrhea. A cautiously performed transanal contrast study reveals an "apple-core" configuration in the rectosigmoid. Appropriate management at this time would include

(A) colonoscopic decompression and rectal tube placement
(B) saline enemas and digital disimpaction of fecal matter from the rectum
(C) colon resection and sigmoid colostomy
(D) oral administration of metronidazole and checking a *Clostridium difficile* titer
(E) evaluation of an electrocardiogram and obtaining an angiogram to evaluate for colonic mesenteric ischemia

8-19. A 4-month-old child is brought to the emergency room. The parents have noted that the child's scrotum is enlarged. The physician found the mass non-tender, smooth, and firm. The scrotum was distended but not taut. Using his penlight, he determined that the mass transilluminated. The most likely diagnosis is

(A) scrotal carcinoma
(B) spermatocele
(C) varicocele
(D) hydrocele
(E) epididymitis

8-20. A 39-year-old woman, gravida 3, para 3, complains of progressive secondary dysmenorrhea and menorrhagia. Pelvic examination demonstrates a firm, diffusely enlarged uterus. Results of endometrial biopsy are normal. This patient most likely has

(A) endometriosis
(B) endometritis
(C) adenomyosis
(D) uterine sarcoma
(E) leiomyoma

8-21. A 2-year-old patient has microscopic and occasionally gross hematuria. His father has hearing loss and end-stage renal disease. The most likely cause of this child's hematuria is

(A) Alport syndrome
(B) Berger nephropathy (IgA nephropathy)
(C) idiopathic hypercalciuria
(D) membranous glomerulopathy
(E) Goodpasture disease

8-22. A 20-year-old man complains of diarrhea, burning of the throat, and difficulty swallowing over 2 months. On examination he has mild jaundice and transverse white striae of the fingernails. There is also evidence of peripheral neuropathy. The best diagnostic study would be

(A) liver biopsy
(B) arsenic level
(C) antinuclear antibody
(D) endoscopy

Items 8-23 through 8-25

For each stage in the treatment of the patient below, select the appropriate next step.

(A) Left hemicolectomy
(B) Right hemicolectomy
(C) Subtotal colectomy
(D) Total colectomy
(E) Hepatic wedge resection
(F) External beam irradiation
(G) 5-Fluorouracil and leucovorin
(H) External beam irradiation and chemotherapy
(I) Abdominal MRI
(J) No further treatment

8-23. A 65-year-old man is admitted to the hospital with complaints of intermittent constipation and microcytic anemia. Barium enema reveals a nonobstructing "apple-core" lesion of the proximal sigmoid colon. Colonoscopy confirms the location of the mass and reveals no other synchronous lesions.
(SELECT 1 STEP)

8-24. The patient undergoes surgery and recovers uneventfully. Pathology of the resected specimen is reported as Dukes C with negative surgical margins.
(SELECT 1 STEP)

8-25. In 6-month follow-up an abdominal CT scan shows a 2-cm isolated lesion in the right lobe of the liver. Repeat colonoscopy shows no evidence of recurrent or metachronous lesions. Chest x-ray and bone scan are normal.
(SELECT 1 STEP)

YOU SHOULD HAVE COMPLETED APPROXIMATELY
25 QUESTIONS AND HAVE 30 MINUTES REMAINING.

8-26. A young man presents to your office after suffering blunt trauma to his right eye. Examination of the eye reveals normal pupillary response, but blood in the anterior chamber. This condition is called

(A) external hordeolum
(B) internal hordeolum
(C) chalazion
(D) hyphema
(E) cataract

8-27. A 40-year-old man has a history of three duodenal ulcers with prompt recurrence. Symptoms have been associated with severe diarrhea. One of the ulcers occurred close to the jejunum. Serum gastrin levels have been 200 pg/mL. The most useful test in this patient is

(A) colonoscopy
(B) endoscopic retrograde cholangiogram
(C) CT scan of abdomen
(D) secretin injection test
(E) upper gastrointestinal series

8-28. A newborn has puffy eyelids, red conjunctivae, and a small amount of clear ocular discharge 6 h after birth. The most likely diagnosis is

(A) dacryocystitis
(B) chemical conjunctivitis
(C) pneumococcal ophthalmia
(D) gonococcal ophthalmia
(E) chlamydial conjunctivitis

8-29. A 40-year-old man is arrested and sent for observation after repeatedly disrupting the local IRS office with accusations that it is an arm of the Central Intelligence Agency and it is spying on him with the intent of assassination because he has relatives living in Russia. His mental status examination is unremarkable except for delusional thinking about the IRS. When his wife visits, she is found to have a somewhat passive relationship with her husband, clearly holds the same convictions that led to his arrest, and otherwise displays an unremarkable mental status. The most likely diagnosis for this man's wife is

(A) paranoid schizophrenia
(B) shared psychotic disorder
(C) paranoid personality disorder
(D) obsessive-compulsive disorder
(E) avoidant personality disorder

8-30. A 1-week-old previously healthy infant presents to the emergency room with the acute onset of bilious vomiting. The abdominal plain film shows evidence of obstruction at the duodenum. Barium enema reveals the cecum to be malpositioned. The most likely diagnosis for this patient is

(A) jejunal atresia
(B) hypertrophic pyloric stenosis
(C) malrotation of the intestines with volvulus
(D) appendicitis
(E) intussusception

8-31. A 52-year-old man complains of impotence. On physical examination he has an elevated jugular venous pulse, S_3 gallop, and hepatomegaly. He also appears tanned, with pigmentation along joint folds. His left knee is swollen and tender. The plasma glucose is 250 mg/dL, and liver enzymes are elevated. Your next study to establish the diagnosis should be

(A) detection of nocturnal penile tumescence
(B) determination of serum ferritin
(C) determination of serum copper
(D) detection of hepatitis B surface antigen
(E) echocardiography

8-32. A 37-year-old man presents after 3 days of feeling weak. He drinks alcohol daily. He had to come in when he felt chest palpitations. He has shortness of breath and lightheadedness with any exertion. His pulse feels irregularly irregular. The most likely diagnosis is

(A) sinus tachycardia
(B) sinus bradycardia
(C) ventricular premature beats
(D) atrial fibrillation
(E) ventricular fibrillation

8-33. An elderly pedestrian collides with a bicycle-riding pizza delivery man and suffers a unilateral fracture of his pelvis through the obturator foramen. You would manage this injury by

(A) external pelvic fixation
(B) angiographic visualization of the obturator artery with surgical exploration if the artery is injured or constricted
(C) direct surgical approach with internal fixation of the ischial ramus
(D) short-term bed rest with gradual ambulation as pain allows after 3 days
(E) hip spica

8-34. A 3-year-old boy has a young puppy and a history of pica. He has had the recent onset of wheezing, hepatomegaly, and marked eosinophilia (80 percent eosinophils). The test most likely to produce a specific diagnosis is

(A) tuberculin skin test
(B) histoplasmin test
(C) ELISA for *Toxocara*
(D) silver stain of gastric aspirate
(E) stool examination for ova and parasites

8-35. A 55-year-old man presents to the hospital with the complaint of severe intermittent pain in his right lower back that radiates around his trunk into his lower quadrant and upper right thigh. The most likely diagnosis is

(A) hepatitis
(B) appendicitis
(C) a ureteral stone
(D) pyelonephritis
(E) biliary obstruction

8-36. A 25-year-old man is brought to the emergency room after sustaining burns during a fire in his apartment. He has blistering and erythema of his face, left upper extremity, and chest with frank charring of his right upper extremity. He is agitated, hypotensive, and tachycardiac. Which one of the following statements concerning this patient's initial wound management is correct?

(A) Topical antibiotics should not be used, as they will encourage growth of resistant organisms
(B) Early excision of facial and hand burns is especially important
(C) Escharotomy should only be performed if neurologic impairment is imminent
(D) Excision of areas of third-degree or of deep second-degree burns usually takes place 3 to 7 days after injury
(E) Split thickness skin grafts over the eschar of third-degree burns should be performed immediately in order to prevent fluid loss

8-37. A psychiatrist finds himself annoyed with a quarrelsome patient for no apparent reason, and later notes that the patient reminds him of his quarrelsome and disliked sibling. This is an example of

(A) reaction formation
(B) projection
(C) countertransference
(D) identification with the aggressor
(E) illusion

8-38. A 2-year-old child with minimal cyanosis has a quadruple rhythm, a systolic murmur in the pulmonic area, and a middiastolic murmur along the lower left sternal border. An electrocardiogram shows right atrial hypertrophy and a ventricular block pattern in the right chest leads. The child most likely has

(A) tricuspid regurgitation and pulmonic stenosis
(B) pulmonic stenosis and a ventricular septal defect (tetralogy of Fallot)
(C) an atrioventricular canal
(D) Ebstein's anomaly
(E) Wolff-Parkinson-White syndrome

8-39. A 19-year-old woman comes to the emergency room and reports that she had fainted at work earlier in the day. She has mild vaginal bleeding. Her abdomen is diffusely tender and distended. In addition, she complains of shoulder and abdominal pain. Her temperature is 36.4°C (97.6°F); pulse rate, 120 beats per minute; and blood pressure, 96/50 mmHg. To confirm the diagnosis suggested by the available clinical data, the best diagnostic procedure would be

(A) a pregnancy test
(B) posterior colpotomy
(C) dilation and curettage
(D) culdocentesis
(E) laparoscopy

8-40. A 3-year-old girl has had a low-grade fever, "raspy" cough, and clear rhinorrhea for 3 days. She does not improve and begins to develop difficulty breathing. Vital signs include a temperature of 39.72°C (103.5°F), a pulse of 160 beats per minute, and a respiratory rate of 36 breaths per minute. Auscultation reveals bilateral rhonchi, wheezing, and some mild stridor. The most appropriate diagnosis is

(A) asthma
(B) epiglottitis
(C) laryngotracheobronchitis
(D) tonsillitis
(E) pneumonia

Items 8-41 through 8-42

A 23-year-old woman is brought to the emergency room from a halfway house, where she had apparently swallowed a handful of pills. The patient complains of shortness of breath and tinnitus, but refuses to identify the pills she ingested. Pertinent laboratory values are as follows:

Arterial blood gases: pH 7.45; P_{O_2} 126 torr; P_{CO_2} 12 torr

Serum electrolytes (meq/L): Na^+ 138; K^+ 4.8; Cl^- 102; HCO_3^- 8

8-41. The patient's acid-base disturbance is best characterized by which of the following descriptions?

(A) Acute respiratory alkalosis, compensated
(B) Chronic respiratory alkalosis, compensated
(C) Metabolic acidosis, compensated
(D) Mixed metabolic acidosis and respiratory alkalosis
(E) Mixed metabolic acidosis and respiratory acidosis

8-42. The most likely cause of the disturbance in this patient is an overdose of

(A) phenformin
(B) aspirin
(C) barbiturates
(D) methanol
(E) diazepam (Valium)

8-43. A 42-year-old man is admitted to the hospital from the emergency room, brought in by a passerby who found him wandering, complaining of intense abdominal pain, strange sensations in his hands, and "amnesia." Physical examination reveals seven scars from previous abdominal surgery. He seems to relish the sick role and attention from the nurses, one of whom recognized him as someone who had appeared in several other hospital emergency rooms with complaints of abdominal pain. It was discovered that he was lying about his amnesia. He is demanding multiple diagnostic tests, including a liver biopsy. The mental status examination is unremarkable. The most likely diagnosis is

(A) acute intermittent porphyria
(B) Munchausen syndrome
(C) malingering
(D) schizophrenia
(E) psychotic depression

8-44. A 4-month-old baby boy has just arrived in the emergency room and is cold and stiff. History from the parents is that the healthy infant had been placed in his crib for the night and when they next saw him in the morning he was dead. Physical examination is uninformative. Routine whole-body x-rays show three fractures in different stages of healing. The most likely diagnosis is

(A) scurvy
(B) syphilis
(C) sudden infant death syndrome (SIDS)
(D) osteogenesis imperfecta
(E) battery

8-45. A 43-year-old woman complains of lancinating pains radiating into the right side of her jaw. This discomfort has been present for more than 3 years and has started occurring more than once a week. The pain is paroxysmal and routinely triggered by cold stimuli, such as ice cream and cold drinks. She has sought relief with multiple dental procedures and has already had two teeth extracted. Multiple neuroimaging studies reveal no structural lesions in her head. Assuming there are no contraindications to the treatment, a reasonable next step would be to prescribe

(A) clonazepam (Klonopin) 1 mg orally (PO) three times daily
(B) diazepam (Valium) 5 mg PO two times daily
(C) divalproex sodium (Depakote) 250 mg PO three times daily
(D) indomethacin (Indocin) 10 mg PO three times daily
(E) carbamazepine (Tegretol) 100 mg PO three times daily

8-46. About 12 days after a mild upper respiratory infection, a 12-year-old boy complains of weakness in his lower extremities. Over several days the weakness progresses to include his trunk. On physical examination he has the weakness described and no lower extremity deep tendon reflexes, muscle atrophy, or pain. Spinal fluid studies are notable for elevated protein only. The most likely diagnosis in this patient is

(A) Bell's palsy
(B) muscular dystrophy
(C) Guillain-Barré syndrome
(D) Charcot-Marie-Tooth disease
(E) Werdnig-Hoffmann disease

8-47. A 30-year-old woman is found to have a low serum thyroxine level after being evaluated for fatigue. Five years ago she had been treated for Graves' disease with radioactive iodine. The diagnostic test of choice is

(A) serum thyroid-stimulating hormone (TSH)
(B) serum tri-iodothyronine (T_3)
(C) thyrotropin-releasing hormone (TRH) stimulation test
(D) radioactive iodine uptake (RAIU)

8-48. A 56-year-old woman with a history of a 15-pound weight loss in the last 5 weeks complains that her meals are getting stuck in her "chest," and not only has this symptom been getting progressively worse, the feeling persists throughout the day. The most probable diagnosis is

(A) lower esophageal ring
(B) reflux esophagitis
(C) esophageal carcinoma
(D) paraesophageal hiatal hernia
(E) autonomic nervous system dysfunction

Items 8-49 through 8-50

A 20-year-old female college student presents with a 5-day history of cough, low-grade fever (37.78°C [100°F]), sore throat, and coryza. On examination, there is mild conjunctivitis and pharyngitis. Tympanic membranes are inflamed and one bullous lesion is seen. Chest examination reveals few basilar rales, and a chest x-ray shows bilateral, patchy infiltrates of the lower lobe. Laboratory findings are as follows:

Hct: 38
WBC: 12,000/mm^3
Lymphocytes: 50 percent
Mean corpuscular volume
   (MCV): 83 mm^3
Reticulocytes: 3 percent
   of red cells

8-49. The sputum Gram stain is likely to show

(A) gram-positive diplococci
(B) tiny gram-negative coccobacilli
(C) white blood cells without organisms
(D) tubercle bacilli

8-50. This patient is likely to have

(A) high titers of adenovirus
(B) high titers of IgM cold agglutinins
(C) a positive silver methenamine stain
(D) a positive blood culture for *S. pneumoniae*

BLOCK I

Answers

I-1. The answer is B. (*Isselbacher, 13/e, pp 272, 561–563.*) Impetigo is a contagious staphylococcal or streptococcal infection of the epidermis. It presents initially as a vesicle or bulla, which ruptures to generate a honey-colored, crusted exudate. Cellulitis may also be caused by staphylococcus or streptococcus, but entails a dermal or subcutaneous infection that presents as a hot, tender, and erythematous region of skin without an exudate. Miliaria, or "prickly heat," is a macular rash caused by occlusion of sweat ducts. Seborrheic dermatitis, or "cradle cap," is a scaly, erythematous lesion that may also be crusted but is generally localized to the scalp and intertriginous areas.

I-2. The answer is B. (*Isselbacher, 13/e, p 7.*) The patient's autonomy as directed by the living will must be respected. This autonomy is not transferred to a surrogate decision maker, even one who is very credible. A family conference in this case would not change the overriding issue: a valid living will is in effect.

I-3. The answer is C. (*Schwartz, 6/e, pp 1485–1487.*) Hematomas of the rectus sheath are more common in women and present most often in the fifth decade. A history of trauma, sudden muscular exertion, or anticoagulation can usually be elicited. The pain is of sudden onset and is sharp in nature. The hematoma is most common in the right lower quadrant and irritation of the peritoneum leads to fever, leukocytosis, anorexia, and nausea. Preoperatively the diagnosis can be established with an ultrasound or CT scan showing a mass within the rectus sheath. Management is conservative unless symptoms are severe and bleeding persists, in which case surgical evacuation of the hematoma and ligation of bleeding vessels is required.

I-4. The answer is D. (*Hales, 2/e, p 939.*) Excessive stimulation of the serotoninergic system can result in the serotonin syndrome. It most commonly occurs in patients treated with two serotoninergic drugs, such as an SSRI and an MAO inhibitor. The usual symptoms include lethargy, restlessness, confusion, flushing, diaphoresis, tremor, and myoclonic jerks. Hyperthermia, myoclonus, and rigor may develop. Medication must be discontinued immediately, and emergency medical treatment undertaken because the condition has the potential to progress to rhabdomyolysis, acidosis, respiratory compromise, and renal failure secondary to myoglobinuria.

I-5. The answer is C. (*Schwartz, 6/e, p 1381.*) Gallstone ileus is due to erosion of a stone from the gallbladder into the gastrointestinal tract (most commonly into the duodenum). The stone becomes lodged in the small bowel (usually in the terminal ileum) and causes small-bowel obstruction. Plain films of the abdomen that demonstrate small-bowel obstruction and air in the biliary tract are diagnostic of the condition. Treatment consists of ileotomy, removal of the stone, and cholecystectomy if it is technically safe. If there is significant inflammation of the right upper quadrant, ileotomy for stone extraction followed by an interval cholecystectomy is often a safer alternative.

I-6. The answer is C. (*Isselbacher, 13/e, p 1079.*) Variant (Prinzmetal's) angina differs from stable (exertional) angina in that it usually occurs at rest. The onset is sudden and frightening and causes chest discomfort and shortness of breath. The pathophysiology is vasospasm of proximal epicardial coronary arteries, and most of the time there is atherosclerosis, which is the focus for the spasm.

I-7. The answer is C. (*Fitzpatrick, 4/e, pp 1572–1573.*) The patient has the typical areas of involvement of seborrheic dermatitis. This common dermatitis appears to be worse in many neurologic diseases. It is also very common and severe in patients with AIDS. In general, symptoms are worse in the winter. *Pityrosporum ovale* appears to play a role in seborrheic dermatitis and dandruff, and the symptoms improve with the use of certain antifungal preparations (e.g., ketoconazole) that decrease this yeast. Mild topical steroids also produce an excellent clinical response.

I-8. The answer is B. (*Mishell, 3/e, pp 229–232.*) In patients with abnormal bleeding who are not responding to standard therapy, a hysteroscopy should be performed. The hysteroscopy can rule out endometrial polyps or small fibroids, which, if present, can be resected. In patients with heavy abnormal bleeding who no longer desire fertility, an endometrial ablation can be performed. If a patient had completed child bearing and was having significant abnormal bleeding, a hysteroscopy rather than a hysterectomy would still be the procedure of choice to rule out easily treated disease. Treatment with a GnRH agonist would only temporarily relieve symptoms.

I-9. The answer is C. (*Schwartz, 6/e, pp 933–940.*) Most abdominal aortic aneurysms are asymptomatic and are discovered on palpation by a physician. A radiograph of the abdomen is useful in demonstrating the aneurysm if there is calcification in the walls. Ultrasound is generally the first diagnostic procedure in confirming the presence of an aneurysm with arteriography performed if the aneurysm is considered large enough to require resection (greater than 5 cm in diameter). Recently CT scan has been useful as a preoperative study in patients suspected of having aneurysms. Surgery should be performed despite the absence of symptoms and can be carried out with a mortality of less than 5 percent. With leaking or ruptured aneurysms, the operative mortality associated with this emergency situation is upwards of 75 percent. The patient's age is not a contraindication to surgery since several studies have demonstrated a low mortality (less than 5 percent) and satisfactory long-term survival and quality of life in elderly, even octogenarian patients.

I-10. The answer is D. (*Rudolph, 20/e, p 2105.*) Although all the listed options can produce the symptoms described, the family history supports the diagnosis of retinoblastoma, the most common intraocular tumor in children. Early detection can result in a survival rate of over 75 percent. The pattern of inheritance of retinoblastoma is complicated: the hereditary form of the disease can be transmitted by means of autosomal dominant inheritance from an affected parent, or from an unaffected parent carrying the gene, or from a new germinal mutation. Familial occurrences are usually bilateral. A second primary tumor develops in 15 percent of survivors of bilateral retinoblastoma, the most common of which is osteosarcoma. Retinoblastoma is associated with a deletion of the long arm of chromosome 13. In addition to specialized ophthalmologic care, management of retinoblastoma includes molecular genetic investigation of the family to identify those who have inherited the tumor-predisposing retinoblastoma gene.

I-11. The answer is E. (*Rudolph, 20/e, pp 530–535, 544–548, 573–580.*) Unsuspected bacteremia due to *Haemophilus influenzae* type b or *Streptococcus pneumoniae* should be considered before prescribing treatment for otitis media in a young, febrile, toxic-appearing infant. Blood culture should be performed before antibiotic therapy is initiated, and examination of the cerebrospinal fluid is indicated if meningitis is suspected. The classic signs of meningitis are found with increasing reliability in children over the age of 6 months. Nevertheless, a febrile, irritable, inconsolable infant with an altered state of alertness deserves a lumbar puncture even in the absence of meningeal signs. A petechial rash, characteristically associated with meningococcal infection, has been known to occur with other bacterial infections as well. Organisms may be identified on smear of these lesions.

A fever accompanied by inability to flex rather than rotate the neck immediately suggests meningitis. An indolent clinical course does not rule out bacterial meningitis: *Haemophilus influenzae* may produce meningeal symptoms (fever, headache, and stiff neck or back) that are so mild that several days can elapse before medical advice is sought. A lumbar puncture is of prime diagnostic importance in determining the presence of bacterial meningitis, which requires immediate antibiotic therapy. A delay in treatment of even 1 h may lead to such complications as cerebrovascular thrombosis, obstructive hydrocephalus, cerebritis with seizures or acute increased intracranial pressure, coma, or death.

1-12–1-14. The answers are 1-12 C, 1-13 A, 1-14 C. (*Isselbacher, 13/e, pp 790–793.*) This young man presents with classic signs and symptoms of infectious mononucleosis. In a young patient with fever, pharyngitis, lymphadenopathy, and lymphocytosis, the peripheral blood smear should be evaluated for atypical lymphocytes. A heterophil antibody test should be performed. The symptoms described in association with atypical lymphocytes and a positive heterophil test are virtually always due to Epstein-Barr virus. Neither liver biopsy nor lymph node biopsy is necessary. Work-up for toxoplasmosis, cytomegalovirus infection, or hepatitis B and C would be considered in heterophil-negative patients. Hepatitis does not occur in the setting of rheumatic fever and an antistreptolysin-O titer is not indicated. Corticosteroids are indicated in the treatment of infectious mononucleosis when severe hemolytic anemia is demonstrated or when airway obstruction occurs. Neither fatigue nor the complication of hepatitis is an indication for corticosteroid therapy. Steroids are not appropriate for the treatment of hepatitis B.

I-15. The answer is D. (*Lynch, 3/e, pp 67–68, 122–126, 138–140, 320–324.*) This history is classic for scabies. Contact dermatitis is unlikely in this location and cutaneous larva migrans typically presents with large erythematous, serpiginous tracts. Lesions of dermatitis herpetiformis can appear in the intertriginous area, but there are no burrows and the infection is often associated with a gluten-sensitive enteropathy. Impetigo is an infectious skin disease seen most frequently on the face; it is characterized by discrete vesicles that rupture and form a yellowish crust.

I-16. The answer is C. (*Benenson, 16/e, pp 347–351.*) Pertussis has been recognized with increased frequency in the U.S. among young adults and adolescents who were previously immunized. The immunity provided by the vaccine is limited and fades over time. The infection can be particularly severe in children under the age of 1. Antibiotic prophylaxis with erythromycin is recommended for close contacts to prevent disease and outbreaks. The symptoms are not typical of influenza, legionellosis, or pneumonia due to streptococci. Prophylaxis of contacts is not recommended for mycoplasma infections; it is much less contagious than pertussis.

I-17. The answer is B. (*Delp, 9/e, p 165. Vaughan, 13/e, pp 21–54.*) A pinhole test allows only paraxial parallel light rays through and improves visual acuity if refractory errors are present. The slit-lamp examination is a direct visualization of the eye and its components. The pseudochromatic plate test detects color blindness. Schiotz tonometry measures intraocular pressure. Visual field testing determines if there are any blind spots.

I-18. The answer is D. (*Hardy, 2/e, pp 454–456. Schwartz, 6/e, pp 1426–1427.*) Insulin-secreting *beta*-cell tumors of the pancreas produce paroxysmal nervous system manifestations that may be a consequence of hypoglycemia, although the blood glucose level may bear little relation to the severity of the symptoms, even in the same patient from episode to episode. Most insulinomas are single discrete tumors. Patients with insulinoma in the setting of the MEN-I syndrome (synchronous islet cell tumors of the pancreas, pituitary hyperplasia or adenomas, and parathyroid chief cell hyperplasia), however, are more likely to have multiple tumors throughout the pancreas. If a careful examination of the pancreas reveals one or more specific adenomas, these can be locally excised. Excision of these tumors may be difficult in MEN-I, when the tumors are small and multiple (10 to 15 percent of cases). The finding of an elevated serum calcium level would raise the suspicion of MEN-I and parathyroid hyperplasia. Insulinomas are not associated with MEN-II, which comprises coexistent medullary thyroid cancer, parathyroid hyperplasia, and pheochromocytoma. About one in seven of these tumors is malignant. Streptozotocin, a potent antibiotic that selectively destroys islet cells, can be useful in controlling symptoms from unresectable malignant tumors of the islet cells but probably has little to offer in the definitive management of the typical benign islet cell insulinoma.

1-19. The answer is D. (*Rudolph, 20/e, pp 1933–1934.*) The history, signs, and symptoms as outlined in the question are characteristic of a basilar skull fracture. Those patients with rupture of the tympanic membrane allowing otorrhea and those with rhinorrhea after the injury are at increased risk of complications of infection. For these children, a semi-upright position and observation for 72 h for evidence of increased intracranial pressure or infection without use of prophylactic antibiotics is appropriate. CSF drainage frequently stops within 72 h. Drainage beyond 72 h may require surgical closure; the risk of complications such as infection increases after this time.

1-20. The answer is A. (*Kaplan, 6/e, p 2757.*) There is no legal obligation to accept any patient for therapy, but once the doctor-patient relationship is established, there are legal and ethical obligations on the doctor to keep informed about the patient's condition and to provide needed care. Abandonment that results in injury may establish grounds for malpractice. The safety and welfare of the patient is paramount. To simply provide medication does not account for the fact that the patient may decompensate and injure himself during the period of time it takes to find a new psychiatrist. The therapist may terminate treatment with an uncooperative or noncompliant patient, but only if assistance is given in finding a new therapist.

1-21. The answer is C. (*Lynch, 3/e, pp 138–140.*) Impetigo is typically caused by *Staphylococcus aureus* or ß-hemolytic streptococci and usually occurs in children but can occur in adults as well. Many of the strains that cause impetigo are nephritogenic and can result in acute glomerulonephritis. Treatment is with antibiotics, preferably a penicillinase-resistant drug, as many strains are ß-lactamase-positive. The lesions of staphylococcal scalded-skin syndrome are usually sterile.

1-22. The answer is E. *(Lechtenberg, Multiple Sclerosis, p 123.)* Trigeminal neuralgia (tic douloureux) develops in MS patients independently of acute exacerbations in the disease. It may persist long after other signs of demyelination have remitted. Oral carbamazepine (Tegretol) is often successful in reducing the pain. The effective dose is usually 200 to 400 mg three to four times daily. ACTH is useful in abbreviating the duration of exacerbations in MS, but it does not limit the deficits experienced by the patient on a long-term basis. Methylprednisolone has a similar effect on optic neuritis secondary to multiple sclerosis.

1-23. The answer is A. *(Seidel, 3/e, pp 605–619.)* Orchitis is an uncommon occurrence except as a sequela of infection with mumps in young males. It is most often unilateral and testicular atrophy occurs in 50 percent of cases. Testicular tumors are the most common neoplasm in men 15 to 30 years of age. The tumors do not transilluminate, they are not tender, they are fixed to the testicle, and most are malignant. Epididymitis presents as an enlarged, very erythematous, extremely tender scrotum and is usually associated with a urinary tract infection. A varicocele is usually a left-sided swelling of the scrotal sac, which when palpated feels like "a bag of worms." A spermatocele is a swelling of the epididymis; it does transilluminate, but remains localized to the epididymis.

1-24. The answer is A. *(Adams, 6/e, pp 172–178.)* Classic migraine is usually familial, involves a unilateral, throbbing head pain, and diminishes in frequency with age. The blind spot, or scotoma, that may develop as part of the aura of a classic migraine attack will involve the same visual field in both eyes. This defect usually changes over the course of minutes. It typically enlarges and may intrude upon central vision. The margin of the blind spot is often scintillating or dazzling. If this margin has a pattern like the battlement of a castle, it is called a *fortification spectrum,* or *teichopsia.* Homonymous hemianopic defects of the sort that develop during the aura of a classic migraine indicate an irritative lesion that is affecting one part of the occipital cortex in one hemisphere of the brain. The changes in the scotoma over the course of minutes indicates that the irritative phenomenon sets off a cascade of events in the visual cortex that temporarily disturbs vision in a progressively larger area. Other focal neurologic phenomena may precede classic migraine, the most common being tingling of the face or hand, mild confusion, transient hemiparesis, and ataxia. Fatigue, irritability, and easy distractibility often develop before a migraine. Affected persons usually also have hypersensitivity to light and noise during the attack.

1-25. The answer is D. (*Lechtenberg, Synopsis, pp 114–115.*) Trigeminal neuralgia may develop in the context of multiple sclerosis. This woman's other neurologic problems suggest multiple sclerosis. The development of trigeminal neuralgia (tic douloureux) indicates that demyelination has probably extended to the brainstem and may be involving trigeminal nerve connections. A more detailed history would probably reveal that she had pain in the eye that now has disturbed vision. This is expected with the optic neuritis typically associated with multiple sclerosis. Other symptoms commonly reported at this age by patients with previously undiagnosed multiple sclerosis include bedwetting (enuresis), changes in speech (dysarthria), and gait instability (ataxia).

1-26. The answer is B. (*Adams, 6/e, pp 180–182.*) The term *cluster headache* refers to the tendency of these headaches to cluster in time. They may be distinctly seasonal, but the triggering event is unknown. The pain of cluster headache is usually described as originating in the eye and spreading over the temporal area as the headache evolves. In contrast to migraine, men are more often affected than women, and extreme irritability may accompany the headache. The pain usually abates in less than an hour. Affected persons routinely have autonomic phenomena associated with the headache that include unilateral nasal congestion, tearing from one eye, conjunctival injection, and pupillary constriction. The autonomic phenomena are on the same side of the face as the pain. These phenomena are similar to those elicited by the local action of histamine and gave rise to the now largely abandoned term of *Horton's histamine headaches.*

1-27. The answer is F. (*Adams, 6/e, p 185.*) Both men and women are at risk for temporal arteritis, and the greatest risk to both is loss of vision in association with the headache. The erythrocyte sedimentation rate is usually dramatically elevated and the abolition of symptoms with corticosteroid therapy is equally dramatic. Temporal arteritis is largely nonexistent in persons under 50 years of age and rare in those under 60. Many patients exhibit persistent fevers and progressive weight loss. The temporal arteries are likely to be pulseless or at least thickened. Biopsy of the artery often reveals a giant cell arteritis.

I-28. The answer is J. *(Isselbacher, 13/e, pp 788–789.)* The rash preceding the facial pain was probably caused by herpes zoster, a virus that erupts in the severely ill elderly and in immunosuppressed persons. The virus is manifested earlier in life as chickenpox and remains dormant for decades in most people. Tricyclic drugs, such as imipramine, are often more useful than analgesics in suppressing the pain associated with this postviral syndrome.

I-29. The answer is E. *(Behrman, 15/e, p 1700.)* The child in this question most likely has breath-holding spells. Two forms exist. Cyanotic spells consist of the symptoms outlined and are predictable upon upsetting or scolding the child. They are rare before 6 months of age, peak at about 2 years of age, and resolve by about 5 years of age. Avoidance of reinforcing this behavior is all that is necessary. Pallid breath-holding spells are less common and are usually caused by a painful experience (such as a fall). With these events, the child will stop breathing, lose consciousness, become pale and hypotonic, and may have a brief tonic seizure. These, too, resolve spontaneously. Again, avoidance of reinforcing behavior is indicated.

I-30. The answer is C. *(Schwartz, 6/e, pp 1011–1013.)* This patient is at high risk for developing cellulitis of her right foot because her underlying problem is unilateral primary lymphedema. Hypoplasia of the lymphatic system of the lower extremity accounts for greater than 90 percent of patients with primary lymphedema. If edema is present at birth it is referred to as congenital, but if it starts early in life (as in this woman) it is called praecox, and if it appears after age 35 it is tarda. The inadequacy of the lymphatic system accounts for the repeated episodes of cellulitis that these patients experience. Swelling is not seen with acute arterial insufficiency or with popliteal entrapment syndrome. Deep venous thrombophlebitis will result in tenderness and is generally not a predisposing factor for cellulitis of the foot.

I-31. The answer is A. *(Henderson, Am J Med 86:559–567, 1989.)* The presence of air in the mediastinum after an episode of vomiting and retching is virtually pathognomonic of spontaneous rupture of the esophagus (Boerhaave's syndrome). The evidence is overwhelming that without prompt surgical exploration of the mediastinum by left thoracotomy, the patient has little chance for a short-term outcome of low morbidity. The aspiration of highly acidic gastric contents into the mediastinum creates havoc in the tissues exposed to it. The surgical procedure must include extensive opening of the mediastinal pleura and removal of any particulate debris that might have been aspirated into the thorax from the stomach. Closure of the esophageal laceration with reinforcement by a pleural flap and secure chest tube drainage of the pleural space are mandatory. If the operation is delayed beyond the first 8 to 24 h, the mortality rises sharply and survival will only follow prolonged intensive care and multiple operations. This catastrophic event is one of the few in which prompt diagnosis and intervention is crucial to success. Because the findings are classic and the diagnosis is so important, Boerhaave's syndrome justifiably receives emphasis in educational programs for emergency physicians, internists, radiologists, and surgeons alike.

1-32–1-34. The answers are 1-32 D, 1-33 D, 1-34 B. (*Rundell, pp 387–390.*) This patient displays some of the classic findings in conversion disorder. She has an alteration of physical functioning that suggests a physical disorder, the altered function was precipitated by a psychological event, the pattern (glove-like anesthesia) cannot readily be explained by a known disorder, and physical findings are negative. Patients with body dysmorphic disorder are preoccupied with imagined defects in their appearance, which is normal. The term hysteria is used pejoratively to mean that the symptoms are not real, but it is not an actual diagnosis. Patients with a parietal tumor would likely have other signs and symptoms.

The patient's lack of anxiety and awareness of the existence and significance of the conflict with her brother is a classic finding in conversion disorder. It is an example of "primary gain." This refers to keeping an internal conflict or need out of awareness, reducing the anxiety associated with it, and finding a partial solution to the underlying conflict. The enjoyment of attention from her family is an example of "secondary gain," which serves to reinforce the symptom. There is no such thing as "tertiary gain," and suppression refers to placing something into the preconscious rather than the unconscious. The indifference reaction is associated with right hemispheric lesions and consists of symptoms of indifference toward failures, lack of interest in family and friends, enjoyment of foolish jokes, and minimizing physical difficulties.

1-35. The answer is C. (*Isselbacher, 13/e, p 408.*) Propylthiouracil can cause a mild or severe leukopenia. When the leukocyte count is less than

1500 cells per cubic millimeter, the drug should be discontinued. In the patient described, a white blood cell count must be determined in order to further manage the patient. Blood culture may also be in order but is not the most important initial step.

I-36. The answer is D. *(Isselbacher, 13/e, p 2069.)* Hemochromatosis is a disorder of iron storage that results in deposition of iron in parenchymal cells. The liver is usually enlarged, and excessive skin pigmentation is seen in 90 percent of symptomatic patients at the time of diagnosis. Diabetes occurs secondary to direct damage of the pancreas by iron deposition. Arthropathy develops in 25 to 50 percent of cases. The other diagnoses listed could not explain all the manifestations of this patient's disease process.

I-37. The answer is B. *(Isselbacher, 13/e, pp 1664–1667.)* Ankylosing spondylitis is a chronic and progressive inflammatory disease that most commonly affects spinal, sacroiliac, and hip joints. Men in the third decade of life are most frequently affected. There is a strong association with HLA-B27. Patients in advanced stages present with a characteristic bent-over posture. A positive Schober test indicates diminished anterior flexion of the lumbar spine. Involvement of the costovertebral joints limits chest expansion.

I-38. The answer is C. *(Berkow, 16/e, pp 1022, 1106, 1122.)* Diabetic ketoacidosis (blood pH 7.2 or lower) induces a distinctive respiratory pattern known as Kussmaul's breathing, which consists of slow and deep respirations that increase the tidal volume. Since the breathing capacity is not hampered, the patient rarely complains of dyspnea. The uremic patient will often complain of dyspnea due to the severe panting brought on by combinations of acidosis, heart failure, pulmonary edema, and anemia. Cerebral lesions, such as intracranial hemorrhage, are often associated with intense hyperventilation that is sometimes noisy and stertorous and also has unpredictable, irregular periods of apnea alternating with periods in which four or five breaths of similar depth are taken; this breathing pattern is known as Biot's respiration. Periodic, or Cheyne-Stokes, respiration has a rhythmic, alternating, gradually changing pattern of apnea and hyperpnea that may be of CNS or cardiac origin. Slowing of the circulation, as happens in heart failure, is the cause most often seen. Both acidosis and hypoxia affect the respiratory centers in the medulla oblongata, and together they can create the respiratory pattern associated with Cheyne-Stokes.

1-39. The answer is D. (*Schwartz, 6/e, pp 1203–1207.*) Cecal diverticula must be differentiated from the more common variety of diverticula that are usually found in the left colon. Cecal diverticula are thought to be a congenital entity. The cecal diverticulum is often solitary and involves all layers of the bowel wall; therefore, cecal diverticula are true diverticula. Diverticula elsewhere in the colon are almost always multiple and are thought to be an acquired disorder. These acquired diverticula are really herniations of mucosa through weakened areas of the muscularis propria of the colon wall. The preoperative diagnosis in the case of cecal diverticulitis is "acute appendicitis" about 80 percent of the time. If there is extensive inflammation involving much of the cecum, an ileocolectomy is indicated. If the inflammation is well localized to the area of the diverticulum, a simple diverticulectomy with closure of the defect is the procedure of choice. To avoid diagnostic confusion in the future, the appendix should be removed whenever an incision is made in the right lower quadrant, unless operatively contraindicated.

1-40. The answer is C. (*Reece, pp 1068–1070.*) The most probable diagnosis in this case is acute pancreatitis. The pain caused by a myoma in degeneration is more localized to the uterine wall. Low-grade fever and mild leukocytosis may appear with a degenerating myoma, but liver function tests are usually normal. The other "obstetric" cause of epigastric pain, severe preeclamptic toxemia (PET), may exhibit disturbed liver function (sometimes associated with the HELLP syndrome), but this patient has only mild elevation of blood pressure and no proteinuria. Acute appendicitis in pregnancy is one of the more common nonobstetric causes of abdominal pain. In pregnancy symptoms of acute appendicitis are similar to those of nonpregnant patients, but the pain is more vague and poorly localized and the point of maximal tenderness moves with advancing gestation to the right upper quadrant. Liver function tests are normal with acute appendicitis. Acute cholecystitis may cause fever, leukocytosis, and pain of the right upper quadrant with abnormal liver function tests, but amylase levels would be only mildly elevated, if at all, and the pain would be less severe than described in this patient. The diagnosis that fits the clinical description and the laboratory findings is acute pancreatitis. This disorder may be more common during pregnancy with an incidence of 1:100 to 1:10,000 pregnancies. Cholelithiasis, chronic alcoholism, infection, abdominal trauma, some medications, and pregnancy-induced hypertension are known predisposing factors. Patients with pancreatitis are usually in acute distress—the classic finding is a person who is rocking with knees drawn up and trunk flexed in agony. Fever, tachypnea, hypotension, ascites, and pleural effusion may be observed. Hypotonic bowel sounds, epigastric tenderness, and signs of peritonitis may be demonstrated on examination.

Leukocytosis, hemoconcentration, and abnormal liver function tests are common laboratory findings in acute pancreatitis. The most important laboratory finding is, however, an elevation of serum amylase levels, which appears 12 to 24 h after onset of clinical disease. Values may exceed 200 U/dL (normal values 50 to 160 U/dL). A useful diagnostic tool in the pregnant patient with only modest elevation of amylase values is the amylase/creatinine ratio. In patients with acute pancreatitis, the ratio of amylase clearance to creatinine clearance is always greater than 5 to 6 percent.

Treatment considerations for the pregnant patient with acute pancreatitis are similar to those in nonpregnant patients. IV hydration, nasogastric suction, enteric rest, and correction of electrolyte imbalance and of hyperglycemia are the mainstays of therapy. Careful attention to tissue perfusion, volume expansion, and transfusions to maintain a stable cardiovascular performance are critical. Gradual recovery occurs over 5 to 6 days.

I-41. The answer is C. (_Hall, pp 1818–1825._) Whenever significant bleeding is noted in the early postoperative period, the presumption should always be that it is due to an error in surgical control of blood vessels in the operative field. Hematologic disorders that are not apparent during the long operation are most unlikely to surface as problems postoperatively. Blood transfusion reactions can cause diffuse loss of clot integrity; the sudden appearance of diffuse bleeding during an operation may be the only evidence of an intraoperative transfusion reaction. In the postoperative period, transfusion reactions usually present as unexplained fever, apprehension, and headache—all symptoms difficult to interpret in the early postoperative period. Factor VIII deficiency (hemophilia) would almost certainly be known by history in a 65-year-old man, but if not, intraoperative bleeding would have been a problem earlier in this long operation. Severely hypothermic patients will not be able to form clots effectively, but clot dissolution does not occur. Care should be taken to prevent the development of hypothermia during long operations through the use of warmed intravenous fluid, gas humidifiers, and insulated skin barriers.

I-42. The answer is A. (_Behrman, 15/e, pp 1060–1062._) A history of non-bilious vomiting of 10 days' duration in a child who does not look ill points to infantile hypertrophic pyloric stenosis as the most likely diagnosis. The incidence of this condition in infants is between 1:250 and 1:750, with males affected more often than females. Although there is no specific pattern of inheritance, a familial incidence has been observed in about 15 percent of patients. The prevalence of pyloric stenosis is also higher in first-born infants. White infants have a higher incidence of pyloric stenosis than African-American and Asian infants. Metabolic alkalosis with low serum potassium and chloride levels is frequently seen in pyloric stenosis as a result of loss of gastric contents from vomiting.

1-43. The answer is D. (*Schwartz, 6/e, pp 196–198.*) Gunshot wounds to the lower chest are often associated with intraabdominal injuries. The diaphragm can rise to the level of T4 during maximal expiration. Therefore, any patient with a gunshot wound below the level of T4 should be subjected to abdominal exploration. Exploratory thoracotomy is not indicated because most parenchymal lung injuries will stop bleeding and heal spontaneously with the use of tube thoracostomy alone. Indication for thoracic exploration for bleeding is usually in the range of 100 to 150 mL/h over several hours. Peritoneal lavage is not indicated even though the abdominal examination is unremarkable. As many as 25 percent of patients with negative physical findings and negative peritoneal lavage will have significant intraabdominal injuries in this setting. These injuries include damage to the colon, kidney, pancreas, aorta, and diaphragm. Local wound exploration is not recommended because the determination of diaphragmatic injury with this technique is unreliable.

1-44. The answer is D. (*Schwartz, 6/e, pp 526–527.*) The survival of patients with malignant melanoma correlates with the depth of invasion (Clark) and the thickness of the lesion (Breslow). It is widely held that patients with thin lesions (<0.76 mm) and Clark's level I and II lesions are adequately managed by wide local excision. The incidence of nodal metastases rises with increasing Clark's level of invasion such that a level IV lesion has a 30 to 50 percent incidence of nodal metastases. The assumption that removal of microscopic foci of disease is beneficial, in conjunction with retrospective data indicating improved survival in patients who have undergone removal of clinically negative but pathologically positive nodes, has led to the widely held belief that prophylactic node dissections are indicated for melanoma. Prospective data have challenged this concept. Veronesi and Sim have found that patients undergoing prophylactic node dissections survived no longer than those who were followed closely and underwent node dissections only after nodes became palpable. The subject remains controversial and further study and follow-up are necessary. Immunotherapy has not been successful in controlling widespread metastatic melanoma even when added to chemotherapy. Intralesional administration of BCG has been demonstrated to control local skin lesions in only 20 percent of patients. Dinitrochlorobenzene (DNCB) can also be used.

I-45. The answer is A. (*Isselbacher, 13/e, pp 1976–1978.*) A hypertensive crisis in this young woman suggests a secondary cause of hypertension. In the setting of palpitations, apprehension, and hyperglycemia, pheochromocytoma should be considered. Unexplained hypotension associated with surgery or trauma may also suggest the disease. The patient's hypoglycemia is a result of a catecholamine effect of insulin suppression and stimulation of hepatic glucose output. Hypercalcemia has been attributed to ectopic secretion of parathormone-related protein. Renal artery stenosis can cause severe hypertension but would not explain the systemic symptoms or laboratory abnormalities in this case.

I-46. The answer is E. (*Isselbacher, 13/e, pp 1509–1512.*) This reaction is a positive Murphy's sign and is found in patients with acute cholecystitis. The anterior abdominal wall is inverted below the right costal margin by the examiner's digital pressure. The liver and gallbladder move inferiorly as the diaphragm contracts on deep inspiration. The inferior movement of the diaphragm causes the inflamed gallbladder to become compressed against the inverted wall. The patient will experience sharp pain and abruptly halt inspiration.

I-47. The answer is B. (*Behrman, 15/e, p 1192.*) Maxillary and ethmoid sinuses are large enough to harbor infections from infancy. Frontal sinuses are rarely large enough to harbor infections until the 6th to 10th year of life. Sphenoid sinuses do not become large until about the 3rd to 5th year of life. In general, a cold lasting longer than about 10 days with fever and face pain is indicative of sinusitis. Examination of the nose may reveal pus draining from the middle meatus in maxillary, frontal, or anterior ethmoid sinusitis. Pus in the superior meatus indicates sphenoid or posterior ethmoid sinuses. Diagnosis is on clinical grounds and is difficult; CT scans are the preferred route. Sinus films are very difficult to interpret. The treatment is usually oral antibiotics for 14 to 21 days. Decongestants and antihistamines are useless.

I-48. The answer is A. *(Isselbacher, 13/e, pp 251–253.)* The electrocardiogram exhibited in the question demonstrates changes that are essentially diagnostic of severe hyperkalemia. Correct treatment for the affected patient includes administration of a source of calcium ions (which will immediately oppose the neuromuscular effect of potassium) and administration of sodium bicarb ions (which, by producing a mild alkalosis, will shift potassium into cells); each will temporarily reduce serum potassium concentration. Infusion of glucose and insulin would also effect a temporary transcellular shift of potassium. However, these maneuvers are only temporarily effective; definitive treatment calls for removal of potassium from the body. The sodium-potassium exchange resin sodium polystyrene sulfonate (Kayexalate) would accomplish this removal but over a period of hours and at the price of adding a sodium ion for each potassium ion that is removed. Hemodialysis or peritoneal dialysis is probably required for this patient, since these procedures also rectify the other consequences of acute renal failure, but would not be the first line of therapy given the acute need to reduce the potassium level. Both lidocaine and digoxin would not only be ineffective but contraindicated, since they would further depress the myocardial conduction system.

I-49. The answer is D. *(Isselbacher, 13/e, pp 1194–1197.)* This is a typical clinical presentation of cystic fibrosis. There is nearly always a history of recurrent respiratory infections (90 percent) with a persistent cough between attacks and failure to thrive (85 percent). A history of meconium ileus occurs in 5 percent of cases. The most common organisms responsible for the respiratory infections are *Staphylococcus aureus* and *Pseudomonas aeruginosa*, both of which produce the large amounts of mucus that cause the earliest obstructive lesions in the bronchi and bronchioles.

I-50. The answer is B. *(Behrman, 15/e, pp 661–670.)* Juvenile rheumatoid arthritis frequently causes spindle-shaped swelling of finger joints and may involve unusual joints such as the sternoclavicular joint. This disorder can be associated with spiking high fevers, which are not a feature of rheumatic fever, toxic synovitis, septic arthritis, or osteoarthritis. Although septic arthritis may affect any joint, it would not be likely to affect finger joints by causing spindle-shaped swellings; in this respect, septic arthritis resembles acute rheumatic fever. Toxic synovitis usually involves hip joints in boys, and osteoarthritis is not a disease of childhood.

BLOCK 2

Answers

2-1. The answer is B. *(Isselbacher, 13/e, p 572.)* Erysipeloid occurs in persons employed as fish or meat handlers. The causative organism is *Erysipelothrix rhusiopathiae*. Arthritis and endocarditis can occur as a result of infection, as well as a septicemia. The most common manifestation is that of a localized violaceous or purple lesion that spreads peripherally with a clearing center. There is a lack of constitutional symptoms, which differentiates erysipeloid from erysipelas.

2-2. The answer is D. *(Schwartz, 6/e, pp 1673–1674.)* Postthyroidectomy hypocalcemia is usually due to transient ischemia of the parathyroid glands and is self-limited. When it becomes symptomatic, it should be treated with intravenous infusions of calcium. In most cases the problem is resolved in several days. If hypocalcemia persists, oral therapy is then added with calcium gluconate. Vitamin D preparations are only used if hypocalcemia is prolonged and permanent hypocalcemia is suspected. There is no role for thyroid hormone replacement or magnesium sulfate in the treatment of hypocalcemia.

2-3. The answer is B. *(Adams, 6/e, p 261.)* Vascular disease may produce bilateral injury to the MLF in the elderly, but it is an unlikely explanation in the young adult. Injury to the MLF in multiple sclerosis is demyelinating. Bilateral MLF syndromes associated with optic atrophy are virtually diagnostic of multiple sclerosis in persons under 40 years of age.

2-4. The answer is E. *(Isselbacher, 13/e, pp 787–790.)* Shingles is a disease that usually occurs many years after an initial infection of chickenpox, which is caused by herpes zoster. For unknown reasons, the virus, which had been latent in the nerve, reactivates and expresses itself along the dermatome. The painful dermatomic lesions begin as erythema then progress to vesicular and pustular eruptions, which burst and crust over. Open wounds are contagious. The pain appears to be worse in the elderly and immunocompromised.

2-5. The answer is A. *(Goroll, 3/e, pp 13–16.)* Assessing serum cholesterol is an important part of the screening health examination. Interventions that lower serum cholesterol and LDL cholesterol result in decreased risk of coronary artery disease. Lipoprotein electrophoresis would not be indicated as a screening test but might be used in a patient with high or borderline cholesterol levels to evaluate LDL and HDL cholesterol. An electrocardiogram in this asymptomatic patient without hypertension is not recommended as a screening procedure. Serum electrolytes or other routine biochemical tests are also not useful as screening tests.

2-6. The answer is B. *(Benenson, 16/e, pp 245–251. Greenberg, 2/e, ch 5, p 70.)* Antigenic drift is most likely the cause of changes in the strain that allowed infection despite adequate vaccination. Partial immunity or mutation to a less virulent strain (also due to antigenic drift) could be responsible for the less severe symptoms noted in this outbreak. Antigenic drift is a slow and progressive change in the antigenic composition of microorganisms. This alters the immunological responses of individuals and a population's susceptibility to that microorganism. Antigenic shift is a sudden change in the molecular structure of a microorganism and produces new strains. This results in little or no acquired immunity to these new strains and is the explanation for new epidemics or pandemics. Vaccine failure would result in influenza cases with high case fatality rates seen previously with this strain. Herd immunity would decrease the rate of infection by decreasing the probability that a susceptible person would come into contact with an infected person. This would not affect the clinical presentation of those infected. Influenza is not a rhinovirus and there is no cross-immunity between the two.

2-7. The answer is A. *(Kaplan, 6/e, p 2145.)* Seasonal depression, which is associated with decreased daylight hours, typically occurs at the onset of winter and fades in the spring. It often has the symptoms of an atypical depression with weight gain and hypersomnia. It is commonly treated with the MAO inhibitor antidepressant drugs or the SSRIs. The phototherapy of exposure to very bright light of 2500 lux or more is believed to be effective. Benzodiazepines, biofeedback, and steroid medication are not employed to treat major depressive symptoms. Electroconvulsive therapy would not commonly be considered for such a patient.

2-8. The answer is B. *(Rudolph, 20/e, pp 1635–1638.)* Recurrent pneumonias in an otherwise healthy child should indicate the potential for anatomic blockage of an airway. In the patient in this question, the findings on clinical examination suggest a foreign body in the airway. Inspiratory and expiratory films may be helpful. Routine inspiratory films are likely to appear normal or near normal (as outlined in the question). Expiratory films will identify air trapping behind the foreign body. It is uncommon for the foreign body to be visible on the plain radiograph; a high index of suspicion is necessary to make the diagnosis. Suspected foreign bodies in the airway are potentially diagnosed with fluoroscopy, but rigid bronchoscopy is not only diagnostic but also the treatment of choice for removal of the foreign body.

2-9. The answer is B. *(Isselbacher, 13/e, p 1042.)* Patent ductus arteriosus is a condition in which the ductus arteriosus fails to close properly after birth. Physical examination will reveal a characteristic machinery-type murmur at the left upper sternal border. The runoff of blood through the ductus causes the widened pulse pressure and the bounding peripheral pulses.

2-10. The answer is D. *(Adams, 6/e, p 1373.)* This patient has weakness of the left face and the contralateral (right) arm and leg, commonly called a "crossed hemiplegia." Such crossed syndromes are characteristic of brainstem lesions. In this case the lesion is an infarct localized to the left inferior pons and caused by occlusion of a branch of the basilar artery. The infarct has damaged the left sixth and seventh cranial nerves or nuclei in the left pons with resultant diplopia on left lateral gaze and left facial weakness. Also damaged in the left pons is the left corticospinal tract, proximal to its decussation in the medulla; this damage causes weakness in the right arm and leg. This classic presentation has been called the Millard-Gubler syndrome.

2-11. The answer is A. *(Kaplan, 6/e, p 2710.)* Using points, tokens, or credits to reinforce desired behaviors and token "fines" to discourage undesirable behavior is called a token economy. It may be used to reinforce social skills training or participation in therapeutic activities. To be effective, the entire staff must be united and consistent in providing positive and negative consequences for target behaviors.

2-12. The answer is D. *(Behrman, 15/e, pp 1345–1348.)* The presentation of infective endocarditis can be quite variable, ranging from prolonged fever with few other symptoms to an acute and severe course with early toxicity. A high index of suspicion is necessary to make the diagnosis quickly. Identification of the causative organism (frequently *Streptococcus viridans*) through multiple blood cultures is imperative for appropriate treatment. Echocardiography may identify valvular vegetations and may be predictive of impending embolic events. Treatment usually consists of 4 to 6 weeks of appropriate antimicrobial therapy. Bed rest should only be instituted for heart failure. Antimicrobial prophylaxis prior to and after dental cleaning is indicated.

2-13–2-16. The answers are 2-13 B, 2-14 D, 2-15 C, 2-16 A. (*Cameron, 4/e, pp 53–57.*) Gastric ulcers have been classified as type I (incisura or most inferior portion of lesser curvature), type II (gastric and duodenal), type III (pyloric and prepyloric), and type IV (juxtacardial). Indications for surgery are intractability, perforation, obstruction, and bleeding. A patient with an intractable type I ulcer can be treated with an antrectomy alone or with a proximal gastric vagotomy. If done properly, antrectomy offers slightly lower recurrence rates and a higher incidence of postoperative sequelae as compared with a proximal gastric vagotomy. However, significant scarring along the lesser curvature makes a proximal gastric vagotomy technically unfeasible.

Gastric outlet obstruction and severe inflammation around the pylorus and duodenum make resection a difficult and dangerous option. Similarly, pyloroplasty is often not adequate in the setting of gastric outlet obstruction to provide adequate drainage. Vagotomy and gastrojejunostomy, although associated with the highest recurrence rate, offers the best choice in the described setting.

In an elderly patient with a bleeding duodenal ulcer, recurrence rates are less of a consideration and thus the simplest and most expedient operation offers the best surgical outcome. Vagotomy and pyloroplasty with oversewing of the ulcer is the best choice in this setting.

Finally, in a young patient with intractable type III ulcers, antrectomy with vagotomy offers the best long-term outcome. Recurrence rates following this procedure are about 2 to 3 percent as compared with 7.4 percent for vagotomy and drainage and from 10 to 31 percent in patients receiving a proximal gastric vagotomy only.

2-17. The answer is C. (*Hall, pp 984–985.*) Because of the ease with which carbon dioxide diffuses across the alveolar membranes, the Pa_{CO_2} is a highly reliable indicator of alveolar ventilation. In this postoperative patient with respiratory acidosis and hypoxemia, the hypercarbia is diagnostic of alveolar hypoventilation. Acute hypoxemia can occur with pulmonary embolism, pulmonary edema, and significant atelectasis, but in all those situations the CO_2 partial pressures should be normal or reduced as the patient hyperventilates to improve oxygenation. The absorption of gas from the peritoneal cavity may affect transiently the Pa_{CO_2}, but should have no effect on oxygenation.

2-18. The answer is B. (Berg, p 916. Toole, 4/e, p 482.) This young man almost certainly has numerous problems associated with his intravenous drug abuse, but the cause of his current complaints is most likely bleeding from a mycotic aneurysm. Aneurysms are especially likely to bleed during exertion, such as that associated with sexual intercourse or defecation. That the lesion appeared largely the same on unenhanced and enhanced CT scans suggests that it is a hematoma. HIV antibody testing might reveal evidence of exposure to the human immunodeficiency virus, but aside from establishing that he was at increased risk of opportunistic infections, that test would provide little insight into the cause of the acute neurologic syndrome. The cerebrospinal fluid would be expected to be xanthochromic (yellow) with many (>20 RBCs/mm^3) red blood cells or grossly bloody, thereby providing evidence of a recent subarachnoid hemorrhage. Electroencephalography would undoubtedly reveal an asymmetric pattern associated with the left hemispheric lesion, but this too would provide little insight into the cause of the problem. Nerve conduction studies would not clarify the basis for a lesion of the central nervous system because they only examine structures of the peripheral nervous system. Cardiac catheterization might reveal valvular abnormalities, but these need not be associated with disease of the central nervous system.

2-19. The answer is A. (Berg, p 916. Toole, 4/e, p 482.) The most likely explanation for this patient's deficits is bleeding from a mycotic aneurysm. This type of aneurysm is usually relatively small and might not be evident on CT scanning or even on arteriography. An arteriogram would miss the lesion if it had destroyed itself when it bled or if the aneurysmal sac was completely thrombosed. The name *mycotic* is misleading. It suggests a fungal etiology, but it actually refers to the appearance of these aneurysms, which tend to be multiple. These aneurysms occur with either grampositive or gram-negative infections, but the responsible organisms usually have relatively low virulence. Mycotic aneurysms form over the cerebral convexities with subacute bacterial endocarditis. The aneurysm develops from an infected embolus originating on the diseased heart valves and lodging in the arterial wall. Bleeding from these small aneurysms is largely directed into the subarachnoid space. More virulent organisms that produce valvular heart disease are more likely to produce a meningitis or multifocal brain abscess with seeding of infected emboli to the brain. With acquired immunodeficiency syndrome (AIDS), a fungus could be the causative agent, but patients with endocarditis more typically have streptococcal or staphylococcal infections. Even if mycotic aneurysms form with endocarditis, they need not inevitably become symptomatic.

2-20. The answer is C. (*Berg, p 916. Toole, 4/e, p 482.*) Vasospasm routinely occurs with subarachnoid hemorrhage. This man obviously had intraparenchymal extension of his hemorrhage, but the small mass in his parietal lobe would not explain the extensive weakness evident on his initial examination. Cerebral infarction may occur if this subarachnoid blood produces significant vasoconstriction in an artery supplying the cerebrum, but vasospasm may remit before infarction occurs. If infarction does occur, it may be associated with edema, but this edema will not usually remit sufficiently with diuresis to produce reversal of major neurologic deficits. An encephalitis might remit if it were viral in origin, but the pattern and time course described would be improbable with most viral encephalitides. Cerebral infarction sometimes occurs because the embolus that originates on the infected heart valve is sufficiently stable to produce persistent occlusion of the cerebral vessel in which it lodges. Thrombolytic agents might lyse this intraarterial thrombus, but they would be inappropriate in a patient with an obvious intracranial hemorrhage. The thrombolytic agent would exacerbate the hemorrhage. If the embolus results in abscess formation, the abscess may drain spontaneously into the subarachnoid space or into the ventricles, but such spontaneous drainage usually results in a dramatic deterioration, rather than improvement.

2-21. The answer is D. (*Berg, p 917.*) Anticoagulation with warfarin or heparin and thrombolysis with r-tPA or urokinase are contraindicated in anyone with an intracranial hemorrhage. The risk of focal seizures that secondarily generalize after an intracerebral or subarachnoid hemorrhage is high and is appropriately treated with an antiepileptic drug, such as phenytoin (Dilantin). In fact, the risk of seizure activity is so high that many physicians give intravenous phenytoin prophylactically. That the patient had weakness after the obvious seizure activity is evidence of postictal deficits. Postictal weakness does not suggest extension of the bleeding or new areas of cerebrocortical damage.

2-22. The answer is E. (*Rudolph, 20/e, p 620.*) The tuberculin skin test is based on the detection of delayed hypersensitivity to the antigen of *Mycobacterium tuberculosis.* Two to ten weeks after infection, the intradermal injection of antigen will result in a positive response indicated by induration. The tine test, a multipuncture skin test used widely for mass screening because of its ease of administration, uses a plastic unit with four stainless steel blades treated with a crude filtrate of culture medium containing old tuberculin (OT). The tine test has a number of problems such as no standardization and variable results. Their use is discouraged, especially if TB is suspected. Retesting positive or doubtful tine reactions with the Mantoux test is indicated. The Mantoux intracutaneous tuberculin test uses a protein precipitate derived from OT (purified protein derivative, PPD) and is the preferred skin test. It is a more reliable test because of the efforts used in its preparation to standardize and preserve potency and because it delivers a defined amount of the antigen. The most appropriate next step in managing an asymptomatic, thriving child with a positive tine test is to administer a Mantoux test.

2-23. The answer is D. (*McCullough, pp 26–27.*) There are two intrascrotal appendages that may suffer torsion. The appendix testis and the appendix epididymidis are embryonic ductal system remnants. Torsion can occur at any time, but the peak occurrence is between the ages of 10 and 15 years. Onset of pain can be sudden or gradual. The infarcted appendage can often be seen as a "blue dot" on the superior pole of the testis. Reactive hydrocele or scrotal erythema may mask the blue dot, whereas transillumination may highlight its appearance.

2-24. The answer is B. (*Isselbacher, 13/e, p 2071.*) Patients with hemochromatosis and cirrhosis have a very high incidence of hepatocellular carcinoma. The incidence of this complication is 30 percent and increases with age. Weight loss and abdominal pain suggest hepatoma in this patient. A CT scan or ultrasound would be indicated. The picture of pain in the right upper quadrant and elevated alkaline phosphatase would not suggest acute hepatitis or worsening of the cirrhosis caused by hemochromatosis. Primary biliary cirrhosis can cause an obstructive biliary disease but would be much less likely in this patient.

2-25. The answer is C. *(Bartlett, 7/e, pp 110–111.)* Postexposure prophylaxis is recommended for *any* physical contact with bats. Bites or scratches may be too small to be visible to the naked eye. Both human rabies immunoglobulin (HRIG) and vaccine should be administered to persons who have not been previously vaccinated. HRIG is never recommended as only prophylaxis. It provides rapid passive protection with a half-life of 21 days. Active immunization induces response after 7 to 10 days and persists for at least 2 years. Only the vaccine is necessary if the person has a history of previous vaccination with documented antibody response. Consulting public health authorities before an intervention may be appropriate if the contact did not involve animals known to be a reservoir for rabies. Animals known to be reservoirs are the bat, woodchuck, skunk, raccoon, fox, bobcat, coyote, and other wild carnivores.

2-26. The answer is A. *(DSM-IV, pp 650–654.)* All the patient's personality traits are typical of borderline personality disorder. These patients frantically avoid real or imagined abandonment, have unstable interpersonal relations, and demonstrate impulsivity, emptiness, and inappropriate anger and affective instability. In paranoid and narcissistic personality disorder, there is a relative lack of self-destructiveness, impulsivity, and abandonment fears. Antisocial personalities are also manipulative, but they manipulate to obtain profit rather than to gain the attention of caretakers. Persons with dependent personality tend to react with appeasement and submissiveness and to seek out alternative supports when faced with fears of abandonment.

Persons with borderline personality disorder often undermine themselves when they are about to achieve a goal and typically react to stress with psychotic-like symptoms. These include transient hallucinations, distortion of body image, ideas of reference, and hypnagogic phenomena. The patient's history usually displays chaotic behavior, including suicide attempts or gestures, disrupted relationships, and a poor occupational history.

2-27. The answer is D. *(Kaplan, 6/e, p 1056.)* These symptoms are characteristic of koro, which appears suddenly and is associated with intense fear. There are marked somatic anxiety symptoms, including palpitations, skin pallor, weakness, or fainting. The patient often clutches his penis desperately or uses strings or clamps to prevent the retraction. This condition is primarily seen in Southeast Asia, particularly among the Chinese population. Often the patient believes the problem to have been caused by sexual excesses. Sporadic cases are seen in western countries, but are usually not associated with a fear of impending death, and most often are but one manifestation of an axis I psychosis.

2-28. The answer is B. (*Behrman, 15/e, pp 1745–1748.*) The most common form of muscular dystrophy is Duchenne muscular dystrophy. It is inherited as an X-linked recessive trait. Male infants are rarely diagnosed at birth or early infancy since they often reach gross milestones at the expected age. Early after walking, however, the features of this disease become more evident. While these children walk at the appropriate age, the hip girdle weakness is seen by age 2. Increased lordosis when standing is evidence of gluteal weakness. Gowers' sign is seen by 3 to 5 years of age as is the hip waddle gait. Ambulation remains common through about 7 to 12 years, after which use of a wheelchair is common. Associated features include mental impairment and cardiomyopathy. Death due to respiratory failure, heart failure, pneumonia, or aspiration is common by 18 years of age.

2-29. The answer is C. (*Schwartz, 6/e, pp 1134–1142.*) Perforation of a duodenal ulcer is an indication for emergency celiotomy and closure of the perforation. In patients with no prior history of peptic ulcer disease, simple closure with an omental patch is recommended. Seventy-two percent of patients who are asymptomatic preoperatively will remain so postoperatively. Patients with long-standing ulcer disease require a definitive acid-reducing procedure, except in high-risk situations. The choice of procedure is made by weighing the risk of recurrence against the incidence of undesirable side effects of the procedure, and considerable controversy persists about this issue. Antrectomy and truncal vagotomy offers a recurrence rate of 1 percent, but carries a 15 to 25 percent incidence of sequelae such as diarrhea, dumping syndrome, bloating, and gastric stasis. Highly selective vagotomy, if technically feasible, offers a 1 to 5 percent incidence of side effects but carries a recurrence rate of 10 to 13 percent in some series, although results are better when gastric and prepyloric ulcers are excluded. In general, definitive acid-reducing procedures should be postponed if the perforation is more than 12 h old, or if there is extensive peritoneal soilage.

Pyloroplasty and truncal vagotomy carries intermediate rates of recurrence and side effects, but has the advantage of speed in the setting of very ill patients with acute perforation.

2-30. The answer is B. *(Sawyers, Am J Surg 159:8–14, 1990.)* Though reminiscent of the carcinoid syndrome, this patient's complaints in the context of recent gastric surgery are highly suggestive of "the dumping syndrome," seen after gastroenteric bypass such as antrectomy and gastrojejunostomy. Dumping syndrome presents as vasomotor symptoms (weakness, sweating, syncope) and intestinal symptoms (bloating, cramping, diarrhea). The etiology of dumping has best been attributed to the rapid influx of fluid with a high osmotic gradient into the small intestine from the gastric remnant. Medical management consists of reassurance and frequent small meals that are low in carbohydrates (to limit the osmotic load). Antispasmodic medications are sometimes used if dietary adjustments are unsuccessful. The majority of cases will resolve within 3 months of operation on this regimen. Surgery for intractable dumping consists of creation of an antiperistaltic limb of jejunum distal to the gastrojejunostomy.

2-31. The answer is C. *(Mishell, 3/e, pp 330–339.)* Although there is an increased risk of spontaneous abortion, and a small risk of infection, an intrauterine pregnancy can occur and continue successfully to term with an IUD in place. However, if the patient wishes to keep the pregnancy and if the strings are visible, the IUD should be removed in an attempt to reduce the risk of infection, abortion, or both. Although the percentage of ectopic pregnancies may be increased, the majority of pregnancies occurring with an IUD are intrauterine. Therefore, in the absence of signs and symptoms suggestive of an ectopic pregnancy, laparoscopy is not indicated.

2-32. The answer is B. *(Seidel, 3/e, pp 604–605.)* Phimosis is the condition in which the foreskin in an uncircumcised patient cannot be retracted; this may occur normally during the first 6 years of life. Phimosis is usually congenital, but may be due to recurrent infections or balanoposthitis (inflammation of the glans penis and prepuce). Balanitis is inflammation of the glans penis and occurs only in uncircumcised persons. Escutcheon is the hair pattern associated with the genitalia. Smegma is a white, cheesy material that collects around the glans penis in an uncircumcised patient. Priapism is a prolonged penile erection, which is often painful.

2-33. The answer is C. (*Burnside, 17/e, p 232.*) Vascular sounds in the abdomen indicate areas of turbulent flow, which can be found in dilated, constricted, or tortuous vessels. Where the bruit is heard best can be a good indicator of the source of the bruit; however, definitive localization of the bruit is dependent upon arteriography. Bruits of the aorta are heard best in the right hypochondrium. Bruits of the splenic artery are heard best in the left hypochondrium. Renal artery bruits are heard best in the umbilical region, in the flanks, and occasionally in the costovertebral angles. In patients with hypertension, these bruits may indicate renal artery stenosis. Finally, vascular bruits can be distinguished from transmitted heart murmurs by simultaneously palpating the cardiac apex while listening to the bruit. The transmitted murmur will be synchronous with the impulse, whereas a local bruit occurs somewhat later.

2-34. The answer is D. (*Bennett, 20/e, pp 1223–1226. Felig, 3/e, pp 402– 412. Isselbacher, 13/e, pp 1923–1928.*) Metastatic tumors rarely cause diabetes insipidus, but of the tumors that may cause it, carcinoma of the breast is by far the most common. In the patient discussed in the question, the diagnosis of diabetes insipidus is suggested by hypernatremia and a low urine osmolality. Psychogenic polydipsia is an unlikely diagnosis since serum sodium is usually mildly reduced in this condition. Renal glycosuria would be expected to induce a higher urine osmolality than this patient has because of the osmotic effect of glucose. While nephrocalcinosis secondary to hypercalcemia may produce polyuria, hypercalciuria does not. Finally, the findings of inappropriate antidiuretic hormone syndrome are the opposite of those observed in diabetes insipidus and thus incompatible with the clinical picture in this patient.

2-35–2-36. The answers are 2-35 B, 2-36 B. (*Isselbacher, 13/e, pp 1046– 1052.*) This 18-year-old presents with classic features of rheumatic fever. His clinical manifestations include arthritis, fever, and murmur. A subcutaneous nodule is noted and a rash of erythema marginatum is described. These subcutaneous nodules are pea-sized and usually seen over extensor tendons. The rash is usually pink with clear centers and serpiginous margins. Laboratory data show an elevated erythrocyte sedimentation rate as usually occurs in rheumatic fever. The ECG shows evidence of first-degree AV block. An antistreptolysin O antibody is necessary to diagnose the disease by documenting prior streptococcal infection.

Most experts recommend the use of glucocorticoids when carditis is part of the picture of rheumatic fever. Hence, in this patient with first-degree AV block, corticosteroids would be indicated. Penicillin should also be given to eradicate group A beta-hemolytic streptococci.

2-37. The answer is A. *(Behrman, 15/e, p 1548.)* The majority of all cases of acute scrotal pain and swelling in boys under 6 years of age are caused by testicular torsion. If surgical exploration occurs within 6 h, the testes can be saved 90 percent of the time. Too often, delay caused by scheduling of various imaging modalities and laboratory tests results in an unsalvageable gonad.

2-38. The answer is C. *(Behrman, 15/e, pp 471, 1186.)* It is important to make the diagnosis of choanal atresia quickly in that it responds to treatment but may be lethal if unrecognized and untreated. Most neonates are obligate nose breathers since they cannot breathe adequately through their mouths. Infants with choanal atresia have increased breathing difficulty during feeding and sleeping and improve when crying. A variety of temporizing measures to maintain an open airway have been used, including oropharyngeal airways, positioning, tongue fixation, and endotracheal intubation, but surgical correction with placement of nasal tubes is most effective.

2-39. The answer is C. *(Polk, 4/e, pp 386–388.)* Most clinicians would recommend aspiration and cytologic examination of the cyst fluid in this situation. Cysts are common lesions in the breasts of women in their thirties and forties; malignancies are relatively rare. All such lesions justify attention, however, and physicians must not underestimate the fear associated with the discovery of a mass in the breast, even in low-risk situations. If the lesion does not completely disappear after aspiration, excision is advised. In young women the breast parenchyma is dense, which limits the diagnostic value of mammography. The American Cancer Society (ACS) does not suggest a baseline mammographic examination until age 35 unless a suspicious lesion exists.

2-40. The answer is C. *(Behrman, 15/e, pp 678–680.)* Many conditions can be associated with prolonged fever, a limp caused by arthralgia, exanthem, adenopathy, and pharyngitis. Conjunctivitis, however, is suggestive of Kawasaki disease. The fissured lips, while common in Kawasaki disease, could occur after a long period of fever from any cause if the child became dehydrated. The predominance of neutrophils and high sedimentation rate are common to all. An increase in platelets, however, is found only in Kawasaki disease. Kawasaki disease presents a picture of prolonged fever, rash, epidermal peeling on the hands and feet (especially around the fingertips), conjunctivitis, lymphadenopathy, fissured lips, oropharyngeal mucosal erythema, and arthralgia or arthritis. The diagnosis is still possible in the absence of one or two of these physical findings. Coronary artery aneurysms may develop.

2-41. The answer is C. (*Way, 9/e, pp 1140–1141.*) The motor components of the median nerve maintain the muscular function of most of the long flexors of the hand as well as the pronators of the forearm and the thenar muscles. It is also an extremely important sensory innervator of the hand and commonly described as the "eye of the hand" since the palm, the thumb, and the index and middle fingers all receive their sensation via the median nerve.

2-42. The answer is E. (*DSM-IV, pp 345–349.*) Dysthymia is a chronic depression that lasts at least 2 years; it usually begins in late adolescence or early adulthood. Sometimes patients describe being depressed for as long as they can remember. Symptoms fluctuate but are usually not severe. Such patients are commonly concerned with their perceived failures or interpersonal disappointments. The somatic symptoms characteristic of major depression or melancholia are less prominent in dysthymia.

2-43. The answer is D. (*Isselbacher, 13/e, p 1232. Seidel, 3/e, p 360.*) With a penetrating wound to the thorax and deviation of the trachea away from the involved side, the physician can assume tension pneumothorax. Breath sounds will be distant, the percussion note will be hyperresonant, and fremitus will be decreased. There will not be rales or rhonchi on the affected side because the lung will be collapsed. The increased air on the affected side is in the pleural space, not in the lung. As an attempt is made to inflate the lung, air moves into the pleural space from the puncture site. This results in a collapsed lung with a large pleural space.

2-44. The answer is C. (*Schwartz, 6/e, pp 1181–1182.*) Most enterocutaneous fistulas result from trauma sustained during surgical procedures. Irradiated, obstructed, and inflamed intestine is prone to fistulization.

Complications of fistulas include fluid and electrolyte depletion, skin necrosis, and malnutrition. Fistulas are classified according to their location and the volume of output, as these factors influence prognosis and treatment. When the patient is stable, a barium swallow is obtained to determine (1) the location of the fistula, (2) the relation of the fistula to other hollow intraabdominal organs, and (3) whether there is distal obstruction. Proximal small-bowel fistulas tend to produce a high output of intestinal fluid and are less likely to close with conservative management than are distal, low-output fistulas. Small-bowel fistulas that communicate with other organs, particularly the ureter and bladder, may need aggressive surgical repair because of the risk of associated infections. The presence of obstruction distal to the fistula (e.g., an anastomotic stricture) can be diagnosed by barium contrast study and mandates correction of the obstruction. When these poor prognostic factors for stabilization and spontaneous closure are observed, early surgical intervention must be undertaken. The patient in the question, however, appears to have a low-output, distal enterocutaneous fistula. Control of the fistulous drainage should be provided by percutaneous intubation of the tract with a soft catheter. This is usually accomplished under fluoroscopic guidance. Antispasmodic drugs have not been proved effective; somatostatin has been used with mixed success in the setting of high-output (greater than 500 mL/day) fistulas. There is no indication for antibiotics in the absence of sepsis. Total parenteral nutrition (TPN) is given to maintain or restore the patient's nutritional balance, while minimizing the quantity of dietary fluids and endogenous secretions in the gastrointestinal tract. A period of 4 to 6 weeks' TPN therapy is warranted to allow for spontaneous closure of a low-output, distal fistula. Should conservative management fail, surgical closure of the fistula is performed.

2-45. The answer is C. (*Hathaway, 11/e, p 751.*) The most likely diagnosis is torticollis. This is a condition in which the sternomastoid muscle is shortened by muscle spasm or fibrosis. The shortening of the sternomastoid muscle pulls the head down toward the affected side and causes rotation of the head to the opposite side of the involved muscle.

2-46. The answer is B. (*Hall, pp 1930–1933.*) Acute severe hyponatremia sometimes occurs following elective surgical procedures. It is usually the result of the combination of appropriate postoperative stimulation of antidiuretic hormone and injudicious administration of excess free water in the first few postoperative days. Totally sodium-free intravenous fluids (e.g., dextrose and water) should be given with great caution postoperatively, since occasionally the resulting hyponatremia can be associated with sudden death from a flaccid heart or with severe permanent brain damage. The condition is usually best treated by withholding free water and allowing the patient to reequilibrate. At levels below 115 meq/L seizures or mental obtundation may mandate hypertonic sodium solutions. This must be done with extreme care since the risk of fluid overload with acute pulmonary or cerebral edema is high.

2-47. The answer is C. (*Wold, pp 2–7.*) A history of pain that increases in severity, worsens at night, and is relieved by aspirin should suggest osteoid osteoma as a potential diagnosis. It is three times more common in males. Patients in their second decade of life are most commonly affected. The proximal femur is the most common location. Osteoarthritis is a common cause of hip pain in elderly patients. A septic hip joint is typically very acute with other constitutional signs of infection. Only osteoid osteoma has a classic history of relief with aspirin.

2-48. The answer is C. (*Isselbacher, 13/e, pp 1679–1684.*) Sarcoidosis is a systemic illness of unknown etiology. Many patients have respiratory symptoms including cough and dyspnea. Hilar and peripheral lymphadenopathy is common. Hepatomegaly is seen in 20 to 30 percent of patients. The chest x-ray shows symmetric hilar lymphadenopathy. The diagnostic method of choice is transbronchial biopsy, which will show a mononuclear cell granulomatous inflammatory process. While liver and scalene node biopsies are often positive, noncaseating granulomas are so frequent in these sites that they are not considered acceptable for primary diagnosis. ACE levels are elevated in two-thirds of patients, but false positive values are common in other granulomatous disease processes.

2-49. The answer is C. (*Hales, 2/e, p 213.*) An illusion is a misinterpretation of an actual sensory stimulus. A person's emotional state and personality needs can play an important role in determining the presence and type of an illusion. For example, perhaps the girl described in the question thought she saw a bear in her room because the hospital is a frightening, hostile environment for her. Systemic disease states associated with confusion (certain types of poisoning, for instance) also can produce misperceptions of sensory images by interfering with proper functioning of the brain.

2-50. The answer is C. *(Isselbacher, 13/e, p 519.)* With the development of hoarseness, breathing difficulty, and stridor, this patient is likely to have developed acute epiglottitis. Because of the possibility of impending airway obstruction, the patient should be admitted to an intensive care unit for close monitoring. The diagnosis can be confirmed by indirect laryngoscopy or soft tissue x-rays of the neck, which may show an enlarged epiglottis. Otolaryngologic consultation should be obtained. *Haemophilus influenzae* is the most likely causative organism. Many of these organisms are beta-lactamase producing and would be resistant to ampicillin.

The clinical findings are not consistent with the presentation of streptococcal pharyngitis. A lateral neck film would be more useful than a chest x-ray.

BLOCK 3

Answers

3-1. The answer is E. (*Cunningham, 20/e, pp 540, 551.*) Bloody lochia can persist for up to 2 weeks without indicating an underlying pathology; however, if bleeding continues beyond 2 weeks, it may indicate placental site subinvolution, retention of small placental fragments, or both. At this point, appropriate diagnostic and therapeutic measures should be initiated. The physician should first estimate the blood loss and then perform a pelvic examination in search of uterine subinvolution or tenderness. Excessive bleeding or tenderness should lead the physician to suspect retained placental fragments or endometritis. A larger-than-expected but otherwise asymptomatic uterus supports the diagnosis of subinvolution.

3-2. The answer is C. (*Adams, 6/e, pp 162–163.*) The patient who has a lesion of the posterior column will have a loss of the position and vibratory sense below the level of the lesion, but pain and temperature sensation remain intact or only mildly affected. Lesions of the medulla produce a crossed disturbance consisting of a loss of pain and temperature sensation on one side of the face and the opposite side of the body. This pattern is due to a lateral medullary infarction that affects the trigeminal tract or nucleus and the lateral spinothalamic tract. Infarction of the anterior spinal artery will produce motor paralysis and loss of pain and temperature sensation below the lesion with relative or absolute sparing of proprioception; the lesion often affects the ventral part of the cord and the corticospinal tracts along with the ventral gray matter. A lesion of the nucleus ventralis posterolateralis of the thalamus is most often vascular, although tumor is a possibility. The lesion results in loss or deterioration of all forms of sensation on the opposite side of the body; however, position sense is often more profoundly affected than others. A very high lesion of the central gray matter will affect the fibers conducting pain and temperature as they cross the cord in the anterior commissure; this will affect several dermatomes on one or both sides, but will spare tactile sensation. Syringomyelia is the most common cause of such a lesion.

3-3. The answer is D. *(Rudolph, 20/e, p 329.)* Clinitest tablets react with all reducing substances whereas Clinistix (glucose oxidase) is specific for glucose. A positive reaction with the former and a negative reaction with the latter suggests the presence of a reducing substance other than glucose in the urine. Children who have hereditary fructose intolerance as well as those who have essential fructosuria have reducing substances in their urine. Fructose intolerance, which presents during infancy, causes vomiting, hypoglycemia, and jaundice. Essential (benign) fructosuria (absence of fructokinase) is a rare autosomal recessive disorder that causes no symptoms and requires no therapy.

3-4. The answer is D. *(Schwartz, 6/e, pp 1863, 1880–1881.)* This case illustrates two (among many) conditions that lead to the anterior compartment syndrome, namely, acute arterial occlusion without collateral inflow, and rapid reperfusion of ischemic muscle. Treatment for a compartment syndrome is prompt fasciotomy. Assessing a compartment syndrome and proceeding with fasciotomy are generally based on clinical judgment. Inability to dorsiflex the toes is a grave sign of anterior compartment ischemia. EMG studies and compartment pressure measurements would probably be abnormal, but are unnecessary in view of the known findings and would delay treatment. Mere elevation of the leg would be an ineffective means of relieving compartment pressure, although elevation should accompany fasciotomy. Application of a splint has no role in the acute management of this problem.

3-5. The answer is C. *(Goroll, 3/e, pp 302–306.)* The nicotine patch or gum should only be prescribed in conjunction with a behavioral program. The heavy smoker should be educated about withdrawal symptoms and is a good candidate for nicotine reduction therapy, especially in light of past failures to quit smoking.

3-6. The answer is B. *(Delp, 9/e, pp 137–139.)* Firm, hard, nontender lymph nodes in the neck are often due to distant malignancy. The oral cavity should be examined very carefully for a primary malignancy. Patients with malignancy of the face, lips, oral cavity, and larynx may present with enlarged lymph nodes. Other sources of malignancy are the thyroid, which involves the anterior cervical lymph nodes, and lymphomas, chest malignancies, and abdominal malignancies, which may involve the supraclavicular nodes (Virchow's nodes).

3-7. The answer is C. (*Rudolph, 20/e, pp 1537–1539.*) An important noncardiac manifestation of digitalis toxicity in infants is vomiting. Affected infants also exhibit electrocardiographic changes, including sinus arrhythmia and a wandering pacemaker, paroxysmal tachycardia, and a heart rate of less than 100 beats per minute. The commonly used digitalis preparation in infants is digoxin. Digoxin blood levels of 2 ng/dL or less are usually therapeutic in adults; in contrast, therapeutic digoxin blood levels in infants range from 1 to 5 ng/dL, but the benefit of the higher levels in infants is doubtful.

3-8. The answer is C. (*Lynch, 3/e, pp 279–285.*) Psoriasis is a fairly common skin disorder that affects 2 to 3 percent of some populations. It occurs equally in both sexes, and most commonly is diagnosed in the third decade of life. Lesions can vary from small pinpoints to plaques that cover large portions of the body. Nail changes are common and include pitting, onychodystrophy, and a yellow-to-brown discoloration ("oil spot"). Auspitz's sign (pinpoint spots of bleeding seen when scales are lifted up off the skin) is a specific feature of psoriasis and can be used to differentiate it from other diseases with a similar appearance.

3-9–3-10. The answers are 3-9 D, 3-10 E. (*Cass, Urol Clin North Am 16:213–220, 1989. Zuidema, 4/e, pp 528–534.*) In stable patients with suspected genitourinary tract injury, the first urologic study other than a urinalysis should be the intravenous urogram. The technique of high-dose drip infusion is desirable because the high concentration of contrast achieved greatly facilitates interpretation in an unprepared patient. Intravenous urography should be performed before retrograde cystography to avoid obscuring visualization of the lower ureteral tract. The study also may preclude the need for retrograde urethrography in cases where, unlike the case presented, there is a suspicion of urethral injury. Renal arteriography is not indicated routinely but should be performed to rule out renal pedicle injury when no kidney function is demonstrated by drip infusion urography. Peritoneal lavage is not useful in the diagnosis of genitourinary injuries as the structures are retroperitoneal. Seventy to eighty percent of patients with blunt renal trauma are successfully treated nonsurgically. Bed rest may reduce the likelihood of secondary hemorrhage; antibiotics may reduce the chance of infection's developing in a perirenal hematoma. Failure of conservative treatment is indicated by rising fever, increasing leukocytosis, evidence of secondary hemorrhage, and persistent or increasing pain and tenderness in the region of the kidney.

3-11. The answer is D. *(Fitzpatrick, 4/e, pp 727–735.)* Rosacea is a common problem in middle-aged, fair-skinned people. Sun damage appears to play an important role. Stress, alcohol, and heat cause flushing. Men may develop rhinophyma. Low-dose oral tetracycline, erythromycin, and metronidazole control the symptoms. Topical erythromycin and metronidazole also work well.

3-12. The answer is A. *(Isselbacher, 13/e, pp 2372–2373.)* Guillain-Barré syndrome is characterized by an elevated CSF protein with few if any white blood cells. EMG would show a demyelinating process with nonuniform slowing and conduction block. Arterial blood gases would show a respiratory acidosis secondary to hypoventilation. CPK levels should be normal because there is little involvement of muscle in this disease process.

3-13–3-16. The answers are 3-13 A, 3-14 B, 3-15 A, 3-16 C. *(Andreasen, 2/e, pp 247–288.)* In assessing this patient's presenting symptoms, the presence of a significant stressor (job loss) would necessitate consideration of an adjustment disorder. The presence of dysphoria lasting more than 2 weeks and associated with weight loss, sleep disturbance, decreased libido, and loss of interest necessitates consideration of a major depression. His depression might also be secondary to medication or to undeclared substance abuse. Dysthymia is not a consideration, since the diagnosis requires a depressed mood for at least 2 years.

In the absence of a previous history of impotence, the most likely cause of his current difficulty is either the hypertension medication or the direct effects of his depression. Both are frequent causes of impotence. A core gender identity disturbance would have been manifest since childhood.

Fluoxetine is a selective serotonin reuptake inhibitor (SSRI), a common first choice among available antidepressants. Lithium is used for both mania and depression but is not often the first medication selected in the absence of an indication of bipolar disorder. The other listed medications are not used for the primary treatment of depression.

The differential diagnosis of major depression and depressed mood associated with schizophrenia can be very difficult. In schizophrenia, the onset is usually more gradual. The mood is usually apathetic or empty, in comparison with the painful depressed mood that is more common to major depression. Both diagnoses can be associated with psychosis, but in schizophrenia, the mood disturbance tends to persist even after the psychosis has long disappeared.

3-17. The answer is C. *(Rose, 4/e, pp 845–852.)* This patient presents with severe hyperkalemia. Although potassium elevations can occasionally be spurious (e.g., in hemolysis), the changes on this patient's ECG reflect severe cardiotoxic effects from the hyperkalemia. The ECG shows a typical progression in hyperkalemia with peaked T waves followed by widening of the QRS, loss of P waves, and eventually a sine wave pattern. Therapy of severe hyperkalemia includes intravenous calcium gluconate (to normalize membrane excitability), glucose and insulin, sodium bicarbonate (to drive potassium intracellularly), and potassium exchange resins (to remove potassium). Dialysis may occasionally be necessary, particularly in patients with concomitant renal failure.

3-18. The answer is D. *(Isselbacher, 13/e, p 1423.)* Intestinal ischemia is characterized by the triad of postprandial pain, anorexia (from fear of eating), and weight loss. The pain is typically intermittent and often occurs 30 min after eating and persists from 20 min to 3 h.

3-19. The answer is B. *(Rudolph, 20/e, pp 612–614.)* The patient should receive a booster immunization with adult Td, which should be given every 10 years to maintain immunity against both diphtheria and tetanus. He does not need passive immunization with tetanus immune globulin because the wound is superficial and there appears to be little or no risk of tetanus. As of 1993, pertussis immunization is discontinued at age 7.

3-20. The answer is A. *(Rudolph, 20/e, pp 654–655, 661–666, 668–669, 679–681, 907.)* Symptoms of rubella, usually a mild disease, include a diffuse maculopapular rash that lasts for 3 days, marked enlargement of the posterior cervical and occipital lymph nodes, low-grade fever, mild sore throat, and, occasionally, conjunctivitis, arthralgia, or arthritis. Persons with rubeola develop a severe cough, coryza, photophobia, conjunctivitis, and a high fever that reaches its peak at the height of the generalized macular rash, which typically lasts for 5 days. Koplik's spots on the buccal mucosa are diagnostic. Roseola is a viral exanthem of infants in which the high fever abruptly abates as a rash appears. Erythema infectiosum (fifth disease) begins with bright erythema on the cheeks ("slapped cheek" sign), followed by a red maculopapular rash on the trunk and extremities, which fades centrally at first. Erythema multiforme is a poorly understood syndrome consisting of skin lesions and involvement of mucous membranes. A number of infectious agents and drugs have been associated with this syndrome.

3-21–3-25. The answers are 3-21 C, 3-22 B, 3-23-B, 3-24 E, 3-25 D. (*Schwartz, 6/e, pp 557–559.*) The American Joint Committee on Cancer has defined a four-tiered staging system for breast cancer based on the clinical criteria of tumor size, involvement of lymph nodes, and metastatic disease. In one version of this system, a separate category is reserved for inflammatory breast cancer. While the grouping of breast cancers into stages provides a useful shorthand for expressing a patient's survival probability, it is noteworthy that considerable heterogeneity exists both with respect to tumor size and nodal characteristics among tumors that are classified within a given stage.

The TNM stage of breast cancer is assigned by measuring the greatest diameter of the tumor ("T"), assessing the axillary and clavicular lymph nodes for enlargement and fixation ("N"), and judging whether metastatic disease is present ("M"). In general, the worst of the three TNM parameters will determine the stage assignment.

Tumors that are not palpable are classified T0; tumors 2 cm or less, T1; tumors greater than 2 but not more than 5 cm, T2; tumors greater than 5 cm, T3; and tumors with extension into the chest wall or skin, T4.

Clinically negative lymph nodes are classified N0; positive, movable ipsilateral axillary nodes, N1; fixed ipsilateral axillary nodes, N2; and clavicular nodes, N3.

Absence of evidence of metastatic disease is classified M0; distant metastatic disease, M1.

The patient in question 276 has a T0, N2, M0 lesion. This is stage III (fixed or matted nodes are a poor prognostic sign).

The patient in question 277 has a T2, N1, M0 lesion. This is stage II.

The patient in question 278 has a T2, N0, M0 lesion. Though smaller than the tumor in question 277 and without clinically involved nodes, this tumor is also stage II.

The patient in question 279 has findings compatible with inflammatory breast cancer. A biopsy of the involved skin and a mammogram would confirm the diagnosis.

The patient in question 280 has a T1, N0, M1 lesion. This is stage IV (stage IV is any T, any N, M1).

3-26. The answer is C. *(Felig, 3/e, pp 546–549. Isselbacher, 13/e, pp 1626–1627, 1949.)* For the patient described in the question, the markedly increased calcitonin levels indicate the diagnosis of medullary carcinoma of the thyroid. In view of the family history, the patient most likely has multiple endocrine neoplasia (MEN) type II, which includes medullary carcinoma of the thyroid gland, pheochromocytoma, and parathyroid hyperplasia. Pheochromocytoma may exist without sustained hypertension as indicated by excessive urinary catecholamines. Before thyroid surgery is performed on this patient, a pheochromocytoma must be ruled out through urinary catecholamine determinations; the presence of such a tumor might expose him to a hypertensive crisis during surgery. The entire thyroid gland must be removed because foci of parafollicular cell hyperplasia, a premalignant lesion, may be scattered throughout the gland. Successful removal of the medullary carcinoma can be monitored with serum calcitonin levels. Hyperparathyroidism, while unlikely in this patient, is probably present in his brother.

3-27. The answer is A. *(Rowland, 8/e, pp 314–315.)* The pineal region is the source of an extraordinarily diverse group of tumor types, ranging from astrocytomas (derived from glial tissue) to chemodectomas (derived from sympathetic nervous tissue). Several different types of germ cell tumors arise from the tissues in this region, presumably from embryonal cell rests. In the U.S., pineal tumors account for only 1 percent of intracranial tumors, but one-third of these pineal tumors are germ cell tumors, including germinomas and choriocarcinomas.

3-28. The answer is D. *(Seidel, 3/e, pp 604–616.)* Hypospadias is a congenital abnormality in which the urethra is situated on the ventral surface of the shaft of the penis. Balanitis can occur in an uncircumcised man and is an inflammation of the glans penis. Priapism is a painful, long-standing erection that most often occurs in patients with leukemia or sickle cell anemia. Paraphimosis is a condition that occurs when the foreskin cannot be returned to the extended position; it may lead to gangrene of the glans penis. Phimosis is the inability to retract the foreskin.

3-29. The answer is B. *(Schwartz, 6/e, pp 199–201.)* Duodenal hematomas result from blunt abdominal trauma. They present as a high bowel obstruction with abdominal pain and occasionally a palpable right upper quadrant mass. An upper gastrointestinal series is almost always diagnostic with the classic coiled spring appearance of the second and third portions of the duodenum secondary to the crowding of the valvulae conniventes (circular folds) by the hematoma. Nonsurgical management is the mainstay of therapy as the vast majority of duodenal hematomas resolve spontaneously. Simple evacuationof the hematoma is the operative procedure of choice. However, bypass procedures and duodenal resection have been performed for this problem. In patients with duodenal obstruction from the superior mesenteric artery syndrome, the obstruction is usually the result of a marked weight loss and, in conjunction with this, loss of the retroperitoneal fat pad that elevates the superior mesenteric artery from the third and fourth portions of the duodenum. Nutritional repletion and replenishment of this fat pad will elevate the artery off the duodenum and relieve the obstruction.

3-30. The answer is E. *(Behrman, 15/e, p 1762.)* Bell's palsy is an acute, unilateral facial nerve palsy that begins about 2 weeks after a viral infection. The exact pathophysiology is unknown, but it is thought to be immune or allergic. Typically, on the affected side the upper and lower face are paretic, the mouth droops, and the patient cannot close the eye. Treatment consists of maintaining moisture to the affected eye (especially at night) to prevent keratitis. Complete, spontaneous resolution occurs in about 85 percent of cases, 10 percent of cases have mild residual disease, and about 5 percent of cases do not resolve.

3-31. The answer is D. *(Isselbacher, 13/e, pp 1158–1159.)* The carbon monoxide (CO) diffusing capacity provides an estimate of the rate at which oxygen moves by diffusion from alveolar gas to combine with hemoglobin in the red blood cells. It is interpreted as an index of the surface area engaged in alveolar-capillary diffusion. Measurement of diffusing capacity of the lung (DL_{CO}) is done by having the person inspire a low concentration of carbon monoxide. The rate of uptake of the gas by the blood is calculated from the difference between the inspired and expired concentrations. The test can be performed during a single 10-s breath-holding or during a minute of steady-state breathing. The diffusing capacity is defined as the amount of carbon monoxide transferred per minute per millimeter of mercury of driving pressure and correlates with oxygen transport from the alveolus into the capillaries. Primary parenchymal disorders, anemia, and removal of lung tissue decrease the diffusing capacity. Conversely, polycythemia, congestive heart failure, and intrapulmonary hemorrhage tend to increase the value for diffusing capacity.

3-32. The answer is B. (*Isselbacher, 13/e, p 819.*) Influenza A is a potentially lethal disease in the elderly and chronically debilitated patient. In institutional settings such as nursing homes, outbreaks are likely to be particularly severe. Hence, prophylaxis is extremely important in this setting. All residents should receive the vaccine unless they have known egg allergy (patients can choose to decline the vaccine). Since protective antibody to the vaccine will not develop for 2 weeks, amantadine can be used for protection against influenza A during the interim. A reduced dose is given to elderly patients.

3-33. The answer is E. (*Adams, 6/e, pp 1205–1217.*) Methacholine is a cholinergic agent and would be expected to worsen the symptoms exhibited by this man. Pyridostigmine, physostigmine, and edrophonium are all cholinesterase inhibitors used in the evaluation or treatment of myasthenia gravis, and they too would only hasten this man's deterioration. Atropine is usually given in combination with pralidoxime. This man is at most immediate risk of severe bronchospasm and diaphragmatic paralysis with subsequent respiratory arrest. Even if the patient does survive the acute poisoning, he is at risk for a delayed deterioration of the motor system, which may itself prove fatal and which does not respond to atropine treatment.

3-34. The answer is B. (*Evarts, 2/e, p 40.*) The signs and symptoms of fat embolism syndrome are those of adult respiratory distress syndrome in association with musculoskeletal trauma. The predominant feature is acute respiratory failure. Petechiae are found in 50 to 60 percent of cases, generally on the anterior chest and neck, axillae, and conjunctivae.

3-35. The answer is C. (*Schwartz, 6/e, pp 65–66.*) A ruptured abdominal aneurysm is a surgical emergency often accompanied by serious hypotension and vascular collapse before surgery and massive fluid shifts with renal failure after surgery. In this case, all the hemodynamic parameters indicate inadequate intravascular volume, and the patient is therefore suffering from hypovolemic hypotension. The low urine output indicates poor renal perfusion, while the high urine specific gravity indicates adequate renal function with compensatory free water conservation. The administration of a vasopressor agent would certainly raise the blood pressure, but it would do so by increasing peripheral vascular resistance and thereby further decrease tissue perfusion. The deleterious effects of shock would be increased. A vasodilating agent to lower the systemic vascular resistance would lead to profound hypotension and possibly complete vascular collapse because of pooling of an already depleted vascular volume. This patient's blood pressure is critically dependent on an elevated systemic vascular resistance. To properly treat this patient, rapid fluid infusion and expansion of the intravascular volume must be undertaken. This can be easily done with lactated Ringer's solution or blood (or both) until improvements in such parameters as the pulmonary capillary wedge pressure, urine output, and blood pressure are noted.

3-36. The answer is E. (*Schwartz, 6/e, p 140.*) This patient has developed pump failure due to a combination of preexisting coronary artery occlusive disease and high preload following a fluid challenge; afterload remains moderately high as well because of systemic vasoconstriction in the presence of cardiogenic shock. Poor myocardial performance is reflected in the low cardiac output and high pulmonary capillary wedge pressure. Therapy must be directed at increasing cardiac output without creating too high a myocardial oxygen demand on the already-failing heart. Administration of nitroglycerin could be expected to reduce both preload and afterload, but if it is given without an inotrope it would create unacceptable hypotension. Nitroprusside similarly would achieve afterload reduction but would result in hypotension if it was not accompanied by an inotropic agent. A beta blocker would act deleteriously by reducing cardiac contractility and slowing the heart rate in a setting in which cardiac output is likely to be rate-dependent. Dobutamine is a synthetic catecholamine that is becoming the inotropic agent of choice in cardiogenic shock. As a beta$_1$-adrenergic agonist, it improves cardiac performance in pump failure both by positive inotropy and peripheral vasodilation. With minimal chronotropic effect, dobutamine only marginally increases myocardial oxygen demand.

3-37. The answer is A. (*Behrman, 15/e, pp 1731–1735.*) A child who has a subacute disorder of the central nervous system that produces cranial-nerve abnormalities (especially of the seventh nerve and the lower bulbar nerves), long-tract signs, unsteady gait secondary to spasticity, and some behavioral changes is most likely to have a pontine glioma. Tumors of the cerebellar hemispheres may in later stages produce long-tract signs, but the gait disturbance would be ataxia. Dysmetria and nystagmus also would be present. Supratentorial tumors are quite uncommon in 6-year-old children; headache and vomiting would be likely presenting symptoms and papilledema a finding on physical examination.

3-38. The answer is C. *(Isselbacher,13/e, p 951.)* An S_3 gallop is among the more specific signs of systolic dysfunction, particularly in an older patient. Ankle edema is commonly found in elderly patients secondary to venous insufficiency and other local factors. Wheezes may be present in patients with left ventricular failure but also occur in asthma and obstructive lung disease.

3-39. The answer is D. *(Adams, 6/e, pp 1405–1406.)* This woman presented with proximal muscle weakness and pain and a heliotrope rash about her eyes. The term *heliotrope* refers to the lilac color of the periorbital rash characteristic of dermatomyositis. This rash surrounds both eyes and may extend onto the malar eminences, the eyelids, the bridge of the nose, and the forehead. It is usually associated with an erythematous rash across the knuckles and at the base of the nails and may be associated with flat-topped purplish nodules over the elbows and knees. Men with dermatomyositis are at higher-than-normal risk of having underlying malignancies. Psoriatic arthritis may be associated with reddish discoloration of the knuckles and muscle weakness, but the heliotrope rash would not be expected with this disorder. The age of onset for a psoriatic myopathy is also atypical. Similarly, the patient's rashes are not suggestive of lupus erythematosus, although a myopathy may occur with this connective tissue disease as well.

3-40. The answer is B. *(Isselbacher, 13/e, pp 761–762.)* This clinical presentation is fairly typical of chlamydial pneumonia. The history of a prior mild conjunctivitis that responded to erythromycin also lends support to a diagnosis of chlamydial infection. Most chlamydial pneumonias will present between the ages of 3 and 11 weeks, and most will present after 1 week of persistent symptoms. The majority will manifest a staccato cough with bilateral rales. This could represent a mild case of pertussis, but in the unimmunized infant pertussis is unlikely to be mild in appearance. An absolute eosinophil count of greater than 400 correlates well with chlamydial pneumonia, whereas you would most likely see a lymphocytosis with pertussis. There are now enzyme-linked immunoassays that can be used on nasopharyngeal specimens, or chlamydial inclusion bodies can be seen with Wright's or Giemsa's stains. Topical erythromycin will eradicate the conjunctivitis, but it will not eradicate the nasopharyngeal carrier state that has been established; therefore, it is now recommended that oral erythromycin be administered at 40 mg per kilogram body weight per day in four doses for 14 days. A bacterial pneumonia, such as group B streptococcal pneumonia, would present more acutely and the patient would appear very ill. Respiratory syncytial viral (RSV) pneumonia appears very much like chlamydial pneumonia, but with this past history of conjunctivitis it is not the most likely diagnosis. Aspiration pneumonia usually does not occur in the healthy child, and when it occurs the chest roentgenograph will usually reveal an alveolar infiltrate.

3-41. The answer is D. *(Isselbacher, 13/e, pp 1197, 1206.)* Owing to destruction of alveolar septa in this patient, there is reduced elastic recoil, which may allow for collapse of the small airways and thereby prolong the expiratory phase of respiration. During this prolonged expiratory phase, the patient will characteristically be exhaling through "pursed lips" to avoid collapse of these small airways. The respiratory rate is increased by having a markedly shortened inspiratory interval. The patient may also be thin and asthenic, have an increased anteroposterior chest diameter, and evidence hypertrophy of the accessory muscles of respiration. The diaphragm may be depressed, and percussion will be hyperresonant.

3-42. The answer is D. *(Isselbacher, 13/e, p 1186.)* Of the organisms listed, only anaerobic infection is likely to cause a necrotizing process. Type III pneumococci have been reported to cause cavitary disease, but this is unusual. The location of the infiltrate suggests aspiration, which also makes anaerobic infection most likely.

3-43. The answer is B. *(Bartlett, 7/e, pp 136–138.)* The Dominican Republic is one area of high risk for malaria where no chloroquine-resistant strains of *Plasmodium falciparum* have been identified. Other areas include Central America west of the Panama Canal Zone, Haiti, Egypt, and most of the Middle

East. Almost all other countries with a high risk for malaria have resistant strains. The drug of choice for prophylaxis in these areas is mefloquine or doxycycline. Primaquine is given to prevent relapses due to *P. vivax* or *P. ovale*.

3-44. The answer is A. (*Hall, pp 1495–1496.*) In a heparinized patient with significant life-threatening hemorrhage, immediate reversal of heparin anticoagulation is indicated. Protamine sulfate is a specific antidote to heparin and should be given as 1 mg for each 100 U heparin if hemorrhage begins shortly after a bolus of heparin. For a patient (such as this) in whom heparin therapy is ongoing, the dose should be based on the half-life of heparin (90 min). Since protamine is also an anticoagulant, only half the calculated circulating heparin should be reversed. The protaminization should be followed by placement of a percutaneous vena cava filter (Greenfield). In this critically ill patient, exploration of the retroperitoneal space would be surgically challenging and meddlesome.

3-45. The answer is B. (*Isselbacher, 13/e, p 1705.*) The clinical picture suggests hypertrophic osteoarthropathy. This process, the pathogenesis of which is unknown, is characterized by clubbing of digits, periosteal new bone formation, and arthritis. Hypertrophic osteoarthropathy is associated with intrathoracic malignancy, suppurative lung disease, and congenital heart problems. Treatment is directed at the underlying disease process. While x-rays may suggest osteomyelitis, the process is usually bilateral and easily distinguishable from osteomyelitis. The first step in evaluation of this patient is to obtain chest x-rays in order to look for lung infection and carcinoma.

3-46. The answer is A. (*Rudolph, 20/e, pp 486–489, 497, 1241–1242, 1271–1275.*) The mean age of presentation of ITP is 6 years. Patients look well except for petechial rash. Patients with acute lymphoblastic leukemia frequently have symptoms of pallor and fever in addition to bleeding. Nearly 50 percent of them have hepatomegaly and splenomegaly. CBC reveals anemia, leukocytosis or leukopenia, and thrombocytopenia. DIC is secondary to a severe underlying disease, such as fulminant bacterial sepsis with hypotension or profound hypoxia. Patients invariably appear ill and have leukocytosis, thrombocytopenia, and abnormal coagulation studies (e.g., prolonged PT, PTT, decreased fibrinogen concentration, and elevated fibrin split products). Patients with Henoch-Schönlein purpura have symptoms of skin rash and abdominal or joint pain. The rash is usually urticarial and purpuric and present over the buttocks or lower extremities. The platelet count is normal or elevated. SLE is very rare in a 3-year-old. Findings include fever, joint pain, and skin rash. CBC may reveal anemia, leukopenia, and thrombocytopenia.

3-47. The answer is E. *(Behrman, 15/e, pp 143, 167–169.)* The syndrome of kwashiorkor is caused by a diet that is deficient in protein leading to low serum albumin, which causes decreased plasma volume and increased interstitial fluid or edema. The term *marasmus* refers to a combined inadequacy of protein and energy in which the deficiency is dominated by the lack of food in general. The minimum requirement for protein is 8 percent of the total daily calories when the protein provided is from high-quality animal sources. These patients have a high death rate from intercurrent infections.

3-48. The answer is B. *(Isselbacher, 13/e, pp 1059–1061.)* Aortic stenosis may exist for several years before becoming clinically significant. There are three cardinal symptoms of aortic stenosis: dyspnea on exertion, syncope, and angina pectoris. The murmur is a rough, low-pitched systolic murmur usually heard at the base of the heart. The apex beat is usually displaced laterally as a reflection of left ventricular hypertrophy.

3-49. The answer is B. *(Behrman, 15/e, p 1058.)* Many types of objects produce esophageal obstruction in young children, including small toys, coins, and food. Most are usually lodged below the cricopharyngeal muscle at the level of the aortic arch. Initially, the foreign body may cause a cough, drooling, and choking. Later pain, avoidance of food (liquids are tolerated better), and shortness of breath may develop. Diagnosis is by history (as outlined in the question) and by radiographs (especially if the object is radiopaque). The usual treatment is removal of the object via esophagoscopy.

3-50. The answer is D. *(Behrman, 15/e, p 1306.)* Mitral valve prolapse occurs with the billowing into the atria of one or both mitral valve leaflets at the end of systole. It is a congenital abnormality that frequently only manifests during adolescence or later. It is more common in girls than in boys and seems to be inherited in an autosomal dominant fashion. On clinical examination, an apical murmur is noted late in systole, which may be preceded by a click. The diagnosis is confirmed with an echocardiogram that shows prolapse of the mitral leaflets during mid to late systole.

BLOCK 4

Answers

4-1. The answer is A. (*Rudolph, 20/e, pp 172–173.*) The adolescent who has attempted suicide should be hospitalized briefly so that a complete medical, psychological, and social evaluation can be performed and an appropriate treatment plan developed. Hospitalization also emphasizes the seriousness of the adolescent's action to her and to her family and the importance of cooperation in carrying out the recommendations for ongoing future therapy. The treatment plan may include continued counseling or supportive therapy with a pediatrician, out-patient psychotherapy with a psychiatrist or other mental health worker, or family therapy.

4-2. The answer is D. (*Schwartz, 6/e, pp 1731–1732.*) Testicular torsion occurs commonly in adolescents. The underlying pathology is secondary to an abnormally narrowed testicular mesentery with tunica vaginalis surrounding the testis and epididymis in a "bell-clapper" deformity. As the testis twists, it comes to lie in a higher position within the scrotum. Urinalysis is usually negative. Elevation will not provide a decrease in pain (negative Prehn's sign); a positive Prehn's sign might indicate epididymitis. A technetium-99m pertechnetate scan may be helpful in clarifying a confusing case; however, operation should not be delayed beyond 4 h from the time of onset of symptoms in order to maximize testicular salvage. This patient's presentation warrants immediate operation. The salvage rate for delay greater than 12 h is less than 20 percent. Both the affected and unaffected testes should undergo orchiopexy. The differential diagnosis between torsion of the testicle and epididymitis is sometimes quite difficult. On occasion, one has to explore a patient with epididymitis just to rule out a torsion of the testicle. Epididymitis usually occurs in sexually active males. Urinalysis is usually positive for inflammatory cells, and urethral discharge is often present. Spermatocele is a cyst of an efferent ductule of the rete testis. It presents as a painless transilluminable cystic mass that is separate from the testes.

4-3. The answer is C. (*Mayo Clinic, 6/e, pp 468–470, 477–480.*) Myasthenia gravis is a muscular weakness that occurs when repetitive use of a muscle results in exhaustion of its contractile power; although a progressive paresis results, rest partially restores muscle strength. Usually the muscles of the eyes and, slightly less commonly, of the jaw, throat, face, and neck are the first to be affected. Muscular dystrophy usually presents by the third year of life with muscle weakness that causes difficulty walking or running and a tendency to fall. Thyrotoxicosis has been associated with periodic paralysis mainly in young males of Japanese and Chinese descent; the periodic paralysis is unrelated to the severity of the thyrotoxicosis. Patients with multiple sclerosis present with weakness of one or more limbs almost 50 percent of the time. Hypokalemic weakness can result from the hypersecretion of aldosterone in primary aldosteronism.

4-4. The answer is A. (Kaplan, 6/e, p 1818.) Hypnosis has been used to treat a wide variety of psychiatric conditions and a wide variety of symptoms. However, it is not employed in the treatment of psychotic patients, and it is generally contraindicated in paranoid patients. Such patients tend to incorporate the hypnosis into their paranoid systems.

4-5. The answer is C. (Narayan, pp 81–82.) This is a rapidly deteriorating patient who probably suffered head trauma. His right-sided weakness and progressive obtundation suggest a lesion on the left side of his brain. The flexion of the right arm and extension of the right leg are probably decorticate posturing associated with an expanding mass. After head trauma, the mass most likely to be expanding at this pace and impinging upon the cortex is an epidural hematoma. This should be readily visible on a precontrast CT scan. The advantage of a precontrast scan over a postcontrast scan is that an enhancing lesion, such as a brain tumor, would be difficult to differentiate from a blood clot on a postcontrast CT scan. The EEG would be abnormal, but this patient is deteriorating too rapidly to justify a test that will not define the nature of the lesion and will use precious time that could be invested in other investigations. The skull x-ray might reveal a fracture but that would not explain the rapid deterioration.

4-6. The answer is E. (Narayan, pp 452–460.) Unfortunately, the emergency room physician chose his investigations poorly and the patient continued to deteriorate. The site of the skull fracture is consistent with an epidural hematoma. A fracture at this site will usually tear the middle meningeal artery and produce an epidural hematoma. Mannitol is administered to transiently lower intracranial pressure. This buys a little time and increases the likelihood that surgical intervention will be feasible before the patient has a transfalcial herniation. Many physicians would also give steroids, but their usefulness is debatable and at the dose proposed would be pointless. Furosemide at this dose would not be expected to have any impact on the increased intracranial pressure associated with the epidural hematoma. Barbiturates may be useful after head trauma, but the dose proposed will only exacerbate the patient's respiratory depression and will not address the problems of expanding intracranial mass and deteriorating neurologic status. The patient has not had a seizure and needs a variety of other measures implemented to save his life before antiepileptic therapy is instituted.

4-7. The answer is B. _(Narayan, pp 452–460.)_ With reasonable support from this point on, there is no reason to expect the patient to suffer a cardiac arrest and consequently there would be no justification for placement of a cardiac pacemaker. The ventricular drainage can be adjusted to help maintain the intracranial pressure at an acceptable level, but even with an intracranial pressure of less than 15 mmHg, brain herniation may occur under the falx cerebri (transfalcial) or through the tentorium cerebelli (transtentorial) or through the foramen magnum (transforaminal). The ventricular drain will be removed as soon as it is evident that the intracranial pressure has stabilized at an acceptable level (less than 20 mmHg). The idea of "respirator brain" is a common misconception among ICU support staff. The brain will deteriorate despite continuing respiratory support, not because of it, if there is a problem with brain perfusion. Some neurosurgeons favor antibiotic treatment after this type of surgery, but the choice and dose of antibiotic are inappropriate for a patient with a recent history of head trauma. Antiepileptic medications are not warranted, although many neurosurgeons would use them prophylactically in situations like this.

4-8. The answer is A. _(Narayan, pp 705–707.)_ This man has two good reasons to have meningitis: he sustained severe head trauma and he underwent neurosurgery. Fever could occur this early after surgery for a variety of noninfectious reasons, including atelectasis of the lungs and subarachnoid blood, but whenever fever develops within a few days of severe head trauma, meningitis must be presumed to be the problem. A rectal biopsy is a reasonable procedure in the assessment of some neurologic problems, such as storage diseases, but would not be expected to be informative in the assessment of this fever. Similarly, bronchoscopy and gastric aspirate cultures have a place in some fever investigations, but the most likely site of infection in this patient is the CSF or the ventricular drain itself. *Streptococcus pneumoniae* is the most likely organism in posttraumatic meningitis that appears within 3 days of the head trauma.

4-9. The answer is D. *(Narayan, pp 704–707.)* The organism most likely responsible for the fever of unknown origin, even in the absence of a positive Gram stain, is *Streptococcus pneumoniae*. This should be highly sensitive to penicillin G 2 million IU IV every 2 h. Metronidazole would be appropriate with some infections, but would be chosen for treatment only after culture results indicated it was appropriate. If meningitis is in fact the problem and the patient does not respond briskly to the penicillin, the ventricular drain may need to be replaced. This is no trivial procedure and simple removal of the drain is a better option. Cooling blankets may help lower the patient's body temperature, but this is a reasonable procedure only when the temperature elevation itself poses a threat to the patient's survival. Reexploration of the hematoma site would only be appropriate if there was reaccumulation of fluid at the site or evidence of an osteomyelitis in the overlying bone.

4-10–4-13. The answers are 4-10 B, 4-11 B, 4-12 D, 4-13 A. *(Isselbacher, 13/e, pp 2414–2417.)* A wide variety of substances can produce psychotic symptoms with either abuse or overdose. The stimulant drugs, notably cocaine and amphetamine, are particularly apt to produce a psychotic disorder with paranoid symptomatology. This psychosis is often hard to distinguish from schizophrenia, though it is usually present for a shorter duration than that required for the diagnosis of schizophrenia.

The patient displays the symptoms of schizophrenia and meets the criterion of a disturbance of at least 6 months' duration with at least 1 month of symptoms, including at least two or more of the following: hallucinations, delusions, disorganized speech or behavior, or negative symptoms. In addition, however, the patient displayed prominent manic symptomatology, such as grandiosity and hyperactivity, during the month prior to hospitalization. The patient therefore meets the criteria for a diagnosis of schizoaffective disorder. Patients with schizoid personality disorder do not show psychotic symptomatology, and patients with delusional disorder do not display bizarre delusions. Bipolar manic disorder is often hard to differentiate from schizophrenia, but such patients generally do not have a history of periods of psychosis that are without prominent mood symptoms.

Many medical illnesses can be associated with psychotic disorders and may at times be confused with schizophrenia, schizoaffective disorder, or mood disorders. These include neoplasms, endocrine disorders, cardiovascular disease, and renal and hepatic disease, as well as a host of other conditions. Asthma is not associated with psychotic symptoms.

Chlorpromazine was one of the earliest antipsychotic medications, and olanzapine is one of the newest. Haloperidol is also commonly prescribed. Lithium is frequently used to treat mood disorders, particularly manic symptomatology. Benzodiazepines may be used to combat anxiety but are not considered antipsychotic medications.

4-14. The answer is B. (*McCullough, pp 24–28.*) Epididymitis in children usually occurs in the preteenage years and is thought to be most often due to reflux of sterile urine that causes an inflammatory reaction in the epididymis. A urinary tract infection is occasionally seen. There is tenderness of the posterolaterally positioned epididymis with a normal testicle palpated anteriorly. When the testicle is elevated and the patient experiences relief from pain this is known as Prehn's sign. This sign is unreliable, and testicular torsion always needs to be ruled out.

4-15. The answer is C. (*Schwartz, 6/e, pp 1574–1578.*) Acute adrenal insufficiency is classically manifest as changing mental status, increased temperature, cardiovascular collapse, hypoglycemia, and hyperkalemia. The diagnosis can be difficult to make and requires a high index of suspicion. Its clinical presentation is similar to that of sepsis; however, sepsis is generally associated with hyperglycemia and no significant change in potassium. The treatment for adrenal crisis is hydrocortisone 100 mg intravenously, volume resuscitation, and other supportive measures to treat any new or ongoing stress. Then, hydrocortisone 200 to 400 mg is administered over the next 24 h followed by a taper of the steroid as tolerated.

4-16–4-20. The answers are 4-16 D, 4-17 A, 4-18 B, 4-19 E, 4-20 C. (*Schwartz, 6/e, pp 1175–1177, 1316.*) Carcinoid tumors are most commonly found in the appendix and small bowel, where they may be multiple. They have a tendency to metastasize, which varies with the size of the tumor. Tumors < 1 cm uncommonly metastasize. Tumors > 2.0 cm are more often found to be metastatic. Metastasis to the liver and beyond may give rise to the carcinoid syndrome. The tumors cause an intense desmoplastic reaction. Spread into the serosal lymphatics does not imply metastatic disease; local resection is potentially curative. When metastatic lesions are found in the liver, they should be resected when technically feasible to limit the symptoms of the carcinoidsyndrome. When extensive hepatic metastases are found, the disease is not curable. Resection of the appendix and cecum may be performed to prevent an early intestinal obstruction by locally encroaching tumor.

4-21. The answer is A. (*Sapira, p 424.*) Patients often present complaining of pain in an area other than the site of the pathologic process. For this reason, the "chief complaint" is often misleading. Pain originating at the hip joint is most often perceived in the groin area, followed by the buttock or posterior aspect of the greater trochanter. Occasionally pain may be referred to the ipsilateral knee.

4-22. The answer is C. (*Isselbacher, 13/e, p 1652.*) Felty's syndrome consists of a triad of rheumatoid arthritis, splenomegaly, and leukopenia. In contrast to the lymphopenia observed in patients who have systemic lupus erythematosus, the leukopenia of Felty's syndrome is related to a reduction in the number of circulating polymorphonuclear leukocytes. The mechanism of the granulocytopenia is poorly understood. Felty's syndrome tends to occur in people who have had active rheumatoid arthritis for a prolonged period. These patients commonly have other systemic features of rheumatoid disease such as nodules, skin ulcerations, the sicca complex, peripheral sensory and motor neuropathy, and arteritic lesions.

4-23. The answer is B. (*Behrman, 15/e, pp 1891–1892.*) Also known as *Ritter disease,* staphylococcal scalded skin disease is seen most commonly in children less than 5 years of age. The rash is preceded by fever, irritability, and extraordinary tenderness of the skin. Circumoral erythema, crusting of the eyes, mouth, and nose, and blisters on the skin may develop. Intraoral mucosal surfaces are not affected. Peeling of the epidermis in response to mild shearing forces (Nikolsky sign) leaves the patient susceptible to problems similar to those of a burn injury, including infection and fluid and electrolyte imbalance. Cultures are frequently negative. Treatment includes antibiotics (to cover resistant *Staphylococcus aureus*) and localized skin care. Recovery without scarring can be expected.

4-24. The answer is C. (*Mishell, 3/e, pp 198–202.*) Although all the procedures mentioned in the question can be helpful in establishing a case of rape in most situations, the expected lack of sperm and the matching blood types in the situation presented would limit their value in this case. Only the finding of 50 units/mL or more of acid phosphatase in this woman's vagina could be taken as evidence of ejaculation. Her introitus probably would not be injured because of her parity. Foreign pubic hair might only indicate close contact.

4-25–4-27. The answers are 4-25 A, 4-26 E, 4-27 B. (*Shires, 3/e, pp 232–236. Walt, 3/e, pp 184–190.*) Closed head injuries may result in cerebral concussion from depression of the reticular formation of the brainstem. This type of injury is usually reversible.

Local bleeding and swelling (intracranial or extracranial) produce an increase in the intracranial pressure. A characteristic symptom pattern occurs initiated by progressive depression of mental status. Increasing intracranial pressure tends to displace brain tissue away from the source of the pressure; if the pressure is sufficient, herniation of the uncal process through the tentorium cerebri occurs.

Pupillary dilatation is caused by compression of the ipsilateral oculomotor nerve and its parasympathetic fibers. If the pressure is not relieved, the contralateral oculomotor nerve will become involved and, ultimately, the brainstem will herniate through the foramen magnum and cause death. Hypertension and bradycardia are preterminal events.

Emergency measures to reduce intracranial pressure while preparing for localization of the clot or for a craniotomy or both include hyperventilation, dexamethasone (Decadron), and mannitol infusion. Of these, hyperventilation produces the most rapid decrease in brain swelling.

4-28. The answer is D. (*Behrman, 15/e, pp 840–841.*) The CT scan with contrast is an excellent modality for diagnosing tuberculous meningitis. Exudate in the basal cisterns that shows enhancement by contrast material is typical; tuberculomas, lucencies, edema, and infarction may be apparent; and hydrocephalus may develop. The x-ray of the chest will be likely to show signs of pulmonary tuberculosis. A high index of suspicion is necessary to diagnose tuberculous meningitis early.

4-29. The answer is B. (*Goroll, 3/e, p 780.*) Asymptomatic hyperuricemia does increase the risk of acute gouty arthritis. However, the cost of lifelong prophylaxis in this patient would be high, and the prevalence of adverse drug reaction would be between 10 and 25 percent. This expense is generally considered high as compared with a more conservative approach of treating an attack when it does occur. Prophylactic therapy would be reserved for patients who already had one or more acute attacks. Although hyperuricemia is associated with arteriosclerotic disease, the association is not felt to be causal, and there is no proven cardiovascular benefit to reducing the uric acid level. In patients with lymphoproliferative disease, prophylaxis for the prevention of renal impairment is recommended. The risk of urolithiasis is sufficiently low that prophylaxis is not necessary until the development of a stone.

4-30. The answer is C. *(Behrman, 15/e, pp 1490–1491.)* Membranoproliferative glomerulonephritis is the most common form of chronic glomerulonephritis in older children and young adults. It is a chronic, diffuse, proliferative nephritis that occurs in two main forms that are indistinguishable histologically. The micrograph shown in the question depicts type I membranoproliferative glomerulonephritis (MPGN type I) with interposition of mesangial matrix between the basement membrane and the endothelial layer. Subendothelial deposits are also seen. Type I MPGN is more common than type II, which is called "dense deposit disease" because dense-appearing deposits occur within the basement membrane. Complement abnormalities are usually found in both MPGN type I and type II. Progressive renal failure may occur in either form.

4-31. The answer is C. *(Behrman, 15/e, pp 1191–1192.)* Suppurative infection of the chain of lymph nodes between the posterior pharyngeal wall and the prevertebral fascia leads to retropharyngeal abscesses. The most common causative organisms are *S. aureus*, group A hemolytic streptococci, and oral anaerobes. Presenting signs and symptoms include a history of pharyngitis, abrupt onset of fever with severe sore throat, refusal of food, drooling, and muffled or noisy breathing. A bulge in the posterior pharyngeal wall is diagnostic, as are radiographs of the lateral neck that reveal the retropharyngeal mass. Palpation (with adequate provision for emergency control of the airway in case of rupture) reveals a fluctuant mass. Treatment should include incision and drainage if fluctuance is present.

4-32. The answer is A. *(Adams, 6/e, pp 1404–1406.)* Polymyositis is an acquired myopathy characterized by subacute symmetric weakness of proximal limb and trunk muscles that progresses over several weeks or months. When a characteristic skin rash occurs, the disease is known as dermatomyositis. In addition to progressive proximal limb weakness, the patient often presents with dysphagia and neck muscle weakness. Up to one-half of cases with polymyositis-dermatomyositis may have, in addition, features of connective tissue diseases (rheumatoid arthritis, lupus erythematosus, scleroderma, Sjögren's syndrome). Laboratory findings include an elevated serum CK level, an EMG showing myopathic potentials with fibrillations, and a muscle biopsy showing necrotic muscle fibers and inflammatory infiltrates. Polymyositis is clinically distinguished from the muscular dystrophies by its less prolonged course and lack of family history. It is distinguished from myasthenia gravis by its lack of ocular muscle involvement, absence of variability in strength over hours or days, and lack of response to cholinesterase inhibitor drugs.

4-33. The answer is C. *(Isselbacher, 13/e, pp 1363–1378.)* A peptic ulcer (duodenal or gastric) presents with epigastric pain 1 to 4 h postprandially with rhythmicity and periodicity. It is relieved by food, H2 blockers, and alkali (antacid tablets). Its attributes are usually diagnostic. (Recall that attributes of pain are commonly described in the "PQRST" format: P = provoking/ palliating factors, Q = quality of the pain, R = region/radiation, S = severity, and T = temporal relations.) A peptic ulcer is commonly provoked by fasting or drinking alcohol or coffee. It is commonly palliated by ingestion of food or alkali. It is usually described as a gnawing, aching, or burning pain. The severity varies from mild to severe. It occurs about 1 to 4 h after meals.

4-34–4-36. The answers are 4-34 D, 4-35 F, 4-36 B. *(Isselbacher, 13/e, pp 1266–1274.)* The 30-year-old woman has clinical symptoms that could result in volume depletion. The high specific gravity of the urine and high urine sodium make prerenal azotemia the most likely diagnosis. The elderly patient with oliguria and lower abdominal pain should be evaluated for urinary tract obstruction, a side effect of many psychotropic medications, particularly in older men with prostatic hypertrophy. The elderly woman has developed acute tubular necrosis secondary to either hypotension or aminoglycoside therapy.

4-37. The answer is D. *(USDHHS, CDC, MMWR 43:1–38, 1994.)* Children who are late in their immunization schedule should be vaccinated when the opportunity arises. Mild acute illness or antibiotic use is not a contraindication to immunization. OPV and MMR are not contraindicated in children of pregnant women. OPV, but not MMR, is contraindicated in any household contact of a severely immunocompromised person; IPV should be administered if indicated. Live and inactivated vaccines can be given at the same time.

4-38. The answer is C. (*Lechtenberg, Synopsis, p 112.*) Although papilledema must be considered evidence of a potentially life-threatening intracranial process, optic nerve bulging in this young woman is most likely from pseudotumor cerebri. This is a relatively benign condition that occasionally develops in obese or pregnant women. CSF pressure is markedly elevated in these patients, but they are not at risk of herniation. The condition is presumed to arise from hormonal problems. Without treatment, the increased intracranial pressure will produce optic nerve damage with loss of visual acuity.

4-39. The answer is C. (*Boland, New Horizons 2:246–260, 1993.*) The development of acute postoperative cholecystitis is an increasingly recognized complication of the severe illnesses that precipitate admissions to the intensive care unit. The causes are obscure but probably lead to a common final pathway of gallbladder ischemia. The diagnosis is often extremely difficult because the signs and symptoms may be those of occult sepsis. Moreover, the patients are often intubated, sedated, or confused as a consequence of the other therapeutic or medical factors. Biochemical tests, though frequently revealing abnormal liver function, are nonspecific and nondiagnostic. Bedside ultrasonography is usually strongly suggestive of the diagnosis when a thickened gallbladder wall or pericholecystic fluid is present, but radiologic findings may also be nondiagnostic. If the diagnosis is delayed, mortality and morbidity are very high. Percutaneous drainage of the gallbladder is usually curative of acalculous cholecystitis and affords stabilizing palliation if calculous cholecystitis is present. Some authors have recommended prophylactic percutaneous drainage of the gallbladder under CT guidance in any ICU patient who is failing to thrive or has other signs of low-grade sepsis after appropriate therapy of the primary illness has been provided. The distractor items in the question are all either too aggressive to be safely done in critically ill patients or too cautious for a patient with a potentially fatal complication.

4-40. The answer is A. (*Behrman, 15/e, pp 1211–1213.*) Of the choices given, bronchiolitis is the most likely, although asthma, pertussis, and bronchopneumonia can present similarly. The family history of upper respiratory infections, the previous upper respiratory illness in the patient, and signs of intrathoracic airway obstruction make the diagnosis of bronchiolitis more likely. Viral croup, epiglottitis, and diphtheria are not reasonable choices because there are no signs of extrathoracic airway obstruction.

The most likely cause of the illness is infection by respiratory syncytial virus, which causes outbreaks of bronchiolitis of varying severity, usually in the winter and spring. Other viruses such as parainfluenza and the adenoviruses have also been implicated in producing bronchiolitis. Treatment is usually supportive in this usually self-limited condition.

4-41. The answer is B. (*Isselbacher, 13/e, pp 1192, 2013.*) Kartagener's syndrome belongs to a group of inheritable disorders known as *immotile cilia syndromes.* Kartagener's syndrome is known by the triad of dextrocardia (or situs inversus), chronic sinusitis (with formation of nasal polyps), and bronchiectasis. There is a defect that causes the cilia within the respiratory tract epithelium to be immotile, as well as the cilia of sperm.

4-42. The answer is B. (*Isselbacher, 13/2, pp 951–954.*) An acquired arteriovenous fistula may be diagnosed by the presence of a continuous murmur and a palpable thrill over an area of previous trauma. The large pulse pressure is an indication that a large portion of the cardiac output is bypassing the systemic vascular resistance through the fistula.

4-43. The answer is A. (*Behrman, 15/e, pp 1288–1290, 1292–1294, 1306. Rudolph, 20/e, pp 1474–1475.*) Most commonly, children with an atrial septal defect are asymptomatic with the lesion found during a routine examination. In older children, exercise intolerance may become noted if the lesion is of significant size. On examination, the pulses are normal, a right ventricular systolic lift at the left sternal border is palpable, and a fixed splitting of the second heart sound is audible. Surgery is indicated for all symptomatic patients and for those who are currently asymptomatic but with a shunt ratio of at least 2:1. Ventricular septal defects commonly present as a harsh or blowing holosystolic murmur best heard along the left lower sternum. Tricuspid regurgitation is a middiastolic rumble at the lower left sternal border. Often a history of birth asphyxia or findings of other cardiac lesions is present. Mitral valve prolapse occurs with the billowing into the atria of one or both mitral valve leaflets at the end of systole. It is a congenital abnormality that frequently only manifests during adolescence or later. It is more common in girls than in boys and seems to be inherited in an autosomal dominant fashion. On clinical examination, an apical murmur is noted late in systole, which may be preceded by a click. The diagnosis is confirmed with an echocardiogram that shows prolapse of the mitral leaflets during mid to late systole. Antibiotic prophylaxis is recommended for dental work as the incidence of endocarditis may be higher in these patients.

4-44. The answer is C. *(Felig, 3/e, p 29. Isselbacher, 13/e, pp 268–270.)* The symptoms of masculinization (e.g., alopecia, deepening of voice, clitoral hypertrophy) in the patient presented in the question are characteristic of active androgen-producing tumors. Such extreme virilization is very rarely observed in polycystic ovary syndrome or in Cushing's syndrome; moreover, the presence of normal cortisol and markedly elevated plasma testosterone levels indicates an ovarian rather than adrenal cause of her findings. Although hilar cell tumors are capable of producing the picture seen in this patient, they are very rare and usually arise in postmenopausal women. Arrhenoblastomas are the most common androgen-producing ovarian tumors. Their incidence is highest during the reproductive years. Composed of varying proportions of Leydig's and Sertoli's cells, they are generally benign. In contrast to arrhenoblastomas, granulosa-theca cell tumors produce feminization, not virilization.

4-45. The answer is A. *(Johnson, 3/e, pp 400–402.)* Men with myotonic dystrophy characteristically exhibit problems with relaxing their grip, hypersomnolence, premature baldness, testicular atrophy, and cataracts. The EMG pattern displayed by these patients is often referred to as the *dive-bomber pattern* because of the characteristic sound produced when the evoked action potentials are heard. The cardiac defect that evolves in these persons usually requires pacemaker implantation to avoid sudden death. Psychiatric problems also develop in many patients with myotonic dystrophy, but their basis is unknown.

4-46. The answer is B. *(Murray, 2/e, pp 2164–2187.)* Classifying a pleural effusion as either a transudate or an exudate is useful in identifying the underlying disorder. Pleural fluid is exudative if it has any one of the following three properties: a ratio of concentration of total protein in pleural fluid to serum greater than 0.5, an absolute value of LDH greater than 200 IU, or a ratio of LDH concentration in pleural fluid to serum greater than 0.6. Causes of exudative effusions include malignancy, pulmonary embolism, pneumonia, tuberculosis, abdominal disease, collagen vascular diseases, uremia, Dressler's syndrome, and chylothorax. Exudative effusions may also be drug-induced. If none of the aforementioned properties are met, the effusion is a transudate. Differential diagnosis includes congestive heart failure, nephrotic syndrome, cirrhosis, Meigs' syndrome, and hydronephrosis.

4-47. The answer is B. *(Isselbacher, 13/e, pp 2204, 2234.)* The patient is describing a transient ischemic attack (TIA). These attacks occur suddenly and produce reversible, unilateral visual loss or neurologic deficits. The attacks last from a few minutes to a few hours. These attacks are produced by emboli that occlude the retinal artery and may be associated with carotid atherosclerosis, which may be the source of emboli. Auscultation of the carotids may reveal a bruit.

4-48. The answer is B. *(Rudolph, 20/e, pp 851–853.)* Poisoning with tricyclic antidepressants is a leading reason for admissions to pediatric intensive care units and the leading cause of fatal drug overdose in adolescents. These preparations produce a variety of pharmacologic effects, including inhibition of muscarinic cholinergic receptors, blockade of norepinephrine and serotonin uptake, and depression of sodium channels responsible for cardiac cell membrane depolarization. The toxic-to-therapeutic ratio is low. Young children often ingest poisons and drugs during times of household disruption. Visitors' handbags are a great temptation for the inquisitive toddler.

4-49. The answer is C. *(Isselbacher, 13/e, p 1220.)* Because the clinical signs of neurologic deterioration and a petechial rash have occurred in the setting of fracture and hypoxia, fat embolism is the most likely diagnosis. This process occurs when neutral fat is introduced into the venous circulation after bone trauma or fracture. The latent period is 12 to 36 h, usually earlier than a pulmonary embolus would occur after trauma.

4-50. The answer is B. *(Rowland, 8/e, p 627.)* More than 10 percent of patients with Friedreich's disease develop diabetes mellitus. A more life-threatening complication of this degenerative disease is the disturbance of the cardiac conduction system that often develops. Visual problems occur with the hyperglycemia of uncontrolled diabetes mellitus, but even patients without diabetes develop optic atrophy late in the course of the degenerative disease.

BLOCK 5

Answers

5-1. The answer is D. *(Isselbacher, 13/e, pp 1899–1902.)* Hypersecretion of growth hormone after epiphyseal fusion produces leathery skin, increased hand and foot size, and increased sweating. It may also lead to hypertrophic arthropathy, peripheral neuropathy, and generalized visceromegaly. The clinical features of acromegaly are distinct from those of other diseases; thus, it is readily diagnosed by observation.

5-2. The answer is D. *(Isselbacher, 13/e, pp 258–260.)* Both the arterial pH and the P_{CO_2} are elevated in the patient presented in the question; the disturbance is alkalosis with hypoventilation. The P_{CO_2} typically increases by 0.5 to 1.0 torr for each meq/L increase in serum bicarbonate. These findings suggest that the hypoventilation is compensatory rather than a primary phenomenon. This assumption is further supported by the absence of clinical lung disease.

5-3. The answer is A. *(Isselbacher, 13/e, pp 258–260.)* The development of a clinically significant metabolic alkalosis in a patient requires not only the loss of acid or addition of alkali, but renal responses that maintain the alkalosis. The normal kidney can tremendously augment its excretion of acid or alkali in response to changes in ingested load. However, in the presence of significant volume depletion and consequent avid salt and water retention, the tubular maximum for bicarbonate reabsorption is increased. Correction of volume depletion alone is usually sufficient to correct the alkalosis, since the kidney will then excrete the excess bicarbonate. HCl infusion is usually unnecessary and can be dangerous. Acetazolamide is unlikely to be effective in the face of distal $Na+$ reabsorption (in exchange for $H+$ secretion). Moreover, to the extent that acetazolamide causes natriuresis, it will exacerbate the volume depletion.

5-4. The answer is E. *(Schlant, 8/e, pp 1895–1904.)* Cor pulmonale is characterized by the presence of pulmonary hypertension and consequent right ventricular dysfunction. Its causes include diseases leading to hypoxic vasoconstriction, as in cystic fibrosis; occlusion of the pulmonary vasculature, as in pulmonary thromboembolism; and parenchymal destruction, as in sarcoidosis. The right ventricle, in the presence of a chronic increase in afterload, becomes hypertrophic, dilates, and fails. The electrocardiographic findings, as illustrated in the question, include tall, peaked P waves in leads II, III, and AVF, which indicate right atrial enlargement; tall R waves in leads V_1 to V_3 and a deep S wave in V_6 with associated ST-T wave changes, which indicate right ventricular hypertrophy; and right axis deviation. Right bundle branch block occurs in 15 percent of patients.

5-5. The answer is C. (*Rudolph, 20/e, pp 1241–1242, 1245–1249, 1251.*) The prolongation of PT, aPTT, and TT excludes the diagnosis of ITP. PT tests principally for factors I, II, V, VII, and X and is not prolonged in hemophilia A (factor VIII deficiency) or hemophilia B (factor IX deficiency). In vitamin K deficiency there is a decrease in the production of factors II, VII, IX, and X, and PT and aPTT are prolonged. However, the thrombin time, which tests for conversion of fibrinogen to fibrin, should be normal and the platelet count should also be normal. In DIC, there is consumption of fibrinogen; factors II, V, and VIII; and platelets. Therefore, there is prolongation of PT, aPTT, and TT and a decrease in factor VIII level and platelet count. In addition, the titer of fibrin split production is usually increased.

5-6. The answer is E. (*Sapira, p 258.*) Clubbing, a hypertrophic osteoarthropathy, may be seen in a multitude of diseases, such as congenital cyanotic heart disease, bacterial endocarditis, biliary cirrhosis, Crohn's disease, severe ulcerative colitis, myelogenous leukemia, chronic renal failure, and Graves' disease. When clubbing is found in association with cyanosis, however, often the most important underlying condition to be aware of is bronchogenic carcinoma. Clubbing is detected as follows: Observe the angle between the nail bed and the base of the finger, the ungual-phalangeal angle (Lovibond's angle). This should be less than 180°. Some physicians have the patient place the right and left fingers against each other, knuckle to knuckle and fingernail tip to fingernail tip. If there is no abnormality of the angle, a definite rhombus will be seen between the distal phalanges; however, if Lovibond's angle is greater than 180°, no such rhombus will be seen.

5-7. The answer is B. (*Isselbacher, 13/e, p 1469.*) The current hepatitis B vaccine is genetically engineered to consist of hepatitis B surface antigen particles. Therefore only antibody to surface antigen will be detected after vaccination. Since the patient has had no exposure to hepatitis B, she should be surface antigen–negative.

5-8. The answer is C. (*AAP, 23/e, pp 345–347.*) Erythema infectiosum (EI), caused by parvovirus type B19, is a mild, limited viral infection characterized by a distinctive rash on the face often called "slapped-cheek" because of its intensity. The infection may cause chronic anemia in immunodeficient persons and aplastic crisis in those with chronic hemolytic anemia. Adenoviruses cause upper respiratory tract infections and occasionally severe pneumonia. Adenovirus types 31, 40, and 41 have been associated with gastroenteritis. Coxsackieviruses cause multiple clinical manifestations. Type A16 causes the hand, foot, and mouth syndrome and type A24 has been associated with hemorrhagic conjunctivitis. Rotaviruses are implicated in diarrheal syndromes, and echovirus 9 in petechial exanthem and meningitis. Coxsackieviruses and echoviruses are nonpolio enteroviruses.

5-9. The answer is B. (*Kaplan, 6/e, p 2755.*) Patients are increasingly aware and concerned about who will make decisions for them if they lose the ability to make their own decisions. This might be from a recurrent mental illness such as bipolar disorder, a medical illness, or later-life vegetative states. The durable power of attorney allows the selection of a decision maker in advance who can then act without the necessity of a court proceeding.

5-10. The answer is D. (*Ryan, 5/e, pp 232–238.*) The photomicrograph accompanying the question shows villi within a tubular structure; the villi are easily identified by the presence of cytotrophoblasts. The diagnosis is tubal ectopic pregnancy. Molar pregnancy, incomplete abortion, and missed abortion also can be associated with the presence of villi, but specimens from these disorders would not be obtained at laparotomy.

5-11–5-12. The answers are 5-11 A, 5-12 E. (*Schwartz, 6/e, pp 1834–1838, 1846–1848.*) Subdural hematomas usually arise from tears in the veins bridging from the cerebral cortex to the dura or venous sinuses, often after only minor head injuries. They can become apparent several days after the initial injury. Treatment is with drainage of the hematoma through a burr hole; a formal craniotomy may be required if the fluid reaccumulates. Significant brain contusions due to blunt trauma are usually associated with at least transient loss of consciousness; similarly, epidural hematomas result in a period of unconsciousness, although a "lucid interval" may follow during which neurologic findings are minimal.

Subarachnoid hemorrhage (SAH) in the absence of antecedent trauma most commonly arises from a ruptured intracranial aneurysm, which typically is found at the bifurcation of the major branches of the circle of Willis. Other less frequent causes include hypertensive hemorrhage, trauma, and bleeding from an arteriovenous malformation. Patients will present with the sudden onset of an excruciating headache. Complaints of a stiff neck and photophobia are common. Loss of consciousness may be transient or evolve into frank coma. Cranial nerve palsies are seen as a consequence both of increased intracranial pressure due to hemorrhage and from pressure of the aneurysm on adjacent cranial nerves. CT scans followed by cerebral arteriography help to confirm the diagnosis as well as to identify the location of the aneurysm. Treatment consists of surgical ligation of the aneurysm by placing a clip across its neck. Early surgical intervention (within 72 h of SAH) may prevent aneurysmal rebleeding and allow aggressive management of posthemorrhage vasospasm.

5-13. The answer is D. *(Isselbacher, 13/e, p 7.)* The principle of autonomy is an overriding issue in this patient, who is competent to make her own decisions about surgery. Consulting a psychiatrist would be inappropriate unless there is some reason to believe the patient is not competent. No such concern is present in this description of the patient. Since the patient is competent, no friend or relative can give permission for the procedure.

5-14. The answer is B. *(Isselbacher, 13/e, pp 519, 653.)* Acute epiglottitis is a progressive cellulitis of the epiglottis and surrounding tissues in the supraglottic airway that can cause acute airway obstruction. In young patients the causative organism is most frequently *Haemophilus influenzae* type b. In adolescents and adults the epiglottitis may not be as fulminant, and the most common organisms isolated in these cases are *Streptococcus pneumoniae* and *Staphylococcus aureus*. Frequent complaints include dysphagia, odynophagia, and a fever that has progressed over 1 to 2 days. Stridor may be present, but hoarseness and loss of voice power are nearly universal. The patient will prefer to lean forward, and drooling may be seen. An edematous, cherry-red epiglottis and surrounding pharyngeal mucosa will be seen upon examination, and this visualization is the best way to confirm the diagnosis in adults. Examination of the pharynx is contraindicated in children because of the risk of laryngospasm and the resultant airway obstruction. In children a lateral x-ray of the neck will show an enlarged epiglottis, the "thumb-print" sign.

5-15. The answer is B. *(Behrman, 15/e, p 1700.)* Night terrors are most common in boys between the ages of 5 and 7 years. The child awakens suddenly, appears frightened and unaware of his surroundings, and has the clinical signs outlined in the question. He cannot be consoled by the parents. After a few minutes, sleep follows and the patient cannot recall the event in the morning. Sleepwalking is common in these children. Exploring the family dynamics for emotional disorders may be helpful; usually pharmacologic therapy is not required.

5-16. The answer is D. *(Isselbacher, 13/e, pp 102, 145, 761, 764, 1942–1946, 2344, 2349–2350.)* A unilateral ptosis is associated with Horner's syndrome, which is caused by interruption of the cervical sympathetic chain. Bilateral drooping of the eyelids may be an early sign of myasthenia gravis. Bell's palsy and hyperthyroidism both tend to cause lid retraction and a staring gaze. Conjunctivitis constitutes part of the classic triad of Reiter's syndrome.

5-17–5-18. The answers are 5-33 B, 5-34 A. *(Isselbacher, 13/e, p 729.)* The diffuse rash involving palms and soles would in itself suggest the possibility of secondary syphilis. The hypertrophic, wartlike lesions around the anal area are called *condyloma lata* and are specific for secondary syphilis. The VDRL slide test will be positive in all patients with secondary syphilis. The Weil-Felix titer has been used as a screening test for rickettsial infection. In this patient who has condyloma and no systemic symptoms, Rocky Mountain spotted fever would be unlikely. No chlamydial infection would present in this way. Blood cultures might be drawn to rule out bacterial infection such as chronic meningococcemia; however, the clinical picture is not consistent with a systemic bacterial infection. Penicillin is the drug of choice for secondary syphilis. Ceftriaxone and tetracycline are usually considered to be alternate therapies. Interferon alpha has been used in the treatment of condyloma acuminata, a lesion that can be mistaken for syphilitic condyloma.

5-19. The answer is B. *(Behrman, 15/e, pp 2029–2030.)* Human bites may pose a significant problem. They may become infected with oropharyngeal bacteria, including *Staphylococcus aureus,* viridans streptococci, *Bacteroides* species, and anaerobes. A patient with an infected human bite of the hand requires hospitalization for appropriate drainage procedures, Gram stain and culture of the exudate, vigorous cleaning, debridement, and appropriate antibiotics. The wound should be left open and allowed to heal by secondary intention.

5-20. The answer is A. *(Adams, 6/e, pp 270–271.)* The fact that vision is preserved excludes optic neuritis and cavernous sinus thrombosis. Optic neuritis will produce pain in the affected eye and may be associated with a normal optic disc, but visual acuity should be deficient and an afferent pupillary defect should be apparent. Cavernous sinus thrombosis usually produces proptosis and pain, but impaired venous drainage from the eye should interfere with acuity, and the retina should appear profoundly disturbed. With a diphtheritic polyneuropathy, an ophthalmoplegia may develop, but this would not be limited to one eye and is not usually associated with facial trauma. Transverse sinus thrombosis may produce cerebrocortical dysfunction or stroke, but ophthalmoplegia would not be a manifestation of this problem.

5-21–5-22. The answers are 5-21 C, 5-22 B. *(Schwartz, 6/e, pp 700–702.)* Chylothorax may occur after intrathoracic surgery, or it may follow malignant invasion or compression of the thoracic duct. Intraoperative recognition of a thoracic duct injury is managed by double ligation of the duct. Direct repair is impractical owing to the extreme friability of the thoracic duct. Injuries not recognized until several days after intrathoracic surgery frequently heal following the institution of a low-fat diet and either repeated thoracentesis or tube thoracostomy drainage. A low-fat, medium-chain triglyceride diet often reduces the flow of chyle. Failure of this treatment modality requires direct surgical ligation of the thoracic duct. This is best approached from below the diaphragm, regardless of the site of intrathoracic injury.

5-23. The answer is B. *(Ransom, p 53.)* Lymphogranuloma venereum (LGV) is a chronic infection produced by *Chlamydia trachomatis.* The primary infection begins as a painless ulcer on the labia or vaginal vestibule; the patient usually consults the physician several weeks after the development of painful adenopathy in the inguinal and perirectal areas. Diagnosis can be established by culture or antibodies to *Chlamydia trachomatis.* The

Frei skin test is no longer used because of its low sensitivity. The differential diagnosis includes syphilis, chancroid, granuloma inguinale, carcinoma, and herpes. Chancroid is a sexually transmitted disease producing a painful and tender ulceration of the vulva. It is caused by *Haemophilus ducreyi*. Donovan bodies are present in patients with granuloma inguinale, which is caused by *Calymmatobacterium granulomatis*. Therapy for both granuloma inguinale and LGV is administration of tetracycline.

5-24. The answer is D. *(Behrman, 15/e, p 1549.)* The description is that of a hydrocele, an accumulation of fluid in the tunica vaginalis. Small hydroceles usually resolve spontaneously in the first year of life. Larger ones or those that have a variable fluid level with time will likely need surgical repair.

5-25. The answer is D. *(McCullough, pp 33–34.)* The presence of a patent processus vaginalis allows communication of intraperitoneal contents with the scrotum. Clear intraperitoneal fluid can form a hydrocele. Purulent material from a ruptured appendix can cause a hot scrotum. There have been unusual cases of scrotal swelling due to meconium in the newborn and due to migration of ventriculoperitoneal shunt tubing. Abdominal trauma, as from a seat belt, can disrupt intraabdominal contents, and the blood can migrate through a patent processus vaginalis. The scrotal blood will not transilluminate and it may be gravity-dependent.

5-26. The answer is D. *(Fitzpatrick, 4/e, pp 2516–2520.)* The patient presents with the classic picture of measles. The coryza, conjunctivitis, cough, and fever characterize the measles prodrome. The pathognomonic Koplik's spots (pinpoint elevations connected by a network of minute vessels on the soft palate) usually precede onset of the rash by 24 to 48 h and may remain for 2 or 3 days. After the prodrome of 1 to 7 days, the discrete, red macules and papules begin behind the ears and spread to the face, trunk, and then distally over the extremities.

5-27. The answer is C. *(Moosa, Arch Surg 125:1028–1031, 1990. Schwartz, 6/e, pp 1386–1387.)* The scenario in the question is a typical course of a patient with iatrogenic injury of the common bile duct. These injuries commonly occur in the proximal portion of the extrahepatic biliary system. The transhepatic cholangiogram documents a biliary stricture, which in this clinical setting is best dealt with surgically. Choledochoduodenostomy generally cannot be performed because of the proximal location of the stricture. The best results are achieved with end-to-side choledochojejunostomy (Roux-en-Y) performed over a stent. Percutaneous transhepatic dilation has been attempted in select cases, but follow-up is too short to make an adequate assessment of this technique. Primary repair of the common bile duct may result in recurrent stricture.

5-28. The answer is E. *(DSM-IV, pp 629–634.)* The patient displays all the features required for a diagnosis of personality disorder. These include an enduring and pervasive pattern of inner experience and behavior that deviates from the expectations of the culture in at least two of the following ways: cognition (e.g., ways of perceiving self and other people), affective responses, interpersonal functioning, and impulse control. He also meets the requirements that the problem appear by early adulthood and cause social, occupational, or other impairment. He does not show signs of psychosis, as measured by the presence of symptoms or findings on the mental status examination, nor does he demonstrate the behavioral patterns associated with posttraumatic stress disorder or obsessive-compulsive disorder.

Personality disorders and mental retardation are recorded on axis II in DSM-IV. Axis I records clinical disorders, and axis III records general medical conditions. Axis IV is used to record psychosocial and environmental problems, while axis V is used to report a global assessment of functioning (GAF).

5-29. The answer is A. *(Behrman, 15/e, pp 1078–1079.)* The presence of nocturnal abdominal pain and gastrointestinal bleeding and a positive family history support a diagnosis of peptic ulcer disease. Pain is the most common symptom. Symptoms often persist for several years before diagnosis. The increased incidence of peptic ulcer disease in families (25 to 50 percent) and concordance in monozygotic twins suggest a genetic basis for the disease. Antibiotic treatment for *Helicobacter pylori* in patients not responding to conventional therapy may cure this disease in some patients. Appendicitis and intussusception are acute events. Pinworms produce perianal pruritus but do not commonly cause abdominal pain or other serious problems. Meckel's diverticulum causes painless rectal bleeding, usually during early childhood.

5-30. The answer is E. *(Toole, 4/e, pp 471, 478–482.)* The clinical picture suggests that a saccular aneurysm became symptomatic by compressing structures about the base of the brain and subsequently leaking. Aneurysms enlarge with age and usually do not bleed until they are several millimeters across. Persons with intracerebral or subarachnoid hemorrhages before the age of 40 are more likely to have their hemorrhages because of arteriovenous malformations rather than aneurysms. Aneurysms occur with equal frequency in men and women below the age of 40, but in the 40s and 50s women are more susceptible to symptomatic aneurysms. This is especially true of aneurysms that develop on the internal carotid on that segment of the artery that lies within the cavernous sinus. An angiogram is useful in establishing the site and character of the aneurysm. A CT scan would be more likely to reveal subarachnoid, intraventricular, or intraparenchymal blood, but it would reveal the structure of an aneurysm only if it were several (more than 5) millimeters across. MRI will reveal relatively large aneurysms if the system is calibrated and programmed to look at blood vessels. This patient had a transfemoral angiogram, a technique that involves the introduction of a catheter into the femoral artery; the catheter is threaded retrograde in the aorta and up into the carotid or other arteries of interest.

5-31. The answer is B. *(Adams, 6/e, p 268.)* The red glass test produces two images because the eyes are not moving in concert. That the red image appears to the left indicates that the eye covered by the red glass is not moving to the left as much as the other eye. A convenient way to remember this is simply to assume that the eye is not moving where the red image appears to be. This assumes that the red glass is over the impaired eye and ocular motor function in the other eye is completely normal. That the patient has pain behind the right eye and that the pupil of this eye reacts less vigorously to light than the pupil of the other eye suggests that the right eye is solely (or at least disproportionately) involved by whatever the problem is.

5-32. The answer is B. *(Adams, 6/e, pp 841–848.)* An aneurysm on the posterior communicating artery is especially likely to compress the oculomotor (third) nerve. Because the pupilloconstrictor fibers lie superficially on this nerve, problems with pupillary activity are routinely early phenomena. An ischemic injury to the third cranial nerve, such as that seen with diabetes mellitus, will usually spare these superficial fibers, presumably because they have a vascular supply that is fairly distinct from that of the rest of the third nerve. The pupillary response to both direct and consensual stimulation will be impaired with compression of these parasympathetic nerve fibers. This means that the pupil in the right eye will not constrict in response to light shining into either the right eye or the left eye. The normal pupil on the left will constrict with light shining into either the left or the right eye because the sensory input from the right eye is unimpaired. As the aneurysm enlarges, it impinges upon the third nerve fibers that supply the medial rectus muscle, weakness of which was responsible for this woman's double vision.

5-33. The answer is C. (*Adams, 6/e, pp 841–848.*) Vasospasm is a relatively common complication of subarachnoid blood and may result in stroke. Nimodipine is used because it decreases the probability of stroke, but it does not prevent it completely. Anticoagulation with heparin or warfarin worsens the patient's prospects because it increases the risk of additional bleeding. Antiepileptic drugs, such as phenytoin and carbamazepine, will reduce the risk of seizure associated with subarachnoid blood, but they are not usually given prophylactically.

5-34. The answer is B. (*Schwartz, 6/e, p 1381.*) The finding of air in the biliary tract of a nonseptic patient is diagnostic of a biliary enteric fistula. When the clinical findings also include small bowel obstruction in an elderly patient without a history of prior abdominal surgery (a "virgin" abdomen), the diagnosis of gallstone ileus can be made with a high degree of certainty. In this condition, a large chronic gallstone mechanically erodes through the wall of the gallbladder into adjacent stomach or duodenum. As the stone moves down the small intestine, mild cramping symptoms are common. When the gallstone arrives in the distal ileum, the caliber of the bowel no longer allows passage and obstruction develops. Surgical removal of the gallstone is necessary. The diseases suggested by each of the other response items (bleeding ulcer, peritoneal infection, pyloric outlet obstruction, pelvic neoplasm) are common in elderly patients, but each of them would probably present with symptoms other than those of small bowel obstruction.

5-35. The answer is E. (*Schwartz, 6/e, pp 148–149, 157–158, 165.*) The significant observation in this question is the description of lymphangitic inflammatory streaking up the inner aspect of the patient's leg. This is highly suggestive of a streptococcal infection and the presumptive therapy should be high doses of a bactericidal antibiotic. Penicillin remains the mainstay of therapy against presumed streptococcal infections. Most streptococcal cellulitis is adequately treated by penicillin, elevation of the infected extremity, and attention to the local wound to ascertain adequate local drainage and absence of any persisting foreign body. However, the clinician must be alert to the possibility of a more fulminant and life- or limb-threatening infection by clostridia, microaerophilic streptococcus, or other potentially synergistic organisms that can produce rapidly progressive deep infections in fascia of muscle. Smears and cultures of drainage fluid or aspirates should be taken. Close observation of the wound is essential, and aggressive debridement in the operating room is mandatory at the slightest suggestion that fasciitis or myonecrosis may be ensuing.

5-36. The answer is B. *(Kaplan, 6/e, p 995.)* Akathisia has not been found to be responsive to the anticholinergic medications used to treat parkinsonism. Benzodiazepines and diphenhydramine (Benadryl) have shown limited usefulness. The medication most commonly used is propranolol in relatively small dosage.

5-37. The answer is C. *(Seidel, 3/e, pp 584, 616, 618.)* Lymphogranuloma venereum is a sexually transmitted disease caused by a chlamydial organism. It initially presents as painless erosions and later may involve the lymphatics. Peyronie's disease is unilateral deviation of the penis caused by a fibrous band in the corpus cavernosum. A syphilitic chancre is painless, with indurated borders and a clear base appearing 2 weeks after exposure. Scrapings from the chancre will reveal spirochetes. Condyloma acuminatum, or venereal warts, are caused by the human papillomavirus (HPV). They occur on skin and mucosal surfaces of external genitalia and perianal areas. They are sexually transmitted, with an incubation period of 1 to 6 months. The lesions are soft, pink-to-red growths on various parts of the penis and can undergo malignant degeneration.

5-38. The answer is A. *(Isselbacher, 13/e, p 1129.)* The most common cause of refractory hypertension is noncompliance. A history from the patient is useful and a pill count is the best compliance check. Cushing's disease, coarctation, and renal artery stenosis are secondary causes that could result in refractory hypertension, but no clues to these diagnoses are apparent on physical examination.

5-39. The answer is D. *(Rudolph, 20/e, pp 576, 1633.)* Epiglottitis is a life-threatening form of infection-produced upper airway obstruction. The course of the illness is brief and prodromal symptoms are lacking. There is a sudden onset of sore throat, high fever, and prostration that is out of proportion to the duration of the illness. Drooling and difficulty in swallowing, a muffled voice, and preference for a characteristic sitting posture with the neck hyperextended may be noted. Unless preparations are available for immediate intubation by skilled personnel, any attempt to visualize the epiglottis should be avoided. Morbidity and mortality are usually related to a delay in establishing an airway early in the disease. Therefore, radiography of the neck, which may delay definitive treatment, is unwise.

5-40. The answer is E. *(Behrman, 15/e, pp 1339–1341, 1359–1363.)* Congestive heart failure from any cause can result in mild cyanosis, even in the absence of a right-to-left shunt, and in poor peripheral pulses when cardiac output is low. Congestive heart failure usually is associated with a rapid pulse rate (up to 200 beats per minute). A pulse rate greater than 200 beats per minute, however, should suggest the presence of a tachyarrhythmia.

5-41. The answer is C. *(Friesen, pp 405–433.)* The constellation of symptoms in this patient is typical of a functional adrenocortical tumor. Masculinization in females is also a common finding. Elevated urine 17-ketosteroids will be found in this patient. Any adrenocortical tumor larger than 6 cm should be considered a carcinoma rather than an adenoma. Treatment should include resection of as much tumor as possible. This would include invaded adjacent organs such as the kidney or the tail of the pancreas. Symptoms related to hormone production can be minimized by complete resection despite the inability to cure advanced disease. The most effective adjuvant therapy is mitotane, which is toxic for functional adrenocortical cells. When mitotane is used, therefore, glucocorticoids must be administered. Ketoconazole has been found to inhibit the production of various steroid hormones and may be useful in the treatment of hormone-related symptoms. The overall 5-year survival of patients with adrenocortical carcinoma treated with resection and mitotane is 20 percent.

5-42. The answer is C. *(Kaplan, 6/e, p 784. Schuckit, 4/e, p 102.)* Alcohol withdrawal delirium (delirium tremens) is the severest form of alcohol withdrawal. Five percent of all hospitalized alcoholics develop delirium tremens during their hospital course. Clinically, delirium tremens usually develops 2 to 7 days after cessation of drinking and is characterized by tachycardia, diaphoresis, hypertension, confusion, insomnia, illusions or visual hallucinations, and tremor. Delirium tremens is most common in people with at least a 5-year drinking history in which binges are common. Initial treatment usually involves chlordiazepoxide, 50 to 100 mg. Phenothiazines should not be used because of neurologic problems and probable preexisting hepatic impairment. Follow-up treatment should include a complete biopsychosocial evaluation. AA is an excellent referral resource.

5-43. The answer is C. *(Isselbacher, 13/e, pp 206–207, 1360–1382.)* Esophageal carcinoma occurs in the elderly with a history of weeks to months of progressive dysphagia associated with weight loss. In younger age groups, carcinoma of the bronchus and lymphomas can cause similar symptoms from enlarged perihilar lymph nodes that compress the esophagus.

5-44. The answer is A. *(Rudolph, 20/e, pp 252–255.)* An infant of 2300 g at 38 weeks would be considered small for gestational age (SGA), a not uncommon consequence of maternal toxemia. Pregnancy-induced hypertension may produce a decrease in uteroplacental blood flow and areas of placental infarction. This can result in fetal nutritional deprivation and intermittent fetal hypoxemia, with a decrease in glycogen storage and a relative erythrocytosis, respectively. Hence neonatal hypoglycemia and polycythemia are common clinical findings in these infants. However, a blood glucose level above 30 mg/dL in a full-term infant is considered normal during the first postnatal day and an infant is very unlikely to have a convulsion as a result of a level of 38 mg. Serum calcium levels usually decline during the first 2 to 3 postnatal days, but will only be considered abnormally low in a term infant when they fall below 7.5 to 8 mg/dL. Neonatal hypermagnesemia is common in an infant whose mother has received $MgSO_4$ therapy, but is usually asymptomatic or produces decreased muscle tone or floppiness. A persistent venous hematocrit of greater than 65 percent in a neonate is regarded as polycythemia and will be accompanied by an increase in blood viscosity. Manifestations of the "hyperviscosity syndrome" include tremulousness or jitteriness that can progress to seizure activity because of sludging of blood in the cerebral microcirculation or frank thrombus formation, renal vein thrombosis, necrotizing enterocolitis, and tachypnea. Therapy by partial exchange transfusion with albumin is probably more likely to be useful if performed prophylactically before significant symptoms have developed.

5-45. The answer is D. (*Greenfield, pp 522–523.*) The patient is experiencing an acute rejection episode. Seventy-four percent of all acute rejection episodes occur between 1 and 6 months after transplantation. For cadaveric renal transplant recipients, 63 percent of patients will never have an acute rejection episode, 17 percent will have only one rejection episode, and 19 percent will have two or more rejections. In order to grade the rejection as well as to follow the response to treatment, a percutaneous renal biopsy should be performed. The three treatment modalities used for acute rejection are high-dose steroids alone, high-dose steroids plus antilymphocyte globulin (equine serum hyperimmunized to human lymphocytes), or high-dose steroids plus OKT3 (murine monoclonal antibody to the human CD3 complex).

5-46. The answer is C. (*Yudofsky, 2/e, p 401.*) In contrast to popular opinion, there is no increase in the rate of depression or somatic symptoms during the menopause. However, complaints of hot flashes, fatigue, irritability, or depressive feelings are by no means uncommon. A complaint of memory lapses is not common in either panic or depressive disorders, and the absence of typical symptoms or history makes major depression or schizophrenia unlikely. This woman should have an EEG examination to rule out possible temporal lobe epilepsy. Her symptoms are consistent with psychomotor epilepsy, a condition that can be exacerbated at menopause.

5-47. The answer is D. (*Isselbacher, 13/e, pp 2041–2043.*) Persons with Klinefelter's syndrome have a 47,XXY karyotype and are typically tall and eunuchoid in appearance, with gynecomastia, testicular atrophy, and a female pattern of hair distribution. Patients with Turner's syndrome are 45,X or are mosaic and have a female phenotype. Trisomy 21 in either sex presents with characteristic facial features and invariable mental retardation. Testicular feminization syndrome results from defective or absent androgen receptors throughout the body. These patients are 46,XY, but have a female phenotype. Destruction of the liver parenchyma may take away a person's ability to fully metabolize endogenous estrogens and thus lead to gynecomastia and testicular atrophy. However, the young age of the patient and his eunuchoid appearance suggest a 47,XXY karyotype (Klinefelter's syndrome).

5-48. The answer is E. (*Isselbacher, 13/e, p 1747.*) This 30-year-old black man has developed a hemolytic anemia secondary to an antimalarial drug. Toxins or drugs such as primaquine, sulfamethoxazole, and nitrofurantoin cause hemolysis in patients with G6PD deficiency. This occurs most commonly in blacks. The process is usually self-limited, and no specific treatment other than stopping the drug is necessary.

5-49. The answer is E. (*O'Driscoll, Clin Orthop 280:186–197, 1992.*) The history and finding of this patient are typical of a patient with posterolateral rotatory instability of the elbow. Posterolateral rotatory subluxation is the first stage of the clinical spectrum of acute and recurrent elbow instability (excluding pure valgus and radioulnar mechanisms). Posterolateral rotatory instability of the elbow results from disruption of the lateral ulnar collateral ligament (ulnar part of radial collateral ligament). This allows transient rotatory subluxation of the radiohumeral joint. The mechanism of injury is an axial load, valgus stress, and forearm supination. The posterolateral rotatory instability test involves supination of the forearm and application of a valgus stress and axial compression force across the elbow while it is flexed from a position of full extension. The elbow is reduced in full extension and is subluxated as it is flexed in order to obtain a positive test result. Flexion of more than about 40° produces a palpable and visible reduction of the radial head. Without anesthesia, apprehension is elicited from the patient.

5-50. The answer is D. (*Tintinalli, 4/e, pp 703–706.*) Carbon monoxide (CO) is the leading cause of toxin-related death in the U.S. It is produced by the incomplete combustion of fossil fuels and is emitted by virtually all gas-powered engines and appliances that burn fossil fuel, e.g., home furnaces, water heaters, stoves, pool heaters, kerosene heaters, and charcoal fires. Tobacco smoke—particularly smoke released from the tip of the cigarette, which has 2.5 times more CO than inhaled smoke—produces a significant amount of the gas; nonsmokers working in closed quarters with smokers may have carboxyhemoglobin (COHb) levels as high as 15 percent, easily enough to cause headache and some impairment of judgment. Fire fighters are at particularly high risk for CO intoxication. The pathophysiology of CO poisoning is unclear. It is known to cause an adverse shift in the oxygen-hemoglobin dissociation curve, to cause direct cardiovascular depression, and to inhibit cytochrome A_3. Tissue hypoxia is the result. Treatment is directed toward increasing the partial pressures of O_2 to which the transalveolar hemoglobin is exposed. In most cases, administering 100% oxygen through a tightly fitted face mask will result in a serum elimination half-life of COHb of 80 min (compared with 520 min when one breathes room air). In severe cases, where coma, seizures, or respiratory failure are present, the partial pressure of O_2 is increased by administering it in a hyperbaric chamber with the atmospheric pressure of 2.8. In this situation the serum elimination half-life is reduced to 23 min. In any case, the oxygen therapy should continue until the COHb levels reach 10 percent.

BLOCK 6

Answers

6-1. The answer is D. *(Isselbacher, 13/e, pp 303, 557, 725, 864.)* This is a classic presentation for sporotrichosis. The organism, *Sporothrix schenckii*, is found in the soil and can occur as a pulmonary infection or as a systemic disease, but these presentations are unusual. The lesion first begins as a painless, unfixed nodule that eventually becomes fixed and necrotic, the sporotrichotic chancre. A few weeks following the initial lesion there can be sequential formation of multiple nodules along lymphatic channels, which results in "pipestem lymphatics"; however, lymph node involvement is rare. Infection is best treated with potassium iodide.

6-2. The answer is B. *(Goroll, 3/e, p 983.)* The lesion described is characteristic of leukoplakia. This is a precancerous lesion that requires biopsy. Histologically, these lesions show hyperkeratosis, acanthosis, and atypia. There are homogeneous and nonhomogeneous types. Homogeneous lesions are much more likely to undergo malignant transformation. Oropharyngeal candidiasis would be unlikely to occur in this patient and would appear as a more diffuse, lacy lesion of the buccal mucosa and oropharynx.

6-3. The answer is C. *(Schwartz, 6/e, pp 1833–1838.)* Epidural hematomas are typically caused by a tear of the middle meningeal artery or vein, or a dural venous sinus. Ninety percent of epidural hematomas are associated with linear skull fractures, usually in the temporal region. *Only 2 percent of patients admitted with craniocerebral trauma suffer epidural hematomas.* The lesion appears as a hyperdense biconvex mass between the skull and brain on CT scan. Clinical presentation is highly variable and outcome largely depends on promptness of diagnosis and surgical evacuation. The typical history is one of head trauma followed by a momentary alteration in consciousness and then a lucid interval lasting for up to a few hours. This is followed by a loss of consciousness, dilatation of the pupil on the side of the epidural hematoma, and then compromise of the brainstem and death. Treatment consists of temporal craniectomy, evaluation of the hemorrhage, and control of the bleeding vessel. The mortality of epidural hematoma is approximately 50 percent.

6-4. The answer is A. *(Rudolph, 20/e, pp 1176–1180.)* Iron-deficiency anemia is the most common nutritional deficiency in children between 9 and 15 months of age. Low availability of dietary iron, impaired absorption of iron related to frequent infections, high requirements for iron for growth, and, occasionally, blood losses, all favor the development of iron deficiency in infants. A history regarding anemia in the family, blood loss, and gestational age and weight may help to establish the cause of an anemia. However, the strong likelihood is that anemia in a 1-year-old child is nutritional in origin and that its cause will be suggested by a detailed nutritional history.

6-5. The answer is B. *(Kaplan, 6/e, p 2755.)* Persons have the right to bequeath their estates to any persons or institutions of their choice. However, for their last will and testament to be valid, they must have testamentary capacity. There is no requirement that they be free of the diagnosis of psychiatric disorder, but testamentary capacity does involve several important criteria. Testators must know who their relatives are and who may have claim to their estate. They must have a reasonable estimate of the extent of their assets, know they are signing a will, and understand the meaning of that act. Undue influence may be grounds for invalidating part or all of a will if it can be shown that the influence was sufficient to lead the testator to make decisions he or she might not otherwise have made. Undue influence relates to voluntariness rather than cognitive capacity and is a distinct and important concept in evaluating a will.

6-6. The answer is D. *(McCullough, p 29.)* Varicocele is dilated veins of the pampiniform plexus. The incidence is rare before 8 years of age, and a plateau is reached at puberty. The cause is venous stasis and reflux into the spermatic vein, which is due to compression of the left renal vein at the level of the aorta. The dilated veins, or "bag of worms," are more easily seen and palpated with the patient standing. Retroperitoneal disease needs to be excluded, and if the testis is diminished in size, then surgery is indicated in an attempt to preserve fertility.

6-7. The answer is B. *(Isselbacher, 13/e, pp 1167–1172.)* Asthma is an airway disease that is characterized by a hyperreactive tracheobronchial tree that manifests physiologically as narrowing of the air passages. The classic triad of symptoms seen in asthma is dyspnea, cough, and wheezing, with the last being the *sine qua non.* In its most typical form, asthma is an episodic disease and attacks occur most often at night, perhaps due to circadian variations in the circulating levels of endogenous catecholamines and histamine. Attacks may also occur abruptly following exposure to a specific allergen, physical exertion, a viral respiratory infection, or emotional excitement. At the onset the patient will sense a constriction about the chest, often with a nonproductive cough. Respiration will become harsh, and wheezing in both phases of respiration will develop. The expiratory phase will become prolonged, and the patient frequently will have tachypnea, tachycardia, and mild systolic hypertension. If the attack is severe or prolonged, the accessory muscles of respiration will be visibly active and frequently a pulsus paradoxus will develop. These two signs correlate well with the degree of obstruction and the probability of hospitalization.

6-8. The answer is C. (*Adams, 6/e, pp 242–247.*) Occlusion of the central retinal artery may be from atheromatous particles, fibrin-platelet emboli, or local retinal artery compression. The visual loss is usually painless and irreversible. Occlusion of the internal carotid artery, the artery from which the ophthalmic and ultimately the retinal arteries originate, need not produce ischemic damage to the retina if collateral supply to the retinal artery is sufficient.

6-9. The answer is D. (*Ransom, pp 53–54.*) Condyloma acuminatum is a sexually transmitted disease caused by the human papillomavirus (HPV). For many years application of podophyllum was the treatment of choice for vulvar warts. Because podophyllum can produce peripheral neuropathy, bone marrow depression, and occasionally death, most physicians recommend the application of trichloroacetic acid to the vulva; however, because of systemic absorption, neither medication should be applied to extensive vaginal lesions. Laser surgery and cryotherapy result in high recurrence rates because of the difficulty of reaching all areas of the vagina. Since the vaginal condylomas are generally flat, optimal medical management includes the topical application of 5% 5-fluorouracil cream.

6-10. The answer is C. (*Ahronheim, pp 219–223.*) The major issues are confidentiality and duty to a third party. When a person initially learns that he or she is HIV-positive, the information in itself is often overwhelming. The patient may not feel capable or willing to inform exposed partners. The best approach is to try to convince the patient of the necessity of this, perhaps at a later visit. Some states have enacted laws to allow the physician to inform third parties of HIV exposure, but *only after efforts by the physician have failed to convince the person to disclose.* These laws protect the physician against legal liability for breach of confidentiality, but they do not obligate the physician to disclose to third parties. Some state law allows only state disease intervention specialists (DIS) to inform third parties after the physician has contacted them. Many states do not have any of these laws, and the only option is to try to convince an infected patient to disclose. As a rule, partner notification is *confidential and voluntary.* DIS cannot inform third parties without the consent of the infected person, even if requested by the physician. They can assist consenting infected persons in informing contacts either by doing it for them (contacts are *never* informed of the source) or coaching them to do it themselves.

6-11. The answer is D. *(Isselbacher, 13/e, p 1066.)* Patients suffering from an acute myocardial infarction are typically anxious and restless secondary to extreme pain. This pain may radiate from the occipital area to the umbilicus, but most commonly can be found in the central portion of the chest or epigastrium or both. Pallor, perspiration, and coolness of the extremities are commonly observed.

6-12–6-13. The answers are 6-12 D, 6-13 B. *(Schwartz, 6/e, pp 1346–1349.)* The diagnosis of bleeding esophageal varices is aided in the adult by stigmata of portal hypertension. Upper gastrointestinal hemorrhage in cirrhotics is due to esophageal varices in less than half of patients. Gastritis and peptic ulcer disease account for the majority of cases. Esophagoscopy is the single most reliable means of establishing the source of bleeding, though variations in transvariceal blood flow may result in nonvisualization of the varices. In addition, endoscopic sclerotherapy is reported to control acute variceal hemorrhage in 80 to 90 percent of cases and carries an acute mortality lower than other procedures. Barium swallow has a high false negative rate and offers no therapeutic advantage. Celiac angiography will rule out arterial hemorrhage and will demonstrate venous collateral circulation, but will not demonstrate variceal bleeding. Parenteral vasopressin controls variceal hemorrhage by constriction of the splanchnic arteriolar bed and a resultant drop in portal pressure. Intraarterial vasopressin offers no advantage over intravenous administration and requires a mesenteric catheter. The reported control rate is 50 to 70 percent. Esophageal balloon tamponade controls variceal hemorrhage in two-thirds of patients, but may also control bleeding ulcers and thereby obscure the diagnosis. Although balloon tamponade has reduced the mortality and morbidity from variceal hemorrhage in good-risk patients, an increased awareness of associated complications (aspiration, asphyxiation, and ulceration at the tamponade site), as well as a rebleeding rate of 40 percent, has reduced its use. It is indicated as a temporary measure when vasopressin and sclerotherapy fail. Emergency portacaval shunt is advised in good-risk cirrhotic patients whose bleeding is not controlled with vasopressin or sclerosis. The mortality for patients with bleeding varices not subjected to shunting is between 66 and 73 percent, whereas operative mortality of emergency shunts ranges from 20 to 50 percent. Esophageal transection with the autostapler carries the same mortality as shunt procedures and the rebleeding rate is estimated to be 50 percent at 1 year.

6-14–6-16. The answers are 6-14 A, 6-15 B, 6-16 D. *(Isselbacher, 13/e, pp 65–71.)* Tension headaches are the leading cause of chronic headaches. Ninety percent are bilateral. They are described as dull, constricting, and bandlike. Tenderness may be present.

Cluster headaches are unilateral, as are migraine headaches and temporal arteritis. They differ from migraines in that they are nonthrobbing and are more common in men.

Temporal arteritis may cause scalp tenderness localized to the involved vessel. It is primarily a disease of the elderly. Blindness caused by occlusion of the ophthalmic artery is the feared complication.

6-17. The answer is B. *(Behrman, 15/e, pp 677–678.)* The rash of anaphylactoid purpura most often involves extensor surfaces of the extremities; the face, soles, palms, and trunk are rarely affected. Both systemic lupus erythematosus and dermatomyositis often are accompanied by typical facial rashes (butterfly and heliotrope, respectively). People who have Takayasu arteritis usually do not present with a rash. The scarlatiniform rash characteristic of streptococcal infections generally does not coincide with the development of poststreptococcal nephritis; impetiginous lesions, however, may still be present.

6-18–6-19. The answers are 6-18 B, 6-19 A. *(Sabiston, 5/e, pp 1314–1331.)* Ventricular septal defect accounts for 20 to 30 percent of all congenital cardiac anomalies. It may lead to cardiac failure and pulmonary hypertension if the defect is larger than 1 cm; or it may be asymptomatic if the defect is small. Surgery is not indicated for the asymptomatic patient with a small defect since a substantial number of these anomalies close spontaneously during the first few years of life. Operation is indicated in infants with congestive heart failure or rising pulmonary vascular resistance (owing to the left-to-right shunt). When symptoms are mild and can be controlled medically, operation is usually delayed until age 4 to 6. Operative mortality ranges from less than 5 percent to more than 20 percent depending on the degree of pulmonary vascular resistance.

Tetralogy of Fallot, transposition, and tricuspid atresia are cyanotic lesions. Congenital cyanosis that persists beyond the age of 2 years is associated, in the vast majority of cases, with a tetralogy of Fallot. Patent ductus arteriosus is associated with the characteristic continuous machinery murmur.

6-20. The answer is B. *(Andreasen, 2/e, p 645.)* Isolation is a defense mechanism for coping with intense emotions. The feelings are stripped away, and what is left is an intellectual and detached discussion of the topic associated with intense emotion. Often the patient will be overly abstract and will have difficulty in recalling or describing past feelings as well. This defense is often found in patients with obsessive-compulsive traits.

6-21. The answer is C. *(Seidel, 3/e, pp 605–609, 616–621.)* Epidermoid, or sebaceous, cysts appear as small lumps in the scrotal skin, which may enlarge and discharge oily material. Molluscum contagiosum is caused by a poxvirus and is sexually transmitted. The lesions are smooth and dome-shaped with discrete margins and occur most commonly on the glans penis.

6-22. The answer is D. *(DSM IV, p 59.)* Patients with Rett's disorder characteristically have normal prenatal and postnatal development until between ages 5 to 30 months, when they begin to lose previously acquired purposeful hand skills and develop stereotyped hand movements such as hand-wringing. They also display poorly coordinated gait or trunk movements and have severely impaired language development. A particular characteristic of this disorder is normal head circumference at birth, with a deceleration of head growth between 5 months and 4 years of age.

6-23. The answer is B. (*Schwartz, 6/e, pp 1166–1167.*) Patients with regional enteritis usually have a chronic and slowly progressive course with intermittent symptom-free periods. The usual symptoms are anorexia, abdominal pain, diarrhea, fever, and weight loss. There are extraintestinal syndromes that may be seen with the disease such as ankylosing spondylitis, polyarthritis, erythema nodosum, pyoderma gangrenosum, gallstones, hepatic fatty infiltration, and fibrosis of the biliary tract, pancreas, and retroperitoneum. However, in about 10 percent of patients, especially those who are young, the onset of the disease is abrupt and may be mistaken for acute appendicitis. Appendectomy is indicated in such patients as long as the cecum at the base of the appendix is not involved, otherwise the risk of fecal fistula must be considered. Interestingly, about 90 percent of patients who present with the acute appendicitis-like form of regional enteritis will not progress to develop the full-blown chronic disease. Thus, resection or bypass of the involved areas is not indicated at this time.

6-24. The answer is C. (*Isselbacher, 13/e, pp 1484–1485.*) The patient's signs and symptoms suggest alcoholic hepatitis. Mallory bodies are alcoholic hyaline seen in damaged hepatocytes. They are likely to be seen in alcoholic hepatitis (but are not specific for the disease). Jugular venous distention should not be part of the process of chronic liver disease (ascites and pedal edema are secondary to hypoalbuminemia and portal hypertension, not increased right-sided pressure). In alcoholic hepatitis, AST to ALT ratios are usually greater than 2, due to the proportionately greater inhibition of ALT synthesis by ethanol. Even after abstinence, clinical recovery is often prolonged.

6-25. The answer is D. (*Berg, pp 924–925. Davis, pp 234–235.*) This patient had encephalofacial angiomatosis (Sturge-Weber syndrome), a congenital disturbance that produces facial cutaneous angiomas with a distinctive and easily recognized appearance, along with intracranial abnormalities, such as leptomeningeal angiomas. Persons with the syndrome may be mentally retarded and often exhibit hemiparesis or hemiatrophy on the side of the body opposite the port wine nevus. Both men and women may be affected and seizures may develop in affected persons. The nevus associated with Sturge-Weber syndrome usually extends over the sensory distribution of V1, the first division of the trigeminal nerve. The lesion usually stays to one side of the face. Affected persons will usually also have an angioma of the choroid of the eye. Intracranial angioma is unlikely if the nevus does not involve the upper face. Deficits develop as the person matures and may be a consequence of focal ischemia in the cerebral cortex that underlies the leptomeningeal angioma.

Hemangioblastomas are vascular tumors seen in association with polycystic disease of the kidney and telangiectasias of the retina (von Hippel-Lindau syndrome). Charcot-Bouchard aneurysms are very small and may be microscopic. They develop in patients with chronic hypertension and most commonly appear in perforating arteries of the brain. The lenticulostriate arteries are most commonly affected. Hemorrhage from these aneurysms is likely and the putamen is the most common site for hematoma formation. Hemorrhage may extend into the ventricles and lead to subarachnoid blood. Other locations commonly affected include the caudate nucleus, thalamus, pons, and the cerebellum. The dentate nucleus of the cerebellum is especially susceptible to the formation of Charcot-Bouchard aneurysms. Fusiform aneurysms are diffusely widened arteries with evaginations along the walls, but without stalks as occur with the typical berry-shaped structures of the saccular aneurysm. This type of aneurysm may be a late consequence of arteriosclerotic damage to the artery wall.

6-26. The answer is A. *(Isselbacher, 13/e, pp 519, 618–619.)* The epiglottis is markedly swollen, cherry-red, and sensitive, such that stimulation of the posterior oral pharynx could precipitate laryngeal spasm and obstruction. Therefore, the diagnosis is made primarily on history and lateral x-rays of the soft tissue of the neck. Other complaints are dysphagia, odynophagia, and fever that has rapidly progressed. Hoarseness and loss of voice power are universal findings. Stridor may be present. The difference between acute epiglottitis and streptococcal pharyngitis is that the onset of streptococcal pharyngitis is slower (days versus hours).

6-27. The answer is A. *(Schwartz, 6/e, pp 1648–1658.)* The patient described is exhibiting classic signs and symptoms of hyperparathyroidism. In addition, if a history is obtainable, frequently the patient will relate a history of renal calculi and bone pain—the syndrome characterized as "groans, stones, and bones." The acute management of the hypercalcemic state includes vigorous hydration to restore intravascular volume, which is invariably diminished. This will establish renal perfusion and thus promote urinary calcium excretion. Thiazide diuretics are contraindicated, as they frequently will cause patients to become hypercalcemic. Instead, diuresis should be promoted with the use of "loop" diuretics such as furosemide (Lasix). The use of intravenous phosphorus infusion is no longer recommended, as precipitation in the lungs, heart, or kidney can lead to serious morbidity. Mithramycin is an antineoplastic agent that in low doses inhibits bone resorption and thus diminishes serum calcium levels; it is used only when other maneuvers fail to decrease the calcium level. Calcitonin is useful at times. Bisphosphonates are newer agents particularly useful for lowering calcium levels in resistant cases, such as those associated with humoral malignancy. Finally, "emergency" neck exploration is seldom warranted. In unprepared patients, the morbidity is unacceptably high.

6-28. The answer is B. (*Hall, pp 2242–2244.*) Shivering is the physiologic effort of the body to generate heat to maintain the core temperature. In healthy persons, shivering will increase the metabolic rate by 3 to 5 times and result in increased oxygen consumption and carbon dioxide production. In critically ill patients these metabolic consequences are almost always counterproductive and should be prevented with other means employed to correct systemic hypothermia. In the presence of vigorous shivering, oxygen debt in the muscles and lactic acidemia develop.

6-29. The answer is A. (*DSM-IV, pp 539–545.*) Amenorrhea, an altered body image, and an energetic striving for thinness compose the "classic triad" associated with anorexia nervosa. The profound cachexia is not recognized in these persons, who instead strive by exercise and diet to achieve even greater thinness and to lose what they consider excess weight. In social phobia there may be embarrassment about eating in public, and in obsessive-compulsive disorder, there may be obsessions and compulsions related to food, but not the severe distortions of body image and denial of cachexia. The diagnosis of body dysmorphic disorder can be made only if the distortion is unrelated to body shape and size, for example, a preoccupation that one's eyes are too large.

These patients usually display a number of clinical and laboratory findings, including bradycardia, elevated serum carotene, leukopenia, hypothermia, and hypercholesterolemia. Hypotension, rather than hypertension, is characteristic. When the condition is associated with induced vomiting, metabolic alkalosis may ensue.

The typical patient with this condition is usually a "good child," very control oriented, and dependent. Even when warned about potential death, there is often prominent denial. Depressive symptoms are often present and may be the consequence of starvation or an underlying depression. Psychotic features are not present, as they would be in schizophrenia.

6-30. The answer is B. *(DSM-IV, pp 532–538.)* In adolescents and young adults, gender identity disorder is characterized by a strong cross-gender identification, a persistent discomfort with his or her sex, and clinically significant distress or impairment. Such patients usually trace their conviction to early childhood, often live as the opposite sex, and seek sex reassignment surgery and endocrine treatment. The patient feels a sense of relief and appropriateness in opposite sex clothing, in contrast to the transvestic fetishist who achieves sexual arousal from the behavior. Homosexuality is not a diagnosis in DSM-IV, and while some cross-dress to seek a same-sex partner, there is no inner conviction that they are truly of the opposite sex, nor do they seek sex reassignment surgery. These patients do not display signs of a psychotic disorder.

6-31. The answer is B. *(Morrissy, 4/e, pp 1055–1061.)* Physiologic bowleg occurs in the first 2 years of life. Lateral bowing of the tibia is seen in the first year and bowleg involving both the tibia and distal femur occurs during the second year. Physiologic knock-knee is most pronounced between 3 and 4 years of age. Physiologic variations are common and most resolve with time. Pathologic forms are uncommon and generally do not resolve. The physician should assess growth, nutrition, symmetry, degree of deformity, and other abnormalities. Blount's disease is tibia vara, which results from abnormal growth of the proximal medial physis and metaphysis. It is more common in blacks and obese children. Medial tibial torsion often accompanies the deformity. An asymmetric deformity with a history of trauma may suggest malunion or partial physeal arrest. Rickets should be suspected in a patient with progressive varus deformity whose stature is below the 5th percentile. The diagnosis is confirmed by a low calcium and phosphorus and high alkaline phosphatase activity.

6-32. The answer is A. *(Holmes, 2/e, p 223. Larsen, Clin Microbiol Rev 8:11–12, 1995.)* Nontreponemal tests (RPR, VDRL) can be negative in up to

30 percent of patients at an initial visit for primary syphilis. The probability of a negative test is increased if the patient presents early in the course of primary syphilis. The FTA-ABS (a treponemal test) is more sensitive and is reactive around the time of appearance of the lesion. The dark-field is the investigation of first choice to confirm a diagnosis of syphilis when a chancre is present. Both nontreponemal and treponemal tests will become reactive within 3 weeks after the chancre has occurred. The incubation period for syphilis is between 10 and 90 days, with an average of 21 days. The lesion typical of chancroid is a large and painful ulcer with undermined borders. Large inguinal adenopathy, often suppurative, is also present. The incubation period is usually between 4 and 7 days. Herpetic lesions are shallow, painful, and multiple. Donovanosis is very rare in developed countries and is characterized by lesions that slowly enlarge, bleed easily on contact, and often have beefy-red granulomatous tissue. Lymphogranuloma venereum is also uncommon. It is primarily a disease of the lymphatic system. Patients often present with complaints related to inguinal adenopathy. The initial lesion, which is small, shallow, and painless, often goes unnoticed.

6-33. The answer is D. (*Schwartz, 6/e, pp 981–982.*) Traumatic arterial injuries can be handled with several techniques. The basic principles of debridement of injured tissue and reestablishment of flow should be observed. Primary end-to-end anastomosis is preferable if this can be accomplished without tension. When 5 cm of artery has been destroyed, it is impossible to perform a tension-free primary anastomosis, and a reversed saphenous vein graft is the repair of choice. Ligation of the artery is to be avoided in order to prevent gangrene and limb loss. The use of prosthetic material (Goretex) in a potentially infected field is also to be avoided as infection at the suture line often leads to delayed hemorrhage. Harvesting an arterial graft of similar diameter from elsewhere in the body is hazardous and unnecessary when vein is available.

6-34. The answer is C. (*Isselbacher, 13/e, p 963.*) Costochondritis, esophageal reflux, cholecystitis, and duodenal ulcer disease can all cause symptoms of substernal chest pain. However, in this 55-year-old woman an ECG shows Q waves and ST-segment elevation in leads II, III, and AVF. These ECG findings and the clinical picture are consistent with an acute inferior myocardial infarction.

6-35. The answer is D. (*Gartland, 4/e, p 122. Isselbacher, 13/e, p 1695.*) Osteoarthritis most often affects large weight-bearing joints and is associated with obesity or other forms of mechanical stress. It is more common in women and onset is usually after the age of 50. Pain often occurs on exertion and is relieved by rest, after which the involved joint may become stiff. Distal interphalangeal joints may be involved with production of Heberden's nodes. Rheumatoid arthritis is inflammatory in nature and is a systemic disease also more common in women, but it has an onset usually before the age of 40. Joint involvement is generally symmetric and often involves proximal interphalangeal and metacarpophalangeal joints. Morning stiffness lasting longer than 30 min is characteristic of rheumatoid arthritis. Ninety-five percent of gouty arthritis occurs in men and often involves the great toe. Aspiration of urate crystals from the joint space or relief following colchicine therapy is diagnostic. Reiter's syndrome is characterized by the triad of arthritis, urethritis, and conjunctivitis. Asymmetric oligoarthritis that involves the knees, ankles, shoulders, or digits of the hands or feet occurs in 50 percent of patients with psoriasis. Nail pitting is generally present in psoriasis.

6-36. The answer is B. (*Behrman, 15/e, pp 1034–1035, 1070–1072.*) Hirschsprung's disease is usually suspected in the chronically constipated child despite the fact that 98 percent of such children have functional constipation. Finding a dilated, stool-filled anal canal with poor tone on the physical examination of a well-grown child supports the diagnosis of functional constipation. The difficulty in treating functional constipation once it has been established emphasizes the need for prompt identification and treatment of problems with defecation and for counseling of parents regarding proper toileting behavior.

6-37–6-41. The answers are 6-37 B, 6-38 B, 6-39 A, 6-40 A, 6-41 A. (*Isselbacher, 13/e, pp 519, 806. Seidel, 3/e, p 363.*) Epiglottitis is a serious infection caused almost invariably by *Haemophilus influenzae* and most common during the ages of 3 to 7 years. Epiglottitis does not have a seasonal preference. The patient will complain of a very sore throat and dysphagia and will often be drooling from the mouth. A fever usually greater than 39.44°C (103°F) and leukocytosis with a left shift will be present. On a lateral soft-tissue x-ray of the neck, one will see the classic "thumb-print" sign, which represents a swollen epiglottis. When epiglottitis is strongly suspected, you should not attempt to examine the epiglottis unless you are adequately prepared for a difficult intubation secondary to the laryngospasm that may ensue.

Viral croup occurs most commonly in the fall and winter, and most often in the age group of 3 months to 3 years. The most common etiologic agent is parainfluenza virus. There will usually be a several-day history of a coryza-like prodrome, with or without a sore throat. The temperature will usually be less than 39.44°C (103°F) and the total white blood cell count will usually be normal. The diagnosis is made by clinical presentation and is one of exclusion. Diagnosis can be aided with an anteroposterior x-ray of the larynx, which will show subglottic narrowing, known as the "steeple sign."

6-42. The answer is C. *(Isselbacher, 13/e, p 1204.)* When stupor and coma develop with CO_2 retention, fatal arrhythmias, seizures, and death are likely to follow. Stopping oxygen is the worst course of action as this will exacerbate life-threatening hypoxia. Intubation is the only good alternative. Bicarbonate plays no role in this acidosis, which is respiratory and caused by hypoventilation.

6-43. The answer is A. *(Behrman, 15/e, pp 1186–1187.)* Small children frequently introduce any number of small objects into their nose ranging from food to small toys. Initially, only local irritation occurs. Later, as prolonged obstruction is seen, symptoms increase to include worsening of pain, and a purulent, malodorous, bloody discharge may be seen. Unilateral nasal discharge in the presence of obstruction suggests the need to examine the patient for a nasal foreign body.

6-44. The answer is B. *(Isselbacher, 13/e, p 1146.)* The diagnosis in this patient is suggested by the physical findings. The findings of poor excursion, flatness of percussion, and decreased fremitus on the right side are all consistent with a right-sided pleural effusion. A large right-sided effusion may shift the trachea to the left. A pneumothorax should result in hyperresonance of the affected side. Atelectasis on the right side would shift the trachea to the right. A consolidated pneumonia would characteristically result in increased fremitus and would not cause tracheal deviation.

6-45. The answer is A. *(Behrman, 15/e, pp 1307–1308, 1351–1353.)* The findings of pallor, dyspnea, tachypnea, tachycardia, and cardiomegaly are common in congestive heart failure regardless of the cause. The lack of echocardiographic findings other than ventricular and left atrial dilatation and poor ventricular function is inconsistent with both glycogen storage disease of the heart, in which there is muscle thickening, and pericarditis, since there is no pericardial effusion. It is also not consistent with an aberrant origin of the left coronary artery although the origin of the coronary arteries may be more easily missed. On electrocardiogram, the voltages of the ventricular complexes seen with aberrant origin of the left coronary artery are not diminished and a pattern of myocardial infarction may be seen. Voltages from the left ventricle are usually high in endocardial fibroelastosis, and both right and left ventricular forces are high in glycogen storage disease of the heart.

6-46. The answer is D. *(Way, 9/e, pp 611–612.)* Any patient who has lost much of the ileum (whether from injury, disease, or elective surgery) is at high risk to develop enteric hyperoxaluria if the colon remains intact. Calcium oxalate stones will develop in at least 10 percent of these patients. The condition results from excessive absorption of oxalate from the colon through two related synergistic mechanisms: unabsorbed fatty acids combine with calcium, which prevents the formation of insoluble calcium oxalate and allows oxalate to remain available for colonic absorption; and unabsorbed fatty acids and bile acids also increase the permeability of the colon to the oxalate.

6-47. The answer is B. *(Behrman, 15/e, pp 446–447.)* It is usually impossible with any combination of parenteral and enteral nutrition to match what the infant would have accumulated in utero. The average, healthy, low-birth-weight infant of this size requires a daily intake of calcium of 173 mg/kg. Breast milk has much less calcium (and phosphorus) than do commercial formulas. One may supplement the breast milk with calcium or mix it with commercial formulas designed for the premature infant.

6-48. The answer is E. *(DSM-IV, pp 684–685.)* Following the death of a loved one, a full depressive syndrome may occur as a normal response to the loss. This usually begins several weeks later and may last for up to a year, though for most it is mostly gone after 4 to 6 months. It is distinguished from major depression by the absence of morbid preoccupation with worthlessness, lesser functional impairment, and the usual absence of marked psychomotor retardation or delusions. For the patient described, dysthymia is an inappropriate diagnosis because of the absence of previous depressive trends. The symptoms are not those that meet the criteria for posttraumatic stress disorder, and bereavement is specifically excluded from the official diagnosis of adjustment disorder. All the indicated treatments are commonly used with the exception of neuroleptics, which are reserved for use as antipsychotic agents.

6-49. The answer is A. *(Yudofsky, 2/e, pp 612–614.)* The possibility of an acute organic brain disorder mandates a careful examination of cognitive function. Acute conditions would be associated with a determination that the patient's cognitive ability had changed. For example, poor calculation skills in a person who had been a functioning accountant would be far more significant than the same findings in someone with a long history of poor school performance. It is the assessment of changes in cognitive function, rather than the specific cognitive disturbance, that is most crucial to a diagnosis of acute organic brain disorder. This is what helps the clinician to differentiate memory or other cognitive deficits of recent onset from those that are long standing.

6-50. The answer is B. *(Rudolph, 20/e, pp 212, 902.)* Mongolian spots are bluish-gray lesions located over the buttock, lower back, and occasionally the extensor surfaces of the extremities. They are common in blacks, Asians, and Latin Americans. They tend to disappear by 1 to 2 years of age, although those on the extremities may not fully resolve. Child abuse is unlikely to present with bruises alone; children frequently present with more extensive injuries. Subcutaneous fat necrosis is usually found as a sharply demarcated, hard lesion on the cheeks, buttocks, and limbs. The lesion usually is red. Hemophilia and vitamin K deficiency rarely present with subcutaneous lesions as described and are more likely to present as a bleeding episode.

BLOCK 7

Answers

7-1. The answer is B. *(Isselbacher, 13/e, p 2470.)* The administration of epinephrine is the best treatment in the acute setting. Epinephrine provides both alpha- and beta-adrenergic effects. Antihistamines and corticosteroids are frequently given as well, although they have little immediate effect. The patient should be offered venom immunotherapy after recovery from the systemic reaction. Removal of an insect stinger without compression is worthwhile but not the primary concern.

7-2. The answer is C. *(Rudolph, 20/e, pp 1338, 1844–1847.)* Hypercalcemia may develop in children who are immobilized following the fracture of a weight-bearing bone. Serious complications of immobilization hypercalcemia and the hypercalciuria that occurs as a result include nephropathy, nephrocalcinosis, hypertensive encephalopathy, and convulsions. The early symptoms of hypercalcemia—namely, constipation, anorexia, occasional vomiting, polyuria, and lethargy—are nonspecific and may be ascribed to the effects of the injury and hospitalization. Therefore, careful monitoring of these patients with serial measurements of the serum ionized calcium and the urinary calcium-creatinine ratio is critical during their immobilization. A ratio of ⩾0.2 establishes a diagnosis of hypercalciuria. Although complete mobilization is curative, additional measures such as vigorous intravenous hydration with a balanced salt solution, dietary restrictions of dairy products, and administration of diuretics may be instituted. For patients who are at risk for symptomatic hypercalcemia, short-term therapy with calcitonin is highly effective in reducing the concentration of serum calcium by inhibiting bone resorption.

7-3. The answer is A. *(Shires, 3/e, pp 354–355.)* If time and the patient's condition permit, primary ureteral reconstruction should be carried out. In the middle third of the ureter, this will usually consist of ureteroureterostomy using absorbable sutures over a stent. If the injury involves the upper third, ureteropyeloplasty may be necessary. In the lower third, ureteral implantation into the bladder using a tunneling technique is preferred. If time does not permit definitive repair, suction drainage adjacent to the injured segment alone is inadequate; either ligation and nephrostomy or placement of a catheter into the proximal ureter is an acceptable alternative that would allow reconstruction to be performed later. The creation of a watertight seal is difficult and nephrectomy may be required if the injury occurs during a procedure in which a vascular prosthesis is being implanted (e.g., an aortic reconstructive procedure) and contamination of the foreign body by urine must be avoided.

7-4–7-7. The answers are 7-4 F, 7-5 A, 7-6 D, 7-7 B. (*Schwartz, 6/e, pp 437–448.*) Routine postoperative immunosuppression for a renal transplant recipient includes cyclosporine, azathioprine, and steroids. Cyclosporine is nephrotoxic and is frequently withheld in the postoperative period until the creatinine returns to normal following transplantation. Azathioprine has bone marrow toxicity as its major side effect and both WBC and platelet counts need to be monitored in the immediate posttransplant period. The patient's decrease in WBCs is secondary to azathioprine toxicity and the most appropriate step is to decrease the dose of azathioprine.

Viral infections are a serious cause of morbidity following transplantation. A "buffy coat" is the supernatant of a centrifuged blood sample that contains the WBCs. Viral cultures from this supernatant as well as localization of inclusion bodies can identify transplant patients infected with cytomegalovirus (CMV). This patient has CMV pneumonitis and needs to be treated with high-dose ganciclovir.

An elevation in creatinine at 3-month follow-up can be secondary to rejection, anastomotic problems, urologic complications, infection, or nephrotoxicity of various medications. With a normal ultrasound, no fever, and no graft tenderness, the most likely cause is cyclosporine-induced nephrotoxicity and the most appropriate step is a reduction in the cyclosporine dose.

Finally at 6 months with graft tenderness, fever, and an edematous kidney on ultrasound, rejection must be suspected. Negative cultures makes infection unlikely and a steroid boost is appropriate. Addition of monoclonal antibodies to CD3 (OKT3) or pooled antibodies against lymphocytes (ALG) is also appropriate in the treatment of a first rejection.

7-8. The answer is C. (*Behrman, 15/e, pp 1432–1433.*) In children, idiopathic or immune thrombocytopenic purpura (ITP) is the most common form of thrombocytopenic purpura. In most cases a preceding viral infection can be noted. No diagnostic test exists for this disease; exclusion of the other diseases listed in the question is necessary. In this disease, the platelet count is frequently less than 20,000, but other laboratory tests yield essentially normal results, including the bone marrow aspiration (if done). Aplastic anemia is unlikely if the other cell lines are normal. Von Willebrand disease might be expected to present with bleeding and not just bruising. It is unlikely that acute leukemia would present with thrombocytopenia only. Thrombotic thrombocytopenic purpura is rare in children.

Treatment for ITP consists of gamma globulin, which frequently results in an adequate rise in platelet count. In more severe cases, steroids are also used. Splenectomy is reserved for the most severe and chronic forms.

7-9. The answer is C. *(Isselbacher, 13/e, p 1097.)* The patient's chest pain is most likely due to pericarditis. An enlarged cardiac silhouette without other chest x-ray findings of heart failure suggests pericardial effusion. Echocardiography is the most sensitive, specific way of determining whether or not pericardial fluid is present. The effusion appears as an echo-free space between the moving epicardium and stationary pericardium. It is unnecessary to perform cardiac catheterization for the purpose of evaluating pericardial effusion. Radionuclide scanning is not a preferred method for demonstrating pericardial fluid.

7-10. The answer is C. *(Isselbacher, 13/e, p 1097.)* The patient has developed cardiac tamponade, a condition in which pericardial fluid under-in-creased pressure impedes diastolic filling, resulting in reduced cardiac output and hypotension. On examination there is elevation of jugular venous pressure. The jugular venous pulse shows a sharp x descent, the inward impulse seen at the time of the carotid pulsation. In contrast to pulmonary edema, the lungs usually are clear. Neither a strong apical beat nor an S_3 gallop would be expected in tamponade.

7-11. The answer is B. *(Lynch, 3/e, pp 67, 287–291.)* This history is most consistent with tinea capitis that involves a *Microsporum* species. The condition can usually be differentiated from other scalp disorders by its characteristic appearance. Although tinea capitis has different appearances according to the organism that causes the infection, the most common forms are those caused by a *Microsporum* species. Wood's lamp and KOH preparation are useful laboratory methods for diagnosis. Although the condition can resolve spontaneously, therapy should consist of a systemic antifungal agent, such as griseofulvin.

7-12. The answer is C. (*Isselbacher, 13/e, pp 1266–1274.*) The initial evaluation in this patient is aimed toward obtaining further information so that the cause of acute renal failure may be characterized as either prerenal, renal, or postrenal (obstruction). Of those tests listed, the urine sodium and urine sediment would be the most helpful. A urine sodium greater than 40 meq/L suggests that acute tubular necrosis is more likely than prerenal azotemia. A urine sediment that shows renal tubular epithelial cells and muddy brown casts is diagnostic for acute tubular necrosis.

7-13. The answer is E. (*Hoskins, 2/e, pp 940–944.*) The survivability of women who have ovarian carcinoma varies inversely with the amount of residual tumor left after the initial surgery. At the time of laparotomy, a maximum effort should be made to determine the sites of tumor spread and to excise all resectable tumor. Although the uterus and ovary may appear grossly normal, there is a relatively high incidence of occult metastases to these organs; for this reason, they should be removed during the initial surgery.

7-14. The answer is E. (*Schwartz, 6/e, pp 176–178.*) Loss of consciousness following head trauma should be assumed to be due to intracranial hemorrhage until proved otherwise. However, a thorough evaluation of the head-injured patient includes assessment for other potentially life-threatening injuries. Rarely, a patient may have sufficient hemorrhage from a scalp laceration to cause hypotension. In the patient described, hypotension and tachycardia should not be uncritically attributed to the head injury, since these findings in the setting of blunt trauma are suggestive of serious thoracic, abdominal, or pelvic hemorrhage. When cardiovascular collapse occurs as a result of rising intracranial pressure, it is generally accompanied by hypertension, bradycardia, and respiratory depression.

7-15. The answer is E. (*Behrman, 15/e, pp 484–485.*) Transient tachypnea of the newborn is usually seen after a normal vaginal or cesarean delivery. These patients have tachypnea, retractions, grunting, and sometimes cyanosis. The chest examination is usually normal; the chest radiograph demonstrates prominent pulmonary vascular markings with fluid in the fissures and hyperexpansion (flat diaphragms). Therapy is supportive with maintenance of normal oxygen saturation. Resolution usually occurs in the first 3 days of life.

7-16. The answer is C. (*Hales, 2/e, pp 495–518. Isselbacher, 13/e, pp 2165–2166.*) The patient displays typical symptoms of a panic attack: sudden onset of intense fear, with at least 4 of a potential 13 somatic or cognitive symptoms, and a duration of usually 5 to 20 min. Panic attacks can occur in a wide variety of psychiatric and medical conditions. The patient is diagnosed with panic disorder only if there are recurrent episodes of panic; there is at least 1 month of persistent concern, worry, or behavioral change associated with the attacks; and they are not due to the direct effect of medical illness or medication or substance abuse, or better accounted for by another psychiatric disorder. While anxiety can be intense in generalized anxiety disorder, major depression, acute psychosis, and hypochondriasis, it does not have the typical form described above. Phobias may be accompanied by situationally precipitated panic attacks.

A number of medical conditions can be accompanied by episodes of panic anxiety. These include pheochromocytoma, both hyper- and hypothyroidism, cardiac arrhythmias and coronary insufficiency, hypoglycemia, and both drug and alcohol withdrawal. Hypoparathyroidism is not associated with panic attacks, though there can be severe mental symptoms, including irritability, depression, and psychosis.

A number of pharmacologic agents have been used successfully in the treatment of patients with panic episodes or panic disorder. These include the tricyclic antidepressants (e.g., imipramine), serotonin reuptake inhibitors (e.g., fluoxetine, sertraline), monoamine oxidase inhibitors (e.g., phenelzine), and high-potency benzodiazepines (e.g., alprazolam, clonazepam). Phenobarbital is not an effective treatment for this condition and is further contraindicated because of concern about its addictive potential and sedative effects.

7-17. The answer is A. (*Rudolph, 20/e, pp 573–580, 674–676, 1633–1634.*) Children who have acute epiglottitis, a life-threatening infection of the hypopharynx and epiglottis caused by *Haemophilus influenzae*, typically present with high fever, extremely sore throat, and a croupy cough. Physical examination characteristically shows a red throat and a red, swollen epiglottis that may be obscured by exudate or so distorted that its identity is misinterpreted. It is important that caution be exercised while attempting to visualize the epiglottis. Abrupt glottic spasm is a well-recognized, potentially fatal complication in these patients. Affected children often are unable to swallow saliva, and because the swollen epiglottis can unpredictably and suddenly cause total and fatal airway obstruction, immediate hospitalization is mandatory, even in the absence of severe respiratory distress. If a diagnosis of acute epiglottitis is uncertain, a lateral x-ray of the neck will differentiate epiglottic from subglottic swelling, the latter being associated with a less serious disease, viral croup.

7-18. The answer is E. *(McCullough, pp 24–25.)* The tunica vaginalis normally attaches the posterolateral surfaces of the testicle to the scrotum, thereby anchoring it and preventing rotation. When these attachments are missing, the testicle is free to rotate around the spermatic cord and the critical vascular pedicle. This is known as *intravaginal torsion* and is most common in patients 10 to 19 years of age. Classically, the testicle will have a transverse lie within the scrotum, known as the "bell-clapper" relationship. Onset of pain is sudden and there are no urinary complaints. Many feel that the initiating factor may be contraction of the cremaster muscle. Loss of cremasteric reflex is almost invariably found in torsion.

7-19. The answer is E. *(MMWR vol 40, no RR-12, 1991.)* If a person has received three doses or more of the Td, and the last dose was given more than 5 years before an injury, a tetanus and diphtheria booster should be given if the wound is contaminated, such as the one described. It is preferable to administer the combined diphtheria and tetanus booster (Td). If the last dose of Td was given in the preceding 5 years, then no further action would be necessary. Td and tetanus immunoglobulin (TIG) is recommended for prophylaxis of contaminated wounds when the history of tetanus toxoid is unknown or the person received less than three doses. TIG is never recommended as sole prophylaxis as prolonged immunity is desired.

7-20. The answer is A. *(Behrman, 15/e, pp 730, 1936–1937, 1940–1942.)* This history is typical of Osgood-Schlatter disease. Microfractures in the area of the insertion of the patellar tendon into the tibial tubercle are common in athletic adolescents. Swelling, tenderness, and increase in size of the tibial tuberosity are found. Radiographs may be necessary to rule out other conditions. Treatment consists of rest.

Legg-Calvé-Perthes disease is avascular necrosis of the femoral head. This condition usually produces mild or intermittent pain in the anterior thigh, but may also present as a painless limp.

Gonococcal arthritis, while common in this age range, is uncommon in this anatomic site. More significant systemic signs and symptoms including chills, fever, migratory polyarthralgias, and rash are commonly seen.

Slipped capital femoral epiphysis is usually seen in a younger, more obese child (mean age about 10 years) or in the thinner, older child who has just undergone a rapid growth spurt. Pain upon movement of the hip is diagnostic.

Popliteal cysts are found on the posterior aspect of the knee.

7-21. The answer is D. (*Schwartz, 6/e, pp 467–468.*) The patient presented in the question is suffering from acute, life-threatening respiratory acidosis that has been compounded, if not produced, by the injudicious administration of a central nervous system depressant. While hypoxemia must also be corrected, the immediate task is to correct the acidosis caused by carbon dioxide accumulation. Both disturbances can be resolved by skillful endotracheal intubation and by ventilatory support. Sodium bicarbonate and high-flow nasal oxygen would both be inappropriate. Bicarbonate should not be administered because buffer reserves already are adequate (serum bicarbonate is still 34 meq/L based on the Henderson-Hasselbalch equation). Nasal oxygen administration is not warranted because both acidemia and hypoxemia are themselves potent stimulants to spontaneous ventilation. Headache, confusion, and papilledema are all signs of acute carbon dioxide retention and do not imply the presence of a structural intracranial lesion.

7-22. The answer is B. (*Fitzpatrick, 4/e, pp 2462–2465.*) The diagnosis is tinea versicolor, which can be easily confirmed by a KOH microscopic examination. Routine fungal cultures will not grow this yeast. A Wood's light examination will often show a green fluorescence, but it may be negative if the patient has recently showered. A Tzanck smear is used on blisters to detect herpes infection. A punch biopsy would show the fungus but is unnecessary, and the fungus might be missed unless special stains are performed.

7-23. The answer is C. (*Isselbacher, 13/e, pp 2372–2373.*) This young man presents with an acute symmetric polyneuropathy characteristic of the patient with Guillain-Barré syndrome. This is a demyelinating polyneuropathy that often precedes a viral illness by 1 to 3 weeks. Characteristically there is little sensory involvement, and about 30 percent of patients require ventilatory assistance. Dermatomyositis usually presents insidiously with proximal muscle weakness. Myasthenia gravis also presents insidiously with muscle weakness that is worsened by repetitive use. Diplopia, ptosis, and facial weakness are common first complaints. Multiple sclerosis causes demyelinating lesions disseminated in time and space and would not occur in this acute, symmetric manner. Diabetes mellitus can cause a variety of neuropathies, but would not be rapidly progressive as in this patient.

7-24. The answer is C. (*Adams, 6/e, p 1495.*) The markedly elevated sedimentation rate, anemia, weight loss, and malaise in a person this age suggest polymyalgia rheumatica, although the same complaints in someone 20 years younger could not be explained on the basis of this disorder. Fever may also be evident in the affected person. This constellation of symptoms also suggests an occult neoplasm or infection, and investigations should be conducted to reduce the likelihood of overlooking one of these diseases. Polymyalgia rheumatica is an arteritis of the elderly and is improbable in someone less than 60 years of age. The normal creatine kinase activity markedly reduces the likelihood that this myalgia is the result of polymyositis or dermatomyositis. The new onset of rheumatoid arthritis at this age is also improbable. A hyperthyroid myopathy in the face of a normal thyroxine level is possible on the basis of an elevated T_3 level but is also much less likely than polymyalgia rheumatica in this age group.

7-25. The answer is A. (*Schwartz, 6/e, pp 1084–1086.*) The diagnostic studies listed reveal minimal reflux esophagitis, normal LES relaxation and pressure, and an incidental small epiphrenic diverticulum. None of these findings justifies treatment and none explains the patient's symptoms. On the other hand the finding of prolonged high amplitude contractions in the body of the esophagus in a highly symptomatic patient is diagnostic of diffuse esophageal spasm. The cause of this hypermotility disorder is unknown but its symptoms can be disabling. The recommended treatment for this relatively rare disorder is a long myotomy guided by the manometric evidence. If the LES is functioning properly, most surgeons would now recommend stopping the myotomy short of the normal lower sphincter. It should continue upward at least to the level of the aortic arch—higher if manometric findings of spasm are noted above that level. Eighty to 90 percent of patients treated in this fashion will experience acceptable relief of symptoms.

7-26. The answer is D. *(Kaplan, 6/e, pp 1922–1923.)* Phenothiazines, tricyclic antidepressants, and antiparkinsonian agents (such as benztropine mesylate) all have anticholinergic properties. The action of these drugs becomes additive when they are administered in combination. It is not uncommon for persons receiving such a combination to show evidence of a mild organic brain syndrome, including difficulty in concentrating, impaired short-term memory, and disorientation, which often is more noticeable at night. Dry skin and palms are especially suggestive of atropinism.

7-27. The answer is E. *(Rudolph, 20/e, pp 1877–1879, 1902–1903, 1924–1925, 1950, 1962–1963.)* The abrupt onset of a hemisyndrome, especially with the eyes looking away from the paralyzed side, strongly indicates a diagnosis of acute infantile hemiplegia. Most frequently this represents a thromboembolic occlusion of the middle cerebral artery or one of its major branches. Hemiplegic migraine commonly occurs in children with a history of migraine headaches. Todd's paralysis follows after a focal or jacksonian seizure and generally does not last more than 24 to 48 h. The clinical onset of supratentorial brain tumor is subacute with repeated headaches and gradually developing weakness. A history of trauma usually precedes the signs of an acute subdural hematoma. Clinical signs of other diseases may appear fairly rapidly, but not often with the abruptness of occlusive vascular disease.

7-28. The answer is A. *(Isselbacher, 13/e, p 556.)* Gonococcal infection is the leading cause of bacterial arthritis in young adults and the most common form of infectious arthritis seen in urban medical centers. In fact, arthritis may be the only presenting complaint. An early tenosynovitis-dermatitis syndrome is typically followed by septic arthritis. The knee, shoulder, wrist and interphalangeal joints of the hand are most commonly affected. The history and examination should focus on the urogenital tract, pharynx, and rectum in search of a primary focus.

7-29. The answer is C. *(Isselbacher, 13/e, p 1928.)* The patient described has hyponatremia, normovolemia, and a concentrated urine. These features are sufficient to make a diagnosis of inappropriate antidiuretic hormone (ADH) secretion. Inappropriate ADH secretion occurs by ectopic production from neoplastic tissue. Treatment necessitates restriction of fluid intake. A negative water balance results in a rise in serum NA^+ and serum osmolality and symptom improvement.

7-30–7-32. The answers are 7-30 C, 7-31 B, 7-32 A. (*Isselbacher, 13/e, p 745–747.*) This patient presents with a symptom complex that includes facial nerve palsies, arthralgia, and first-degree AV block. Facial nerve palsy has been increasingly recognized as a first manifestation of Lyme disease. Within several weeks of the onset of illness, about 8 percent of patients develop cardiac involvement; heart block is the most common manifestation. During this stage of early disseminated infection, musculoskeletal pain is common. The diagnosis of Lyme disease is based on careful history and physical examination with serologic confirmation by detection of antibody to *Borrelia burgdorferi*. Neither CT nor MRI of the head would be indicated as the lesion is a peripheral facial palsy. Sarcoidosis can also cause both facial nerve palsy and AV block, but it is much less likely and the Kveim test is rarely used to pursue this diagnosis. The treatment of choice for Lyme disease at this stage would be penicillin or ceftriaxone.

7-33. The answer is E. (*Seidel, 3/e, p 525.*) This is the clinical picture of a ruptured spleen. Intense pain in the left upper quadrant that radiates to the top of the left shoulder (Kehr's sign) is due to diaphragmatic irritation by blood from the ruptured spleen. The spinal levels supplying most of the sensory fibers of the diaphragm (C3, C4, C5—phrenic nerve) are the same levels as some of the sensory supply to the shoulder; therefore, diaphragmatic irritation will sometimes be perceived as shoulder pain. The blood loss to the abdomen frequently causes signs of shock, including pallor, subnormal temperature, and hypotension. A positive peritoneal lavage is enough to warrant immediate exploratory laparotomy and splenectomy if the ruptured spleen cannot be repaired.

7-34. The answer is A. (*Rudolph, 20/e, pp 1121–1122.*) The causes of pancreatitis in children are varied with about one-fourth of cases without predisposing etiology and about one-third of cases as a feature of another systemic disease. Traumatic cases are usually due to blunt trauma to the abdomen. Acute pancreatitis is difficult to diagnose; a high index of suspicion is necessary. Common clinical features include severe pain with nausea and vomiting. Tenderness, guarding or rebound pain, abdominal distention, and a paralytic ileus are signs and symptoms often seen. No diagnostic test is completely accurate. An elevated total serum amylase with the correct clinical history and signs and symptoms is the best diagnostic tool. Plain films of the abdomen exclude other diagnoses; ultrasonography of the pancreas may reveal enlargement of the pancreas, gallstones, cysts, and pseudocysts. Supportive care is indicated until the condition resolves.

7-35. The answer is E. *(Kaplan, 6/e, p 1803.)* This is an example of biofeedback, used in an attempt to induce relaxation and thereby peripheral vasodilatation, which in turn lowers blood pressure. The peripheral dilatation increases skin temperature, and the audible tone helps the patient learn what he needs to do to achieve that elevation. Some clinicians feel that simple relaxation training can accomplish the same goal.

7-36. The answer is E. *(Rundell, pp 316–321.)* Depressive illness consists of both somatic and psychological components. The somatic components include insomnia, anorexia, weight loss, fatigue, motor retardation or agitation, and decreased sexual interest. The psychological components include depressed mood, pessimism, and feelings of worthlessness and guilt. Not all components are present in every case. Patients who have a masked depression present with primarily somatic symptoms and few or no psychological ones. Diagnosis often is made only after extensive medical evaluation is unrevealing. The woman described in the question did not have any signs of dementia; medical evaluation did not reveal an organic disease process; and although hypochondriasis and chronic anxiety could have caused many of her symptoms, they are not likely to have caused the 11.4-kg weight loss.

7-37. The answer is D. *(Lechtenberg, Synopsis, pp 86–87.)* Huntington's disease is transmitted in an autosomal dominant fashion. The age at which the patient becomes symptomatic is variable and has no effect on the probability of transmitting the disease. The defect underlying this degenerative disease is transmitted on chromosome 4.

7-38. The answer is B. *(Behrman, 15/e, p 550.)* In choanal atresia, the baby looks fine when crying but turns blue when crying stops. It is necessary to maintain the airway, and one way to do this temporarily is to make a large hole in the pacifier. The incidence of unilateral choanal atresia is 1:2500 live births; bilateral choanal atresia occurs in 1:5000 live births. The latter condition warrants immediate surgical correction.

7-39. The answer is C. *(Isselbacher, 13/e, pp 1197–1206.)* The increased anteroposterior thickness of the thorax indicates the presence of a "barrel-chest," which in association with a smoking history and exertional dyspnea is a classic presentation of emphysema. Emphysema due to cigarette smoking nearly always begins as centrilobular emphysema, but as the pack-years increase the emphysema progresses to panlobular in nature. With bronchiectasis there is usually a history of repeated episodes of pneumonia or bronchitis, and a classic presentation would be the long-term production of a foul-smelling sputum. Chylothorax commonly presents secondary to chest trauma or lymphoma or as a postsurgical complication, and the pleural effusion is milky, has normal cholesterol and increased triglyceride content, and stains with Sudan III. Lung abscess occurs frequently in alcoholics from aspiration following unconsciousness, and common complaints include halitosis, foul-smelling sputum, and fever. With a bronchial adenoma there is a paucity of physical findings, but the patient may present with wheezing, recurrent bouts of pneumonia, or hemoptysis.

7-40. The answer is C. *(Schwartz, 6/e, pp 675–677.)* The finding of an air-fluid level in the left lower chest with a nasogastric tube entering it after blunt trauma to the abdomen is diagnostic of diaphragmatic rupture with gastric herniation into the chest. This lesion needs to be fixed immediately. With continuing negative pressure in the chest, each breath sucks more of the abdominal contents into the chest and increases the likelihood of vascular compromise of the herniated viscera. While the diaphragm is easily fixed from the left chest, this injury should be approached from the abdomen. The possibility of injury below the diaphragm after sufficient blunt injury to rupture the diaphragm mandates examination of the intraabdominal solid and hollow viscera; adequate exposure of the diaphragm to allow secure repair is possible from this approach.

7-41. The answer is E. *(Mishell, 3/e, p 1159.)* The symptoms described in the question are common symptoms of menopause. They all result primarily from estrogen withdrawal, and most can be reversed by estrogen therapy. *Climacteric* is actually a better word for this complex of symptoms because the menopause is technically the instant at which menses cease.

7-42. The answer is E. *(Kaplan, 6/e, pp 1298–1299, 1321–1333, 1425–1433.)* There is nothing in the patient's history to suggest the presence of a personality disorder. The hallmark of a personality disorder is the presence of a constellation of behaviors or traits that cause significant impairment in social or occupational functioning or cause subjective distress. There is no history of such distress or dysfunction. While some persons in our society might object to his sexual behavior on moral grounds, such judgments are not a part of the diagnostic process.

The patient gives a history of having an average of 9 to 11 orgasms per week and describes a high sexual drive since his teens. While this frequency is higher than that found in most males in their early thirties, it is neither outside the range of normalcy nor in and of itself pathologic. Similarly, the occurrence of masturbation in married men is not particularly unusual and in and of itself does not suggest a sexual disorder or marital problems. It may be due to a higher desire level than can be satisfied with his partner, it may be a relief for sexual impulses that cannot be otherwise satisfied, or it may simply be an enjoyed alternative release. Since masturbation is sometimes motivated by a desire to reduce anxiety rather than to satisfy sexual drive, it may also be related to his general anxiety. Patients who are manic or hypomanic often have increased sexual drive and frequency of release, but this tends to be episodic rather than consistent and lifelong.

Sexual behavior and fantasies range on a continuum from exclusively heterosexual to exclusively homosexual. There are many men who are predominantly heterosexual but who have engaged in homosexual behavior or have occasional homosexual fantasies, and there are many predominantly homosexual men with capacity for heterosexual arousal. The presence of homosexual desire or behavior is not considered, according to the diagnostic definitions of the American Psychiatric Association, to constitute a sexual disorder. While further therapeutic inquiry may uncover sexual conflict or marital disorder, the current history does not necessarily suggest that will be the case.

7-43. The answer is D. (*Behrman, 15/e, pp 1201–1205.*) The signs of illness described are those involving the airway above the point at which the trachea enters the neck and leaves the thorax, as in croup syndrome. Intrathoracic airway diseases, such as asthma or bronchiolitis, produce breathing difficulty on expiration with expiratory wheezing, prolonged expiration, and signs of air trapping owing to the increased narrowing during expiration as the airways are exposed to the same intrathoracic pressure changes as the alveoli. The extrathoracic airway, to the contrary, tends to collapse on inspiration, producing the characteristic findings this patient demonstrates.

7-44. The answer is D. *(Fitzpatrick, 4/e, pp 15–35.)* Poison ivy (*Rhus dermatitis*) begins 24 to 48 h after exposure to the oil from the plant in an allergic person. Linear blisters are an important clue to the diagnosis.

7-45. The answer is D. *(Isselbacher, 13/e, pp 1052–1056.)* Mitral stenosis is characterized by an opening snap just prior to a low-pitched, rumbling diastolic murmur. Mitral regurgitation is a systolic murmur. Aortic insufficiency is a high-pitched diastolic murmur.

7-46. The answer is C. *(Behrman, 15/e, pp 1316–1317.)* Tricuspid atresia has a hypoplastic right ventricle and therefore the ECG shows left axis deviation and left ventricular hypertrophy. Almost all other forms of cyanotic congenital heart disease are associated with elevated pressures in the right ventricle. In those, therefore, the ECG will show right axis deviation and right ventricular hypertrophy.

7-47. The answer is B. *(Schwartz, 6/e, pp 990–1003.)* This patient has a left iliofemoral vein thrombosis, as evidenced by sudden massive swelling of her entire left lower extremity. Noninvasive venous testing should be quite helpful as the venous obstruction extends above the knee and therefore venography and x-ray exposure are unnecessary. Heparin is the preferred agent because it does not cross the placenta. The vena caval filter is not indicated because there is no contraindication to heparin therapy and there has not been any evidence of pulmonary embolus.

7-48. The answer is B. *(Hathaway, 11/e, pp 440–441.)* Acute otitis externa is the infection of the external auditory canal. The external canal can swell, which makes examination of the tympanic membrane difficult. Pulling on the tragus, or the pinna, extends the canal and causes pain. Palpable lymphadenopathy involving the periauricular and cervical lymph nodes may be present. Debris is often seen in the canal and the patient resists all attempts at speculum examination.

7-49. The answer is C. *(Adams, 6/e, p 1358.)* The musculocutaneous nerve is often damaged with fractures of the humerus. This nerve supplies the biceps brachii, brachialis, and coracobrachialis muscles and carries sensory information from the lateral cutaneous nerve of the forearm. Flexion at the elbow with damage to this nerve is most impaired with the forearm supinated.

7-50. The answer is C. *(Isselbacher, 13/e, pp 1214–1220.)* Most often the only symptom of pulmonary thromboembolism (PTE or PE) is sudden onset of unexplained dyspnea. Pleuritic chest pain and hemoptysis will only be present if pulmonic infarction has occurred. The most reliable symptom, however, is breathlessness. If the dyspnea is severe and persistent, this is an ominous sign because it usually indicates extensive embolic occlusion. An excellent clue to the diagnosis of PTE is deep venous thrombosis (DVT), but absence of signs and symptoms of DVT does not exclude PTE. Tachycardia is a single consistent sign. Common settings for the appearance of pulmonary embolism include prolonged immobilization, recent surgery, congestive heart failure, recent trauma (especially to the lower extremities), previous history of thrombophlebitis, use of oral contraceptives with a high estrogen content, sickle cell anemia, polycythemias, and inherited deficiencies of the anticoagulating proteins (antithrombin III, protein C).

BLOCK 8

Answers

8-1–8-2. The answers are 8-1 E, 8-2 E. *(Hales, 2/e, pp 156–160.)* This is a classic example of the defense mechanism known as splitting. Rather than an integrated ambivalence that recognizes both good and bad aspects of the other person, the person is seen as either all good or all bad.

This defense mechanism is particularly seen in patients with a borderline personality disorder. They respond to frustration or rejection with anger and devaluation, during which time the previous "good aspects" of the therapist or therapy are forgotten. This mechanism leads to chaotic interpersonal relationships.

8-3. The answer is A. *(Behrman, 15/e, pp 1555–1556.)* This common condition is diagnosed when a central line of adherence is noted from the area inferior to the clitoris to the fourchette. It is a common, asymptomatic condition seen in girls less than 6 years of age. Labial adhesions may be responsible for vulvovaginitis and increased urinary tract infections in girls owing to pooling of urine in the vagina. Treatment with topical estrogen cream daily results in resolution of this problem. Mechanical separation is not advisable under normal circumstances.

8-4. The answer is A. *(Hardy, 2/e, pp 166–171.)* Flail chest is diagnosed in the presence of paradoxical respiratory movement in a portion of the chest wall. At least two fractures in each of three adjacent rib or costal cartilages are required to produce this condition. Complications of flail chest include segmental pulmonary hypoventilation with subsequent infection and ultimately respiratory failure. Management of flail chest should be individualized. If adequate pain control and pulmonary toilet can be provided, patients may be managed without stabilization of the flail. Often intercostal nerve blocks and tracheostomy aid in this form of management. If stabilization is required, external methods such as sandbags or towel clips are no longer used. Surgical stabilization with wires is used if thoracotomy is to be performed for another indication. If this is not the case, "internal" stabilization is performed by placing the patient on mechanical ventilation with positive end-expiratory pressure. Tracheostomy is recommended because these patients usually require 10 to 14 days to stabilize their flail segment and postventilation pulmonary toilet is simplified by tracheostomy. Indications for mechanical ventilation include significant impedance to ventilation by the flail segment, large pulmonary contusion, an uncooperative patient (e.g., owing to head injury), general anesthesia for another indication, greater than five ribs fractured, and the development of respiratory failure.

8-5. The answer is A. *(Isselbacher, 13/e, pp 1940–1941.)* Classic hypothyroidism is readily detected by a thorough history and physical examination. Chronic renal disease may also present with a picture of edema and hypothermia that closely resembles hypothyroidism. It may therefore be useful to perform laboratory tests on these patients to determine the possible coexistence of renal disease and hypothyroidism.

8-6. The answer is A. *(Isselbacher 13/e, p. 518.)* Ear pain and drainage in an elderly diabetic patient must raise concern about malignant external otitis. The swelling and inflammation of the external auditory meatus strongly suggests this diagnosis. This infection usually occurs in older diabetics and is almost always caused by *Pseudomonas aeruginosa. Haemophilus influenzae* and *Moraxella catarrhalis* frequently cause otitis media but not external otitis.

8-7. The answer is B. *(Crenshaw, 8/e, pp 2227, 2254, 3109, 3118.)* The radial nerve lies next to the shaft of the humerus in the spiral groove. It may be injured as a result of humeral fractures, particularly those involving the distal third of the humerus. The radial nerve supplies the extensor muscles of the wrist and its damage results in wristdrop, a condition in which the patient is unable to extend the wrist.

8-8. The answer is E. *(Rudolph, 20/e, pp 596–598.)* Clinical manifestations of shigellosis range from watery stools for several days to severe infection with high fever, abdominal pain, and generalized seizures. In general, about 50 percent of these children have emesis, 90 percent have fever, 10 to 35 percent have seizures, and 40 percent have blood in their stool. Often the seizure precedes diarrhea and is the complaint that brings the family to the physician. Fever usually lasts about 72 h and the diarrhea resolves within 1 week. Presumptive diagnosis can be made on the clinical history; confirmation is through stool culture. Supportive care, including adequate fluid and electrolyte support, is the mainstay of therapy. Antibiotic treatment is usually with trimethoprim-sulfamethoxazole, although sensitivity to this antibiotic should be assessed.

8-9. The answer is E. *(Isselbacher, 13/e, pp 1807–1808.)* This patient with gram-negative bacteremia has developed disseminated intravascular coagulation as evidenced by multiple-site bleeding, thrombocytopenia, fragmented RBCs on peripheral smear, prolonged PT and PTT, and reduced fibrinogen levels from depletion of coagulation proteins. Initial treatment is directed at correcting the underlying disorder, in this case infection. The use of heparin is somewhat controversial but generally recommended only in association with acute promyelocytic leukemia.

8-10–8-11. The answers are 8-10 C, 8-11 D. *(Sabiston, 5/e, p 396.)* The incidence of myocardial contusion is about 25 percent in patients with severe blunt injury to the chest. The injury occurs as a result of direct compression of the heart between the sternum and the vertebral column. The right ventricle, being the most anterior portion of the heart, is the most commonly injured portion. The blow causes extravasation of blood into the myocardium and results in a progressive loss of ventricular compliance and decreased cardiac output, which usually peaks by 8 to 24 h after the injury.

The most helpful ECG finding is the presence of a new right bundle branch block, which occurs because of damage to the anterior portion of the interventricular septum; ST-segment and T-wave changes and even the development of new Q waves may be seen. CPK-MB fractions are useful if they are positive; however, frequent false negatives may be seen because of the release of CPK-MM from other contused organs, such as the pectoralis muscles, which can dilute the cardiac CPK-MB to nondiagnostic levels. Echocardiography may be helpful but the right ventricle is often poorly visualized. Radionuclide angiography is most useful by suggesting the degree of myocardial impairment caused by decreased compliance.

Therapy of myocardial contusion is directed at inotropic support of the ventricle; usually, the coronary arteries are intact after the injury and so there is little role for coronary vasodilators and less for coronary artery bypass grafting.

8-12. The answer is A. *(USDHHS, CDC, MMWR 44(50): 929–933, 1994.)* A case-control study conducted with cases from the U.S., France, and the

U.K. demonstrated that the factor associated with the greatest risk of transmission of HIV to the health care worker following a needle stick injury was the depth of the injury (odds ratio 16.1, confidence interval 6.1–44.6). In addition, the presence of blood on the device, terminal illness in the source patient, and a procedure that required placing the needle directly in a vein or artery were also associated with a higher risk of transmission. Postexposure use of zidovudine decreased the risk of transmission. New guidelines on prophylaxis following a percutaneous injury have been issued by the CDC (*MMWR* vol 45, no RR-22, 1996). Overall, the risk of HIV transmission following a percutaneous injury is 0.3 percent.

8-13. The answer is C. (*Lechtenberg, Synopsis, pp 154–155.*) Wernicke's encephalopathy is a potentially fatal consequence of thiamine deficiency, a problem for which this woman was at risk by virtue of being an alcoholic. When she came to the emergency room, intravenous fluids were started that probably contained glucose. The stress of a large glucose load will abruptly deplete the central nervous system of the little thiamine it had available and will precipitate the sort of deterioration evident in this woman. Features characteristic of a Wernicke's encephalopathy include deteriorating level of consciousness, autonomic disturbances, ocular motor problems, and gait difficulty. The autonomic disturbances may include lethal hypotension or profound hypothermia. Hemorrhagic necrosis in periventricular gray matter will be evident in this woman's brain if she dies. The mamillary bodies are especially likely to be extensively damaged.

8-14. The answer is E. (*Lechtenberg, Synopsis, pp 154–155.*) Without rapid replacement of thiamine stores, the patient with acute Wernicke's encephalopathy may die. Usually 50 to 100 mg of thiamine is given intravenously immediately. This is followed over the course of a few days with supplementary thiamine injections of 50 to 100 mg. Without thiamine, the patient will develop periaqueductal and mamillary body lesions, which will be clinically apparent as autonomic failure. With chronic thiamine deficiency, neuronal loss occurs in alcoholic persons at least partly because of this relative vitamin deficiency. Purkinje and other cells in the cerebellar vermis will be lost to so dramatic an extent that gross atrophy of the superior cerebellar vermis will be evident.

8-15. The answer is B. (*Behrman, 15/e, pp 1856–1860, 1863–1868.*) Pityriasis rosea is a benign condition that usually presents with a herald patch, a single round or oval lesion appearing anywhere on the body. Usually about 5 to 10 days after the appearance of the herald patch, a more diffuse rash involving the upper extremities and trunk appears. These lesions are oval or round, slightly raised, and pink to brown in color. The lesion is covered in a fine scale with some central clearing possible. The rash can appear in the Christmas tree pattern on the back identified by the aligning of the long axis of the lesions with the cutaneous cleavage lines. The rash lasts 2 to 12 weeks and may be pruritic. This rash is commonly mistaken for tinea corporis, and the consideration of secondary syphilis is important. Treatment is usually unnecessary but may consist of topical emollients and oral antihistamines as needed. More uncommonly, topical steroids may be helpful if the itching is severe.

Lichen planus is rare in children. It is intensely pruritic and additional lesions can be induced with scratching. The lesion is commonly found on the flexor surfaces of the wrists, forearms, inner thighs, and occasionally on the oral mucosa.

Seborrheic dermatitis can begin anytime during life; it frequently presents as cradle cap in the newborn period. This rash is commonly greasy, scaly, and erythematous and in smaller children involves the face, neck, axilla, and diaper area. In older children the rash may be localized to the scalp and intertriginous areas. Pruritus may be marked.

Contact dermatitis is characterized by redness, weeping, and oozing of the affected skin. The pattern of distribution may be helpful in identification of the offending agent. The rash may be pruritic; removal of the causative agent and use of topical emollients or steroids is curative.

Psoriasis consists of red papules that coalesce to form plaques with sharp edges. A thick, silvery scale develops on the surface and leaves a drop of blood upon its removal (Auspitz sign). Additional lesions develop upon scratching older lesions. Commonly affected sites include scalp, knees, elbows, umbilicus, and genitalia.

8-16. The answer is D. (*Bates, 5/e, pp 485–486.*) Speculum examination of a school-aged child must be performed by an experienced practitioner and should be done with the same respect given the adult woman. Swelling and erythema of vulvar tissue should be a "red flag" for child abuse, especially if associated with bruising or a foul-smelling discharge. A sexually transmitted disease would seem pathognomonic. In addition to the anorectal and genitourinary problems, there can be significant behavioral changes, such as sexually provocative mannerisms, excessive masturbation, inappropriate sexual knowledge, depression, school problems, and weight changes. A straddle injury from a bicycle seat occurs over the symphysis pubis, whereas signs of sexual abuse are more posterior around the perineum. Bubble-bath vaginitis is not uncommon and does not require a speculum examination.

8-17. The answer is D. *(Fitzpatrick, 4/e, pp 1117–1123.)* The description of this papulosquamous disease is that of a classic case of pityriasis rosea. This disease occurs in about 10 percent of the population. It is usually seen in young adults on the trunk and proximal extremities. There is a rare inverse form that occurs in the distal extremities and occasionally the face. Pityriasis rosea is usually asymptomatic, although some patients have an early, mild, viral prodrome (malaise and low-grade fever) and itching may be significant. Drug eruptions, fungal infections, and secondary syphilis are often confused with this disease. Fungal infections are rarely as widespread and sudden in onset; potassium hydroxide (KOH) preparation will be positive. Syphilis usually has adenopathy, oral patches, and lesions on the palms and soles (a VDRL test will be strongly positive at this stage). Psoriasis with its thick, scaly red plaques on extensor surfaces should not cause confusion. A rare condition called guttate parapsoriasis should be suspected if the rash lasts more than 2 months, since pityriasis rosea usually clears spontaneously in 6 weeks.

8-18. The answer is C. *(Schwartz, 6/e, pp 1274–1275.)* A markedly distended colon could have many causes in this 80-year-old man. The contrast study, however, reveals a classic "apple-core" lesion in the distal colon, which is diagnostic of colon cancer. No further diagnostic studies are appropriate prior to relief of this large bowel obstruction. After medical preparation (e.g., hydration, normalization of electrolytes), this patient should undergo prompt surgical management of his mechanical obstruction; conservative management by resection and proximal colostomy would generally be preferred in this elderly patient with an obstructed, unprepared bowel.

8-19. The answer is D. *(Seidel, 3/e, pp 618–620.)* Hydrocele is common in infancy, and if the tunica vaginalis is not patent, the hydrocele will usually resolve during the first 6 months of life. A spermatocele does transilluminate, but it does not grow as large as a hydrocele and remains localized as a cystic swelling on the epididymis. A varicocele is due to torsion of the pampiniform plexus that surrounds the spermatic cord. It usually occurs on the left side in boys or young men and can be quite painful. Epididymitis occurs most frequently in association with urinary tract infections and is very painful. The scrotum may be tense and is usually quite erythematous. Epididymitis can mimic testicular torsion, a surgical emergency.

8-20. The answer is C. (*Mishell, 3/e, pp 537–540.*) Adenomyosis is a condition in which normal endometrial glands are growing into the myometrium. Symptomatic disease primarily occurs in multiparous women over the age of 35 years. Patients complain of dysmenorrhea and menorrhagia. Although patients with endometriosis can have similar complaints, the physical examination of these patients more commonly reveals a fixed, retroverted uterus, with scarring and tenderness along the uterosacral ligaments. Leiomyoma is the most common pelvic tumor, but the majority are asymptomatic and the uterus is irregular in shape. Patients with endometritis can present with abnormal bleeding, but endometrial biopsies show an inflammatory pattern.

8-21. The answer is A. (*Behrman, 15/e, p 1486.*) The most common type of hereditary nephritis is Alport syndrome. Clinically, patients present with asymptomatic microscopic hematuria, but gross hematuria is also possible. Hearing loss eventually leading to deafness is associated with Alport syndrome in a minority of cases. End-stage renal disease is common by the second or third decades of life. This syndrome is thought to be an X-linked dominant disorder, which explains the more severe course in males.

8-22. The answer is B. (*Isselbacher, 13/e, pp 2461–2462.*) While there is no clue to exposure (insecticides, rodenticide, wood preservatives), the clinical picture is characteristic of arsenic poisoning. Manifestations of toxicity are varied but include irritation of the GI tract, resulting in the symptoms described. Arsenic combines with the globin chain of hemoglobin to produce hemolysis. The white transverse lines of the fingernails (Aldrich-Mees lines) are a manifestation of chronic arsenic poisoning.

8-23–8-25. The answers are 8-23 A, 8-24 G, 8-25 E. (*Greenfield, pp 1023–1030.*) The patient has a left colon cancer. In order to resect the tumor with a margin of 3 to 5 cm on its proximal and distal ends as well as to remove the draining lymph node basin, a left hemicolectomy should be performed. A Dukes C tumor is one that extends through the bowel wall and involves adjacent lymph nodes. In a study of 1166 patients with stage B and C colon cancer, the National Surgical Adjuvant Breast and Bowel Project (NSABP) reported an improved survival in patients randomized to receive adjuvant chemotherapy compared with no further treatment after resection. Adjuvant radiation therapy has only been useful in preventing local recurrence in rectal cancers with positive surgical margins.

The liver is the most common site of blood-borne metastases from primary colorectal cancers. In a subgroup of patients the liver may be the only site of disease. Overall, surgical resection is associated with a 25 to 30 percent 5-year survival rate.

8-26 **The answer is D.** *(Hathaway, 11/e, pp 405–406. Vaughan, 13/e, pp 347, 426–429.)* A common sequela of blunt trauma to the eye is a hyphema (blood in the anterior chamber). This is caused by rupture of small blood vessels lying close to the cornea. Chalazion is a granulomatous infection of the meibomian glands that causes a slight discomfort and redness to the eyelid with a small lump on the palpebral surface. An external hordeolum is an abscess of the sebaceous glands on the lid margin; an internal hordeolum is an infection of the meibomian glands that usually appears on the conjunctival surface of the lid. A cataract is opacity of the lens caused by precipitated lens proteins.

8-27. **The answer is D.** *(Isselbacher, 13/e, p 1539.)* A young man with recurrent ulcer disease unresponsive to therapy should be evaluated for Zollinger-Ellison syndrome, which includes gastrin-containing tumors that are usually in the pancreas. The patient's serum gastrin level is elevated, but not diagnostic for gastrinoma (>1000 pg/mL). A secretin injection induces marked increases in gastrin levels in all patients with gastrinoma.

8-28. The answer is B. *(Behrman, 15/e, pp 1779–1780.)* The time of onset of symptoms is somewhat helpful in the diagnosis of ophthalmia neonatorum. Chemical conjunctivitis is a self-limited condition that presents within 6 to 12 h of birth as a consequence of silver nitrate prophylaxis. Gonococcal conjunctivitis has its onset within 2 to 5 days after birth and is the most serious of the bacterial infections. Prompt and aggressive topical treatment and systemic antibiotics are indicated to prevent serious complications. Parents should be treated to avoid the risk to the child of reinfection. Silver nitrate is ineffective prophylaxis against chlamydial conjunctivitis, which occurs 5 to 14 days after birth. To avoid the risk of chlamydial pneumonia, treatment with systemic antibiotics is indicated for the infant as well as both parents.

8-29. The answer is B. (*DSM-IV, pp 303–304. Kaplan, 6/e, p 1044.*) Shared psychotic disorder, often called shared paranoid disorder (or folie à deux), is characterized by the transfer of delusions from the dominant personality to others in a shared and often isolated environment. Typically this involves a spouse and children. The condition is relatively rare. For the diagnosis to be made, the patient must not have had a psychotic disorder prior to adopting the induced delusion. Also, the condition must not be better accounted for by another psychotic disorder, in which case one would find the characteristic psychotic features in the mental status examination. Personality disorders are not associated with delusions.

The most important treatment is to separate the patient from the dominant partner. This provides individual support and relationship with persons who do not share the delusion. Family therapy would be contraindicated; it is not behavior that needs modification; and initial treatment would not usually involve ECT or medication.

8-30. The answer is C. (*Behrman, 15/e, pp 1066–1067.*) Malrotation results when incomplete rotation of the intestines occurs during embryologic development. The most common type of malrotation is failure of the cecum to move to its correct location in the right lower quadrant. Most patients present in the first weeks of life with bilious vomiting indicative of bowel obstruction or intermittent abdominal pain. Acute presentation, similar to that in the question, is caused by a volvulus of the intestines. The diagnosis is confirmed by radiographs; barium enema demonstrates malposition of the cecum in about 90 percent of cases. Upper GI series can confirm the diagnosis when necessary. Treatment is surgical.

8-31. The answer is B. (*Bennett, 20/e, pp 1132–1135.*) Iron overload should be considered among patients who present with any one or a combination of the following: hepatomegaly, weakness, pigmentation, atypical arthritis, diabetes, impotence, unexplained chronic abdominal pain, or cardiomyopathy. Excessive alcohol intake increases the diagnostic probability. Diagnostic suspicions should be particularly high when the family history is positive for similar clinical findings. The most frequent cause of iron overload is a common genetic disorder known as ("idiopathic") hemochromatosis. Secondary iron storage problems can occur in a variety of anemias. The most practical screening test is the determination of serum iron, transferrin saturation, and plasma ferritin. Plasma ferritin values above 300 ng/mL in males and 200 ng/mL in females suggest increased iron stores, and definitive diagnosis can be done by liver biopsy. Determination of serum copper is needed when Wilson's disease is the probable cause of hepatic abnormalities. The clinical picture here is inconsistent with that diagnosis. Nocturnal penile tumescence and echocardiogram can confirm clinical findings but will not help to establish the diagnosis.

8-32. The answer is D. *(Isselbacher, 13/e, pp 1011–1036.)* Atrial fibrillation (AF) is a common dysrhythmia that can occur in normal people, especially during emotional stress, after surgery or exercise, or following an alcoholic binge. It is also seen in hypoxia, hypercapnia, and in some metabolic and hemodynamic disturbances. Chronic AF occurs in patients with cardiovascular disease, especially rheumatic heart disease, mitral valve disease, hypertensive cardiomyopathy, atrial septal defect, and chronic lung disease. AF may be the first finding in thyrotoxicosis. Whenever the pulse is felt to be irregularly irregular, AF is almost always the diagnosis.

8-33. The answer is D. *(Tintinalli, 4/e, pp 987–993.)* Most pelvic fractures are the result of automobile-pedestrian accidents and are a frequent cause of death. The pelvis is extremely vascular with a diffuse blood supply that makes hemorrhage common and surgical control of bleeding difficult. This patient has a type II fracture (single break in pelvic ring) through a non-weight-bearing portion of the pelvis. These fractures are best treated by bed rest until hemodynamic stability is assured and thereafter by gentle ambulation as pain permits. The clinician must watch carefully for associated injuries to bladder, urethra, and colon and be alert to the many other possible concurrent injuries to an elderly patient who has suffered a collision, even a low-velocity attack from a pizza man.

8-34. The answer is C. *(Behrman, 15/e, p 1004.)* The presentation described is characteristic of visceral larva migrans from infestation with a common parasite of dogs, *Toxocara canis*. Dirt-eating children ingest the infectious ova. The larvae penetrate the intestine and migrate to visceral sites, such as the liver, lung, and brain, but do not return to the intestine, so the stools do not contain the ova or parasites. The diagnosis is made by a specific enzyme-linked immunosorbent assay (ELISA) for *Toxocara*.

8-35. The answer is C. *(Isselbacher, 13/e, pp 550, 1313–1334.)* Ureteral obstruction causes a severe colicky pain that often originates in the costo-vertebral angle and radiates around the trunk into the lower quadrant of the abdomen and possibly on into the upper thigh and testicle or labium. Vomiting is usually severe. Micturition may be painful and produce bloody urine.

8-36. The answer is D. *(Schwartz, 6/e, pp 246–250.)* Early wound management is characterized by early excision of areas of devitalized tissue with exception of deep wounds of the palms, soles, genitals, and face. Staged excision of deep partial-thickness or full-thickness burns occurs between 3 and 7 days after the injury. There are several proven advantages to early excision including decreased hospital stay and lower cost. This is especially true of burns encompassing >30 to 40 percent total body surface area. In conjunction with early excision, topical antimicrobials such as silver sulfadiazine are extremely important in delaying colonization of the newly excised or fresh burn wounds. Permanent coverage through split-thickness skin grafting usually occurs greater than 1 week after injury. Skin autograft requires a vascular bed and therefore cannot be placed over eschar. Meticulous attention to deep circumferential burns is crucial in the management of burn patients. Progressive tissue edema may lead to progressive vascular and neurologic compromise. Because the blood supply is the initial system affected, frequent assessment of flow is vital, with longitudinal escharotomy performed at the first sign of vascular compromise. A low threshold should be maintained in performing an escharotomy in the setting of severely burned limbs.

8-37. The answer is C. *(Hales, 2/e, p 1040. Nersessian, p 438.)* Countertransference is the name given to the phenomenon when an interviewer develops feelings about an interviewee based on irrational and often unconscious factors. For example, countertransference may be initiated by the fact that the patient resembles someone in the interviewer's past. Sometimes these feelings are positive, and sometimes they are negative. When the physician or psychotherapist becomes aware of having feelings that are quantitatively or qualitatively inappropriate, it is wise to look for the presence of countertransference. Some analysts use the term more restrictively to refer to an analyst's inappropriate reactions to a patient's transference.

8-38. The answer is D. *(Rudolph, 20/e, pp 1505–1506.)* A quadruple rhythm associated with the murmur of tricuspid regurgitation and a mid-diastolic murmur at the lower left sternum suggests the diagnosis of Ebstein's anomaly (downward displacement of the tricuspid valve). The presence of right atrial hypertrophy and right ventricular conduction defects confirms the diagnosis. Both tricuspid regurgitation with pulmonic stenosis and tetralogy of Fallot give electrocardiographic evidence of right ventricular enlargement. The Wolff-Parkinson-White syndrome, which frequently accompanies Ebstein's malformation, is not associated with murmurs or cyanosis as an isolated entity.

8-39. The answer is D. *(Rock, 8/e, pp 121–122.)* The clinical history presented in this question is a classic one for a ruptured tubal pregnancy accompanied by hemoperitoneum. Because pregnancy tests are negative in almost 50 percent of cases, they are of little practical value in an emergency. Dilation and curettage would not permit rapid-enough diagnosis, and the results obtained by this procedure are variable. Posterior colpotomy requires an operating room, surgical anesthesia, and an experienced operator with a scrubbed and gowned associate. Refined optic and electronic systems have improved the accuracy of laparoscopy, but this new equipment is not always available, and the procedure requires an operating room and, usually, surgical anesthesia. Culdocentesis is a rapid, nonsurgical method to confirm the presence of unclotted, intraabdominal blood from a ruptured tubal pregnancy. Culdocentesis, however, is also not perfect and a negative culdocentesis should not be used as the sole criteria for whether or not to operate on a patient.

8-40. The answer is C. *(Isselbacher, 13/e, pp 519, 806.)* Laryngotracheo-bronchitis (LTB), or croup, is a syndrome produced by acute infection of the lower air passages and most commonly occurs in children 3 years old or younger. The most common causative agent is the parainfluenza virus, but a wide variety of respiratory viruses and *Mycoplasma pneumoniae* can also cause LTB. The clinical hallmark is a barking or brassy cough. The epiglottis is not involved, and croup can easily be distinguished from epiglottitis by examination of a lateral neck x-ray, which will show no epiglottal edema.

Management of LTB requires hospitalization, close observation, humidification, and oxygenation as directed by pulse oximetry. Only rarely will intubation be necessary.

8-41. The answer is D. *(Wilmore, vol 1, sect 1, chap 5, pp 5–7.)* The patient presented in the question is in a state of metabolic acidosis as shown by a markedly increased anion gap of 28 meq unmeasured anions per liter of plasma. However, the respiratory response is greater than can be explained by a compensatory response, since the patient is mildly alkalemic. The disturbance cannot be a pure respiratory alkalosis, since the serum bicarbonate does not drop below 15 meq/L as a result of renal compensation, and the anion gap does not vary more than 1 to 2 meq/L from its normal value of 12 in response to a respiratory disturbance. The renal response to hyperventilation involves wasting of bicarbonate and compensatory retention of chloride; it does not involve a change in the concentration of "unmeasured" anions.

8-42. The answer is B. *(Anderson, Ann Intern Med 85:745–748, 1976. Isselbacher, 13/e, pp 257, 260, 2458.)* The acid-base disturbance in the patient described in the previous question demonstrates the value of extracting all available information from a small amount of rapidly retrievable data, e.g., arterial blood gases. Salicylates directly stimulate the respiratory center and produce respiratory alkalosis. By building up an accumulation of organic acids, salicylates also produce a concomitant metabolic acidosis. Characteristically both disturbances exist simultaneously following massive ingestion of salicylates. If sedative agents have been taken as well, the respiratory alkalosis (and even the respiratory compensation) may be absent. Phenformin and methanol overdoses also produce "high anion-gap" metabolic acidosis, but without the simultaneous respiratory disturbance. In the case presented, the patient's history of tinnitus in conjunction with her mixed metabolic acidosis-respiratory alkalosis is essentially pathognomonic of salicylate intoxication.

8-43. The answer is B. *(Hales, 2/e, pp 623–632.)* Munchausen syndrome is an example of a very severe factitious disorder characterized by pathological lying, recurrent feigned or simulated illness, and wandering. Patients often display multiple scars from previous medical intervention and surgical exploration, and they will gladly submit to diagnostic procedures and operations. Acute intermittent porphyria is associated with abdominal pain, and sometimes psychiatric symptoms, but not those displayed by this patient. The absence of significant mental status findings, and particularly those associated with psychosis, eliminates schizophrenia and psychotic depression.

Factitious disorder is characterized by the feigning of physical or psychological symptoms and the motivation to assume the sick role. Patients with dissociative disorder, somatoform disorder, adjustment disorder, or hysterical personality may derive some secondary gain from their problems, but do not feign their illness. Malingering is the most difficult differential diagnosis. Malingering is distinguished from factitious disorders by the presence of an external incentive such as economic gain or avoidance of legal responsibility.

8-44. The answer is E. (*Rudolph, 20/e, pp 145–151.*) The x-ray showing multiple fractures in various stages of healing indicates trauma at different times. This information should be reported to the medical examiner and appropriate social agencies, including the police, so that investigation may be started and other children that may be in the home or under the care of the same babysitter may be protected. Although an autopsy (and death-scene investigation) should be done in every such case, there sometimes develops a tendency for medical examiners to diagnose SIDS without an autopsy, particularly if the parents object to one, unless further information is provided by the emergency room staff as in this case.

8-45. The answer is E. (*Lechtenberg, Synopsis, pp 114–115.*) This woman probably has trigeminal neuralgia (tic douloureux). The treatment options for this facial pain disorder include carbamazepine (Tegretol). Neutropenia routinely occurs with chronic carbamazepine use, thereby making it inadvisable in a patient with an already low WBC count. Although carbamazepine is a potent antiepileptic medication, other antiepileptic medications, such as phenobarbital and divalproex sodium (Depakote), are usually ineffective in blunting the pain. Phenytoin (Dilantin) is another antiepileptic useful in the management of trigeminal neuralgia. Analgesics and anti-inflammatory drugs, such as indomethacin (Indocin), are notably ineffective in managing this disorder.

8-46. The answer is C. (*Behrman, 15/e, pp 1761–1762.*) The paralysis of Guillain-Barré occurs about 10 days after a nonspecific viral illness. Weakness is gradual over days or weeks beginning in the lower extremities and progresses toward the trunk. Later, the upper limbs and the bulbar muscles may become involved. Involvement of the respiratory muscles is life-threatening. The syndrome seems to be caused by a demyelination in the motor and occasionally the sensory nerves. Spinal fluid protein is helpful in the diagnosis; protein levels are increased to more than twice normal, while glucose and cell counts are normal. Hospitalization for observation is indicated. Treatment may consist of intravenous immunoglobulin, steroids, or plasmapheresis. Recovery is not always complete.

8-47. The answer is A. (*Isselbacher, 13/e, p 1941.*) TSH levels are always increased in patients with untreated hypothyroidism (from primary thyroid disease) and would be the test of choice in this patient. Serum T_3 is not sensitive for hypothyroidism. The TRH stimulation test is useful in some cases of hyperthyroidism. A decreased RAIU is of limited value because of the low value for lower limit of normal. In goitrous hypothyroidism, the RAIU may even be increased.

8-48. The answer is C. (*Isselbacher, 13/e, pp 206, 207, 1383.*) Esophageal dysphagia usually presents as a sticking sensation. When it is intermittent, it is usually associated with a lower esophageal ring; when it is progressive, it is usually due to a tumor. Regurgitation may occur minutes to hours after a meal. Patients find that they have to chew their food more thoroughly and that they require increased fluid consumption to "wash the food down." The length of time taken to consume a meal is prolonged.

8-49–8-50. The answers are 8-49 C, 8-50 B. (*Isselbacher 13/e, p 758.*) This young woman presents with symptoms of both upper and lower respiratory infection. The combination of sore throat, bullous myringitis, and infiltrates on chest x-ray is consistent with infection due to *Mycoplasma pneumoniae*. This minute organism is not seen on Gram stain. Neither *Streptococcus pneumoniae* nor *Haemophilus influenzae* would produce this combination of upper and lower respiratory tract symptoms. The patient is likely to have high titers of IgM cold agglutinins. The low hematocrit and elevated reticulocyte count reflect a hemolytic anemia, which can occur from mycoplasma infection. These IgM class antibodies are directed to the I antigen on the erythrocyte membrane. The treatment of choice for mycoplasma infection is erythromycin.

Bibliography

Bibliography

Adams RD, Victor M. Ropper AH: *Principles of Neurology*, 6/e. New York, McGraw-Hill, 1997.

Ahronheim JC, Moreno J, Zuckerman C: *Ethics in Clinical Practice*. Boston, Little, Brown, 1994.

American Academy of Pediatrics (AAP): 1994 Red Book: Report of the Committee on Infectious Diseases, 23/e. Elk Grove Village, IL, AAP, 1994.

American Psychiatric Association: Diagnostic and Statistical Manual of Mental Disorders, 4/e (DSM-IV). Washington, DC, American Psychiatric Press, 1994.

American Psychiatric Association: *Practice Guidelines*. Washington, DC, American Psychiatric Press, 1996.

Anderson, RJ, et al: Unrecognized adult salicylate intoxication, *Ann Intern Med* 85:745–748, 1976.

Andreasen NC, Blac DW: *Introductory Textbook of Psychiatry*, 2/e. Washington, DC, American Psychiatric Press, 1995.

Badgett RG, Tanaka DJ, Hunt DK, et al: Can moderate chronic obstructive pulmonary disease be diagnosed by historical and physical findings alone? *Am J Med* 94(2): 188–96, 1993.

Bartlett JG: *Pocket Book of Infectious Disease Therapy*, 7/e. Baltimore, Williams & Wilkins, 1996.

Bates B, Hoeckelman RA: *A Guide to Physical Examination and History Taking*, 5/e. Philadelphia, Lippincott, 1991.

Beauchamp TL, Childress JF: *Principles of Biomedical Ethics*, 4/e. New York, Oxford University Press, 1994.

Behrman RE, Vaughan VC (eds): *Nelson Textbook of Pediatrics*, 15/e. Philadelphia, Saunders, 1995.

Belkin M, et al: Intra-arterial fibrinolytic therapy. Efficacy of streptokinase vs. urokinase. *Arch Surg* 121:769–773. 1986.

Benenson AS (ed): *Control of Communicable Disease in Man*, 16/e. Washington, DC. American Public Health Association, 1995.

Berek JS, Hacker NF (eds): *Practical Gynecologic Oncology*. Baltimore, Williams & Wilkins, 1989.

Berg BO: *Principles of Child Neurology*, New York McGraw-Hill, 1996.

Berkow R, Fletcher AJ (eds): *The Merck Manual: General Medicine*, vol 1, 16/e. Rahway, NJ, Merck, 1992.

Braunwald E (ed): *Heart Disease; A Textbook of Cardiovascular Medicine*, 4/e. Philadelphia, Saunders, 1992.

Burnside JW, McGlynn TJ: *Physical Diagnosis*, 17/e. Baltimore, Williams & Wilkins, 1987.

Calkins D, Fernandopulle RJ, Marino BS: *Health Care Policy*, Cambridge, MA, Blackwell Science, 1995.

Cameron JL: *Current Surgical Therapy*, 4/e. St. Louis, Mosby, 1992.

Carr BR, Blackwell RE (eds): *Textbook of Reproductive Medicine*. East Norwalk, CT, Appleton & Lange, 1993.

Cass AS: Renovascular injuries from external trauma. Diagnosis, treatment, and outcome. *Urol Clin North Am* 16:213–220, 1989.

Charlson ME, et al: The preoperative and intraoperative hemodynamic predictors of postoperative myocardial infarction or ischemia in patients undergoing noncardiac surgery. *Ann Surg* 210:637–648, 1989.

Coffey CE, Cummins JL (eds): *American Psychiatric Press Textbook of Geriatric Neuropsychiatry*. Washington, DC, American Psychiatric Press, 1994.

Cosentino CM, et al: Choledochal duct cyst: Resection with physiologic reconstruction. *Surgery* 112:740–748, 1992.

Crenshaw AH (ed): *Campbell's Operative Orthopaedics*, 8/e. St. Louis, Mosby, 1992.

Cummings RA, et al: Pneumopericardium resulting in cardiac tamponade. *Ann Thorac Surgery* 37:511–518, 1984.

Cunningham FG, et al (eds): *Williams Obstetrics*, 20/e. East Norwalk, CT, Appleton & Lange, 1993.

Delp MH, Manning RT: *Major's Physical Diagnosis: An Introduction to the Clinical Process*, 9/e. Philadelphia, Saunders, 1981.

Dietrich NA, et al: A growing spectrum of surgical disease in patients with human immunodeficiency virus/acquired immunodeficiency syndrome, experience with 120 major cases, *Arch Surg* 126:860–866, 1991.

DiSaia PJ, Creasman WT (eds): *Clinical Gynecologic Oncology*, 5/e. St. Louis, Mosby, 1997.

Dutky PA, Stevens SL, Maull KI: Factors affecting rapid fluid resuscitation with large-bore introducer catheters. *J Trauma* 29:856–860, 1989.

Ehrlich O, Brem AS: A prospective comparison of urinary tract infections in patients Treated with either clean intermittent catheterization or urinary diversion. *Pediatrics* 70:665, 1982.

Evans MI (ed): *Reproductive Risks and Prenatal Diagnosis*. East Norwalk, CT, Appleton & Lange, 1992.

Evarts CM (ed): *Surgery of the Musculoskeletal System*, 2/e. New York, Churchill Livingstone,. 1990.

Felig P, Baxter JD, Frohman LA: *Endocrinology and Metabolism*, 3/e. New York, McGraw-Hill, 1995.

Fiore MC, Smith SS, Jorenby DE, Baker TB: The effectiveness of the nicotine patch for smoking cessation: A meta-analysis. *JAMA* 271:1904–1907, 1994.

Fitzpatrick TB, Eisen AZ, Wolff K, et al: *Dermatology in General Medicine*, 4/e. New York, McGraw-Hill, 1993.

Fleisher AC, et al (ed): *Principles and Practice of Ultrasonography in Obstetrics and Gynecology*, 5/e. East Norwalk, CT, Appleton & Lange, 1997.

Friedman SB, Fisher M, Schonberg SK: *Comprehensive Adolescent Health Care*, St. Louis, Quality Medical Publishing, 1992.

Gartland JJ: *Fundamentals of Orthopaedics*, 4/e. Philadelphia, Saunders, 1987.

Gilman S, Bloedel JR, Lechtenberg R: *Disorders of the Cerebellum*, Philadelphia, Davis, 1981.

Gilman S, Winans SS: *Manter and Gatz's Essentials of Clinical Neuro-anatomy and Neurophysiology*, 6/e. Philadelphia, Davis, 1982.

Goroll AH, May LA, Mulley AG Jr, et al (eds): *Primary Care Medicine*, 3/e. Philadelphia, Lippincott, 1995.

Hales RE, Yudofsky SC, Talbott JA (eds): *American Psychiatric Press Textbook of Psychiatry*, 2/e. Washington, DC, American Psychiatric Press, 1994.

Hall JB, Schmidt GA, Wood LDH: *Principles of Critical Care*. New York, McGraw-Hill, 1992.

Hankins GDV, et al (eds): *Operative Obstetrics*. Norwalk, CT, Appleton & Lange, 1995.

Hardman JG, Limbird LE, Molinoff PB, et al (eds): *Goodman and Gilman's The Pharmacological Basis of Therapeutics*, 9/e, New York, McGraw-Hill, 1996.

Hardy JT (ed): *Hardy's Textbook of Surgery*, 2/e. Philadelphia, Lippincott, 1988.

Harrison MR, et al (eds): *The Unborn Patient: Prenatal Diagnosis and Treatment*, 2/e. Philadelphia, Saunders, 1990.

Harvey AM, et al: *The Principles and Practice of Medicine*, 22/e. East Norwalk, CT, Appleton & Lange, 1988.

Hatcher RA, Trussell J, Stewart F, et al: *Contraceptive Technology*, 16/e. New York, Irvington, 1994.

Hathaway WE, Hay WW, Groothuis JR, et al: *Current Pediatric Diagnosis and Treatment*, 11/e. East Norwalk, CT, Appleton & Lange, 1993.

Henderson JA, Peloquin AJ: Boerhaave revisited: Spontaneous esophageal perforation as a diagnostic masquerader. *Am J Med* 86:559–567, 1989.

Hennekens CH, Buring JE: *Epidemiology in Medicine*. Boston, Little, Brown, 1987.

Holliday MA, Barratt TM, Avner ED: *Pediatric Nephrology*, 3/e. Baltimore, Williams & Wilkins, 1994.

Holmes KK, Mardh PE, Sparling PF, et al: *Sexually Transmitted Diseases*, 2/e. New York, McGraw-Hill, 1990.

Isselbacher KJ, Braunwald E, Wilson JD, et al (eds): *Harrison's Principles of Internal Medicine*, 13/e. New York, McGraw-Hill, 1994.

Jaffe R, Warsof SL (eds): *Color Doppler Imaging in Obstetrics and Gynecology*, New York, McGraw-Hill, 1992.

Jones KL (ed): *Smith's Recognizable Patterns of Human Malformations*, 5/e. Philadelphia, Saunders, 1988.

Kaplan H, Sadock J: *Comprehensive Textbook of Psychiatry*, 6/e. Baltimore, Williams & Wilkins, 1996.

Keye WR, et al (eds): *Infertility: Evaluation and Treatment*. Philadelphia, Saunders, 1995.

Ladou J: *Occupational Medicine*. East Norwalk, CT, Appleton & Lange, 1990.

Larsen SA, Steiner BM, Rudolph AH: Laboratory diagnosis and interpretation of tests for syphilis. *Clin Microbiol Rev* 8:1–21, 1995.

Last JM: *Maxcy-Rosenau Public Health and Preventive Medicine*, 13/e. East Norwalk, CT, Appleton & Lange, 1992.

Lechtenberg R (ed): *Handbook of Cerebellar Diseases*. New York, Dekker, 1993.

Lechtenberg R: *Multiple Sclerosis Fact Book*, 2/e. Philadelphia, Davis, 1995.

Lechtenberg R: *The Psychiatrist's Guide to Diseases of the Nervous System*. New York, Wiley & Sons, 1982.

Lechtenberg R: *Seizure Recognition and Treatment*. New York, Churchill- Livingstone, 1990.

Lechtenberg R: *Synopsis of Neurology*. Philadelphia, Lea & Febiger, 1991.

Lechtenberg R, Sher JH: *AIDS in the Nervous System*. New York, Churchill- Livingstone, 1988.

Lynch PJ: *House Officers Series: Dermatology*, 3/e. Baltimore, Williams & Wilkins, 1994.

Magee DJ: *Orthopaedic Physical Assessment*, 2/e. Philadelphia, Saunders, 1992.

Mandell GL, Douglas RG Jr, Bennett JE: *Principles and Practice of Infectious Disease*, 4/e. New York, Churchill Livingstone, 1995.

Markovchick VJ, Pons PT, Wolfe RE: *Emergency Medicine Secrets*. Philadelphia, Hanley & Belfus, 1993.

Mayo Clinic, Department of Neurology: *Clinical Examinations in Neurology*, 6/e. Philadelphia, Saunders, 1991.

McCullough DL (ed): *Difficult Diagnoses in Urology*, New York, Churchill Livingstone, 1988.

Miller FB, Shumate CR, Richardson JD: Myocardial contusion. When can the diagnosis be eliminated? *Arch Surg* 124:805–808, 1989.

Miller MD: *Review of Orthopaedics*, 2/e. Philadelphia, Saunders, 1996.

Miller MD, Cooper DE, Warner JJP: *Review of Sports Medicine and Arthroscopy*, Philadelphia, Saunders, 1995.

Miller RD: *Anesthesia*, 3/e. New York, Churchill Livingstone, 1990.

Mishell Dr, Stenchever MA, Droegenmueller W, Herbst Al (eds): *Comprehensive Gynecology*, 3/e. St. Louis, Mosby, 1997.

Moeller DW: *Environmental Health*. Cambridge, MA, Harvard University Press, 1992.

Moosa AR, Mayer, AD, Stabile B: Iatrogenic injury to the bile duct. Who, how, where? *Arch Surg* 125:1028–1031, 1990.

Morrey BF (ed): *The Elbow and Its Disorders*, 2/e. Philadelphia, Saunders, 1993.

Morrissy RT, Weinstein ST: *Lovell and Winter's Pediatric Orthopaedics*, 4/e. Philadelphia, Lippincott, 1996.

Murray JF, Nadel JA (ed): *Textbook of Respiratory Medicine*, 2/e. Philadelphia, Saunders, 1994.

Nichols DH (ed): *Gynecologic and Obstetric Surgery*. St. Louis, Mosby, 1993.

O'Driscoll SW, Morrey BF, Korinek S, An KN: Elbow subluxation and dislocation: A spectrum of instability. *Clin Orthop* 280:186–197, 1992.

O'Rourke RA, (ed): *Hurst's The Heart*, update 1. New York, McGraw-Hill, 1996.

Osborn AG: *Introduction to Cerebral Angiography*. New York, Harper & Row, 1980.

Pansky B: *Review of Gross Anatomy*, 6/e, New York, McGraw-Hill, 1996.

Porter JT, et al: Diagnosis and management of primary hyperpararthyroidism: Consensus Development Conference Statement. *Ann Intern Med* 114:593–597, 1991.

Remington JS, Klein JO (eds): *Infectious Diseases of the Fetus and Newborn Infant*, 4/e. Philadelphia, Saunders, 1995.

Remoin RL, Connor JM, Pyeritz RE (eds): *Principles and Practice of Medicine Genetics*, 3/e. New York, Churchill Livingstone, 1996.

Rhame FS: Preventing HIV transmission. Strategies to protect clinicians and patients. *Postgrad Med* 91:144, 147–152, 1992.

Roitt IM, Brostoff J, Male DK: *Immunology*, 3/e. St. Louis, Mosby, 1993.

Rose BD: *Clinical Physiology of Acid-Base and Electrolyte Disorders*, 4/e. New York, McGraw-Hill, 1994.

Rudolph AM, Hoffman JIE, Rudolph CD: *Rudolph Pediatrics*, 20/e. East Norwalk, CT, Appleton & Lange, 1996.

Rutherford RB: *Vascular Surgery*, 3/e. Philadelphia, Saunders, 1989.

Ryan KJ, et al: *Kistner's Gynecology; Principles and Practice*, 5/e. Chicago, Year Book Medical, 1990.

Sabiston DC Jr, Spencer FC: *Gibbon's Surgery of the Chest*, 5/e. Philadelphia, Saunders, 1990.

Sawyers JL: Management of postgastrectomy syndromes. *Am J Surg* 159:8–14, 1990.

Sapira JD: *The Art and Science of Bedside Diagnosis*. Baltimore, Urban & Schwarzenberg, 1989.

Schlant RC, Alexander RW, O'Rourke RA, et al (eds): *Hurst's The Heart*, 8/e. New York, McGraw-Hill, 1994.

Schwartz SI, Shires GT, Spencer FC (ed): *Principles of Surgery*, 6/e. New York McGraw-Hill, 1994.

Sherlock S: *Diseases of the Liver and Biliary System*, 9/e. Cambridge, MA, Blackwell Scientific, 1993.

Shoemaker WC, Thompson WL, Holbrook PR. *The Society of Critical Care Medicine: Textbook of Critical Care*, 2/e. Philadelphia, Saunders, 1988.

Siegel AF: *Statistics and Data Analysis: An Introduction*. New York, Wiley, 1988.

Tintinalli JE, Krome RL, Ruiz E (eds): *Emergency Medicine: A Comprehensive Study Guide*, 4/e. New York, McGraw-Hill, 1996.

Torg FS, Conrad W. Kalen V: Clinical diagnosis of anterior cruciate ligament instability to the athlete. *Am J Sports Med* 4:84–93. 1976.

United States Department of Health and Human Services (USDHHS): Healthy People 2000: National Health Promotion and Disease Prevention Objectives, Washington, DC, USDHHS, 1988.

USDHHS, PHS, Centers for Disease Control (CDC): Case-control study of HIV seroconversion in health-care workers after percutaneous exposure to HIV-infected blood. France, United Kingdon, and United States, January 1988-August 1994, *MMWR* 44:929–933, 1995.

Vaughan D, Asbury T: *General Ophthalmology*, 18/e. East Norwalk, CT. Appleton & Lange, 1992.

Way LW: *Current Surgical Diagnosis and Treatment*, 9/e. East Norwalk, CT, Appleton & Lange, 1991

Williams WJ, et al (eds): *Hematology*, 5/e. New York, McGraw-Hill, 1995.

Youmans JR (ed): *Neurological Surgery*, 3/e. Philadelphia, Saunders, 1990.

Yudofsky SC, Hales RE (eds): *American Psychiatric Press Textbook of Neuropsychiatry*, 2/e. Washington, DC, American Psychiatric Press, 1992.

ISBN 0-07-135558-8

9 780071 355582

90000

CLINICAL VIGNETTES FOR
THE USMLE STEP 2